Pakistan
Living with a Nuclear Monkey

.............*Mr. Speaker, We played our role as politicians in Pakistan in many forms to put the country on the right track, but the military generals have done nothing positive, and one day we will bring them to justice. The army dismembered Pakistan but prosecuted Zulfiqar Ali Bhutto, and now they are behind Benazir Bhutto and Nawaz Sharif. In Pakistan's constitution, there are articles 244 and article 6, which propose punishment for the army. Mr. Speaker, today, my nation's bullet-riddled body speaks. Baluchistan, FATA and Waziristan are blood-stained; if Punjab keeps quiet this time, the nation will not tolerate its attitude. In the past, Bengalis were brutally killed by our army, while Punjab was silent and played the role of collaborator, but today, Punjab will no more tolerate atrocities by the armed forces against the Baloch and Pashtun brothers.*

– Foreign Minister of Pakistan Khawaja Muhammad Asif's fascinating budget speech (2006/7) in the National Assembly of Pakistan

.............*Pakistan is alike roundabout or circuitous place where Mullahs are available for Fatwas, leaders and military generals are available for sale. The fact is world treats us as a village of killers, murderers, and mercenaries. Military receive charity from the United States and Saudi Arabia, but kill civilians, rape women, girls, and bomb their houses. What does coalition support fund mean? The United States kill us and we support its illegal war against our country. Mr. Speaker and member of the house please note, our army kills our children, but I want to tell our intelligence agencies that we know the US kill us with your support, humiliate us with your support, and destroy our houses with your support, but please not; one day we will bring you to justice, and you will be punished. Our army is our enemy. Mr. Speaker and members of the house, our army killed innocent women and children in North Waziristan. They were not extremists. Why their houses and market were bulldozed. Why shops of poor people were bulldozed in Miran Shah and Mir Ali districts? Mr. Speaker, there are no RAW and NDS agents operating in Pakistan, our intelligence agencies kill our people, and they have no fear of God. Who are these jihadist and extremist groups dancing in our streets and villages, Mr. Speaker, the fact is our army trains these people for marketing fear and terrorism in Pakistan.*

–Maulana Muhammad Khan Shirani
Member National Assembly of Pakistan and Executive Member of Jamiat-e-Ulema-e-Islam (F) group

.............*In Malakand Division, the army never killed a single terrorist, but killed innocent women and children, and raped young girls. The army commanders gaze tribal elders with rubbernecking, sarcasm and scorn.*

–Senator Maulana Gul Naseeb Khan (Malakand), Exectuve Member of Jamiat-e-Ulema-e-Islam (F) group

Pakistan
Living with a Nuclear Monkey

Musa Khan Jalalzai

Vij Books India Pvt Ltd
New Delhi (India)

Published by

Vij Books India Pvt Ltd
(Publishers, Distributors & Importers)
2/19, Ansari Road
Delhi – 110 002
Phones: 91-11-43596460, 91-11-47340674
Fax: 91-11-47340674
e-mail: vijbooks@rediffmail.com
www.vijbooks.com

ISBN: 978-93-86457-90-5 (Hardback)
ISBN: 978-93-86457-92-9 (ebook)

Contents

Introduction

Pakistan is teetering on the brink. The country's staggering and lurching foreign policy has failed to evolve with changing political and geopolitical developments.[1] The army and ISI lack coherent and long-term approach to national security, international relations and internal security mechanism.[2] The prolixity of the Afghan war and participation of Pakistan's jihadist black-water in it has blighted its social stratification.[3] Its domestic policies are in a grief-stricken state.[4] The two states (Islamic Republic and Military Establishment) have adopted different foreign, domestic and economic policies, and view neighbouring states with different glasses. Military Establishment (Miltablishment) and the state of Pakistan do not interfere in each other financial and industrial matter. The state of Pakistan wants friendly relations with India, and Afghanistan, while the state of military establishment sends mercenaries for jihad. Each state is struggling to control foreign and security policies of Pakistan, but do not interfere in each other's corruption matter.

The state wants social and political integration while the army continues to disintegrate national, social and political stratification by killing and torturing Balochs and Pashtuns. A rogue nuclear state, mother of terror, corrupt, jihadist and many other titles are being attributed to the country by critics, analysts and researchers due its brutal and cacophonous treatment of citizens.[5] The two Pakistani states have been in hot-blooded and protracted war since 1970s.[6] From nuclear black marketing to forced disappearances, and war on its own people in Baluchistan, Waziristan and FATA, miltablishment never trusted democratic government, parliament, civil society and political parties.[7]

Journalist and expert Imad Zafar has painted a hard-featured and ominous image of the army and ISI in his all-inclusive article. He mainly focuses on the army political and bureaucratic role: "As per the constitution of Pakistan every democratic government is answerable to the people of Pakistan. But in reality they are actually answerable to the GHQ. Every single Prime Minister in Pakistan can only do their job smoothly if they completely surrender in the matter of defense, interior strategic decisions and foreign policy. It means the rule for civilian governments are already decided and they have been told to go by the book, not to cross the red-lines defined by the defense establishment. This makes it a "state within a state" who instead of ruling the country from the front, prefers to politicians and civilian governments to implement its decision and exercise power".[8]

Broken-down ethnically, and detached religiously, the garrison-jihadist state has now become a permanent headache of international community.[9] Defeated in Bangladesh, Afghanistan and Kashmir, military general now started business of supplying proxies to regional and sectarian conflicts in Middle East and Persian Gulf, and promote business of soldiers for sale. On 05 December 2015, a pro-miltablishment newspaper, Daily the Nation published a detailed account of how Pakistan illegally occupied Baluchistan.[10] Alike Baluchistan, Sindh, FATA and Waziristan are too in turmoil. Jihadist culture, and contribution of proxies into Afghan war consumed thousands lives of Pakistani citizens and soldiers. Jihadist factories have been producing hundreds of thousands pious soldiers, leaders and commanders-representing Pakistan across the globe.[11]

The miltablishment and its proxies are expanding the matrix of deep state to all institution to gradually undermine democracy in Pakistan, legalize its private criminal enterprise and operations of jihadists' militias. In his Asia Times analysis, Imad Zafar described nexus of jihadists, wealthy individuals and the army in Pakistan: "The nexus of mullah, property tycoons and businesses men and serving and retired bureaucrats and opportunist politicians have all lent their support to the invisible forces in order for the deep state to maintain a successful business enterprise".[12]

In 2017, Prime Minister Nawaz Sharif tried to take control of foreign and internal policy of the country, but disqualified by the Supreme Court.[13] He wanted to lead Pakistan's India and Afghan policy on right direction; he was intercepted, humiliated and threatened and his movements were salami-sliced. He was not allowed a single visit to a nuclear site, and threatened of dire consequence by the ISI and miltablishment.[14] Retrospectively, former President Asif Ali Zardari tried to bring ISI under the control of Interior Ministry; he faced the same threatening situation, and was warned that his crippled and torturous body would be shifted to hospital by an army ambulance. The ISI and the army reprehensibly designed policies, and their intransigencies led the state towards a dangerous destiny, where it cannot survive as a coherent nation state.[15]

The consecutive militarization and Talibanization of society, and instability led to the catastrophe of disintegration and failure of the state, while most part of these challenges was further inflamed by the US war on terrorism, and international involvement in Afghanistan.[16] The fall of Taliban regime in 2001 opened up a new chapter of confrontation between Afghanistan and Pakistan. India signed strategic partnership agreement (2011) with Afghanistan to support stabilization efforts in the country.[17] The lack of Pakistan's constructive and positive diplomatic approach towards Afghanistan prompted deep crisis, including the closure of trade routes and diplomatic impasse.[18]

Moreover, Afghans understand that Pakistan army pursued its own agenda in Afghanistan in ways the country purveys funds and sanctuaries to terrorist groups on its soil. Its support to Haqqani terrorist networks, and ISIS, prolonged the Afghan war and caused catastrophe.[19] These and other misgivings and premonition caused great diplomatic and foreign policy challenges. Today, the country's leadership feels isolation, and no one likes to dance to its tango.[20] These and other afflictions and suffering forced civilian leadership to recalibrate foreign policy of the country. On 28 February 2018, Dawn reported the country's National Security Committee (NSC) decision of recalibrating foreign policy to make it more effective and regionally focused.[21] Pakistan's nuclear smuggling across the globe also caused embarrassment, mortification, and shame. Miltablishment (military establishment) shamelessly pursued dangerous business, and purveyed nuclear materials to all rogue states in Asia and Africa, and proved their Stupidity and preposterousness.[22]

The Miltablishment's nuclear smuggling network prospered for nearly two decades and was linked to middlemen and businesses in over 20 countries.[23] On 24 September 2017, journalist Amit Baruah in his column quoted Russian Ambassador informed his colleagues in Islamabad about the progress of Pakistan nuclear weapons: "In May 1979, the Soviet Ambassador Sarwar Alimzhanovich Azimov informed his socialist colleagues in Islamabad that Pakistan possessed both the "material and intellectual capabilities" to carry out a nuclear explosion. "The execution of the programme is being accelerated by the recent discovery of uranium of a favorable composition near Dera Ghazi Khan. The Soviet Ambassador also stated that the country's nuclear programme, proceeding at an accelerated pace, was "actively supported" by both Saudi Arabia and Libya".[24]

Pakistan's former President Pervez Musharraf remained tight-lip during a ceremony in Islamabad on a question of his country's nuclear smuggling networks, while nuclear scientist Abdul Qadeer Khan alleged that Mr. Musharraf gave-away nuclear secrets to the US and Israel, and called Pervez Musharraf an "American stooge".[25] Mr. Khan incriminated him of transferring "very sensitive information" to the United States. There were speculations cruising in international press that the General handed security of Pakistan's nuclear weapons to the US Special Forces. Mr. Khan also confirmed media reports which cited him as saying that China purveyed Pakistan with weapons-grade uranium and the blueprint for a simple nuclear weapon in 1982.[26]

On 08 March 2004, journalist Seymour M. Hersh in his New Yorker article uncovered the story of secret nuclear links between Pakistan and Iran: "Musharraf has insisted that any dealings between Khan and Iran were independent of, and unknown to, the Pakistan government. But there is evidence to contradict him. On a trip to the Middle East, I was told that a number of years ago the Israeli signals-intelligence agency, known as Unit 8200, broke a sophisticated Iranian code and began monitoring communications that included talk between Iran and Pakistan about Iran's burgeoning nuclear-weapons program. The Israeli intelligence community has many covert contacts inside Iran, stemming from the strong ties it had there before the overthrow of the Shah, in 1979; some of these ties still exist. Israeli intelligence also maintained close contact with many Iranian opposition groups, such as the National Council. A connection was made—directly or indirectly—and the Israeli intelligence about Iran's nuclear program reached the National Council. A senior I.A.E.A. official subsequently told me that he knew that the Council's information had originated with Israeli intelligence, but he refused to say where he had learned that fact".[27]

These facts and figure cannot be repudiated. The story of North Korean's nuclear weapons programme, and its links with Mr. Khan's nuclear smuggling network has proved that Pakistan purveyed nuclear and missiles technology to the country. On 01 December 2007, the Guardian reported Bush administration handed blueprint to seize Pakistan's nuclear arsenal, but some reports confirmed that US Special Commandos had already reached Pakistani to take the control of nuclear sites and the bomb: "Mr. Frederick Kagan, a former West Point military historian, called on White House to consider various options for an unstable Pakistan. "These included sending elite British or US troops to control nuclear weapons capable of being transported out of the country and take them to a secret storage depot in New Mexico or a "remote redoubt" inside Pakistan; sending US troops to Pakistan's North-Western border to fight the Taliban and al-Qaida; and a US military occupation of the capital Islamabad, and the provinces of Punjab, Sindh and Baluchistan if asked for assistance by a fractured Pakistan military, so that the US could shore up President Pervez Musharraf and General Ashfaq Kayani".[28]

The United States has been spending $100 million on the security of Pakistan's nuclear weapons since years, but Miltablishment is denying the fact that its nuclear sites are guarded by US Special Forces. Researcher Lisa Curtis noted in her paper that some observers incorrectly characterized the threat of nuclear terrorism in Pakistan as stemming from the danger of radical Islamists overrunning the country and gaining control of the country's nuclear assets: "However, given that the religious parties lack wide popular support and that President Pervez Musharraf and his senior army commanders largely oppose the Islamist agenda, the probability of this scenario occurring is relatively low. When it comes to preventing terrorists from acquiring nuclear bombs, the more worrisome trend in Pakistan is the links between some retired military and intelligence officials and nuclear scientists to Taliban and al-Qaeda terrorists. U.S. policy should therefore centre on helping to prevent the penetration of the nuclear establishment over time by individuals sympathetic to al-Qaeda goals. Despite Pakistan's arguments that its nuclear weapons are safely guarded, the U.S. must construct and implement policies that proactively thwart the unwelcome possibility of Pakistan's nuclear weapons falling into the wrong hands".[29]

On 31 August 2017, The Nation reported former President Pervez Musharraf's remarks about the CIA evidence against Dr. Abdul Qadeer Khan's involvement in nuclear smuggling. He said when CIA showed him the evidence of nuclear proliferation done by Pakistani nuclear scientist Dr. Abdul Qadeer Khan; it was most disappointed day of his entire life. Dawn (2005) also reported his interview with a private TV Channel, in which Musharraf said; Dr. Khan apologized and asked for his help in a meeting.[30] However, General Pervez Musharraf denied the allegations that transfers of centrifuge designs to North Korea by Dr Abdul Qadeer Khan helped N. Korea in acquiring nuclear weapons.[31] According to a New York Times report, in an interview with Japanese news agency Kyodo, he confirmed that Dr Khan provided centrifuge machines and their designs to North Korea, but said these transfers did not help North Korea acquire a nuclear weapons capability. Mr. Khan confessed in February 2004 to having supplied nuclear technology and expertise to North Korea, Libya and Iran.[32]

Moreover, on 01 September 2017, Dawn reported Veteran politician Javed Hashmi's meeting with Dr Abdul Qadeer Khan who told him that a group in the army was not in favor of Pakistan's nuclear tests. He said there was a group of people who did not want to see Pakistan a nuclear power. "A lobby like Pervez Musharraf was agreed to compromise on country's nuclear programme," he claimed. However, Dawn reported Mr. Hashmi revelation about the 2003 ceremony hosted by the Saudi Arabian embassy. "Dr Qadeer informed audience about the threats he was receiving from Pervez Musharraf. Admiral Abdul Aziz and Syed Mushahid Hussain were also present at that moment," Hashmi said. Mr. Hashmi said at that time Dr Qadeer was disappointed as Musharraf had made life tough for him.[33]

On 30 August 2017, Dawn reported the PPP Senator Farhatullah Babar called for an investigation into nuclear proliferation by Pakistan under the rule of former President Pervez Musharraf. Senator Babar rejected claims Musharraf made during an interview with Dunya News, in which he said that he met with George Tenet, a former Director General of Central Intelligence Agency (CIA) during a trip to the United States at the insistence of former US President George Bush. President Musharraf asserted in his interview that the former CIA agent had shown him photographic evidence of Pakistani nuclear scientist Dr Abdul Qadeer Khan's involvement in the proliferation of nuclear material outside Pakistan.[34]

This concern of the United States was further substantiated by the Taliban and Baloch terrorist attacks on Pakistan's nuclear facilities during the last 15 years. However, on 05 May 2006, Baloch militants attacked the nuclear dumping site near Baghalchur Uranium mine in Dera Ghazi Khan District.[35] In 2007, terrorists also attacked two air force facilities in Sargodha, associated with nuclear installations.[36] On 21 August 2008, Taliban attacked Ordinance Factory in Wah.[37] In July 2009, a suicide bomber struck a bus that carrying A.Q Khan Research Laboratory scientists. In this incident, 30 people received minor injuries.[38] Moreover, two attacks by Baloch militants on suspected Atomic Energy Commission facilities at Dera Ghazi Khan also drew international attention to the safety and insecurity of Pakistan's nuclear weapons.

On 10 October 2009, nine terrorists, and army officers dressed in army uniform—attacked GHQ,[39] while on June 2014, two suicide bombers killed high ranking military officers linked to Pakistan's nuclear program, in Fateh Jang.[40] During the Kargil war (1999), Pakistan once decided to use nuclear weapons against India. These and other vexations forced India to adopt "Cold Start Doctrine" in 2004.[41]

On 2010, the Rand Corporation in its research paper spotlighted important elements caused constriction between the two South Asian states: "India's frustration with Pakistan's use of sub-conventional approaches under the nuclear umbrella and desire to create a conflict space from which to punish Pakistan for its use of proxy elements or deter it from using these elements has resulted in various efforts to promulgate an Indian doctrine of limited war. India's experience with the limited conflict in Kargil suggests to Indian strategic elites that "limited war" is indeed possible."[42]

The gradual radicalization of Pakistan army and its links with worldwide terrorist organizations over the last 50 years, posed a grave danger to the country's nuclear installations in terms of insider attacks. The spectrum of radicalized elements ranging from military officers to employees of Strategic Planning Division, or officers of nuclear forces, posing precarious threat to nuclear weapons.[43] The Islamic State, Kashmiri organizations, al Qaeda and Taliban are still waiting to receive their share. On 13 October 2016, former Indian national security advisor Shivshankar Menon expressed the same concern, and warned that the real threat to Pakistan nuclear weapons is from rogue elements inside its military rather than from the terrorist outfits. "To my mind, the real threat (to Pak nukes) is from insiders, from a Pakistani pilot or a brigadier".[44]

These and other apprehensions can be confirmed in recent article of expert Madhav Nalapat: "Both the nuclear explosions that took place in North Korea this year are "made in Pakistan", according to those silently, and in total secrecy, tracking the nuclear trajectory of the East Asian country. "By end-2005, it was clear that testing of nuclear devices through computer modeling was not yielding operationally significant results", a key analyst based mainly in Hong Kong claimed, adding that from then onwards, a hyper secretive programme of cooperation between the DPRK military and the Pakistan army was begun. In both countries, the men in uniform control the development and production of nuclear devices".[45]

In Pakistan, the threat of nuclear materials falling into the hands of Taliban and Islamic State (ISIS) is all-round and ambidextrous danger, composed of several different scenarios, such as insiders within the Pakistani nuclear sites can proliferate nuclear weapons and knowledge to terrorist groups; a terrorist group can steal nuclear materials and a radical Islamist group can seize control of the Pakistani government and nuclear arsenal, through a coup or democratic elections.[46]

An Indian military intelligence veteran, Vinayak Bhat noted the same concern in his recent analysis about the danger of nuclear weapons falling into the hands of terrorist groups in Pakistan: "The possibility exists that individuals who work at a facility will remove weapons or weapons components without proper authorization. The insiders' objectives may be to control these items for their own use, transfer

Outlook of South Asia: Trends and Challenges.' The seminar was organized by an Islamabad-based think tank, Centre for International Strategic Studies, and a political foundation, the Konrad Adenauer Stiftung of Germany. The sacked nuclear workers could not clear the Personnel Reliability Programme that was started in mid- 2003/04 to screen the employees working on the sensitive programme, Mr. Raza said.[53] But Mr. Raza did not disclose who were these axed people, and to which ethnic group they were belonged? In 2014 and 2015, in some of my Daily Times articles, I warned that employees of Pakistan nuclear weapons programme are a hidden danger.

On 23 June, 2011, BBC reported Brigadier Ali Khan's incarceration. His wife confirmed to journalists that Mr. Khan was against the killing of Osama bin Laden and drone attacks in Waziristan.[54] Former Director General Inter Services Press Relations Major General Athar Abbas also warned in an interview that the trend of jihadism in army and its links with terrorist groups could be harmful for armed forces.[55] On 21 January 2014, PTI news reported the head of Indian Mujahedeen leader, Ahmad Zarar Siddiq, who admitted that he once asked his Pakistan based friend Riyaz Bhaktal in a phone conversation that if he could be given materials for a dirty bomb to use it against India. With this attempt, the security of Pakistan's fissile materials became a leading security concern for the United States.[56]

The test of Pakistan's ballistic missile, Nasr (70k), capable of carrying a nuclear warhead, and India's ballistic missile, Prahaar and others, once again complicated nuclear weapons race in South Asia.[57] On 10 July 2017, analyst Ankit Panda highlighted Pakistan's missiles race in South Asia: "The Nasr is Pakistan's delivery platform for low-yield nuclear weapons (sometimes called "tactical" nuclear weapons) and has been in development since the mid-2000s. The expected nuclear payload of the Nasr is estimated to be in the sub-kiloton range. According to a statement released by Inter Services Public Relations (ISPR), Pakistan concluded "series of training launches and tests" verifying "new technical parameters" for the Nasr systems."[58] India's tactical nuclear weapons are more dangerous than Pakistan. Indian nuclear missiles like Agni-I, Agni-III, VI and V present a bigger threat to the national security of Pakistan. India also launched various military and surveillance satellites to enter into an anti-satellite weapons and ballistic missile Defense race with

China. The availability of nuclear materials in Pakistani black market, specifically in tribal regions, has raised serious questions about the security of the country's nuclear weapons facilities.[59]

The threat of nuclear terrorism in Pakistan is real. Measures to secure these weapons are complicated while the news of rifts between the democratic government and strategic planning division over the security plan, recruitment of nuclear forces, and policy of good and bad Taliban appeared in newspapers in 2016 and 2017. The failure of General Raheel's shepherded operation Zar-b-Azb to bring stability to Pakistan caused the death of thousand army soldiers and officers in North Waziristan. Numerous forums including International Crisis Group (ICG) criticized the shot and kill policy of General Sharif and his resentment towards Pashtuns of North Waziristan. The ICG in its July 2016 report deeply criticized this strategy of Pakistani army and its brutal military operation. "The militarization of counter-terrorism policy puts at risk Pakistan's evolution toward greater civilian rule, which is itself a necessary but not sufficient condition to stabilize the democratic transition", ICG noted.[60]

On 21 June 2014, Dawn reported more than 600,000 people fled Waziristan. They faced grave difficulties because of transport shortages and over pricing. They were being mistreated by the army officers, verbally abused and physically tortured. The army did not allow blood stained women and children to receive medical treatment in hospitals. The FATA Disaster Management Authority (FDMA) said more than 227,049 people, including 100,370 children were registered at the Saidgi checkpoint on the Bannu-Miran-shah road. An official said thousands of families were on way to Bannu.[61]

The internally displaced people faced numerous difficulties, including kidnapping and humiliation at the hands of army officers in various districts. Daily Times in its editorial page reported the difficulties of IDPs who left their houses under the clouds of brutal war: "In the area void of many trees and shade bearing around 42 degrees temperature nowadays, a total of 36904 families and 4570481 internally displaced individuals registered as per PDMA have walked for miles from North Waziristan in the scorching heat to reside in Bannu city and FR Bannu".[62]

In the end of July 2014, the army began a house-to-house search in Miran shah, killed and kidnapped women and children, and enkindled their houses. Both Pakistani and the Afghan Taliban groups were therefore displaced but not neutralized. Eventually, they were relocated and reorganized. In this brutal war led by war criminal General Raheel Sharif, air strikes and artillery bombardment reduced large parts of the township of Miran Shah and Mir Ali to rubble. That military operation of Pakistan army was the worse form of state terrorism and crime against humanity. Residents of North Waziristan rejected the army claims that they were targeting Taliban. In July 2014, in 16 airstrikes, the army killed dozens of children and women. The army did this earlier in Swat and other regions of FATA in 2009. The army claimed that it achieved its goal, but the ground reality was more sobering. Women and children were at risk, and medical treatment was denied to more than 2500 pregnant women.

In Baluchistan province, thousands Baloch dissidents were tortured to death, forcefully disappeared and kidnapped by the state security agencies. On 09 February 2014, Dawn reported provincial Health Minister of Baluchistan admitted that all decomposed and mutilated bodies found in Tootak area of Khuzdar district were of those who had been missing since long. "This is intolerable and a cause of serious consternation, especially among the youths losing all hopes fast. This is a liability of wrong policies left out by the Musharraf regime for the helpless people of Baluchistan to suffer, which is also providing space to the inimical hidden hands to pursue their nefarious designs." the Minister told Dawn.[63]

In the tail-end of operation Zar-b-Azb, police, ISI, IB, Special Branch, CID and military intelligence agencies in Punjab put Pashtun workers and businessmen under strict surveillance. Police arrested, tortured and abused thousands Pashtuns working in offices, markets and private firms. On 22 February 2017, Dawn reported Punjab police started a surveillance of people belonging to the Federally Administered Tribal Areas (FATA) and decided to issue them chip-based national identity cards equipped with security features. A senior police official told Dawn that more than 5,400 Pashtuns living in Rawalpindi were put under strict surveillance. He said police were also considering containing them to a specific place so that they could be keep under a watch.[64]

On 01 March 2017, Dawn reported informal orders from administrations in some districts argued citizens to keep an eye on Pashtuns. Rawalpindi police began conducting surveillance of people from the tribal areas living within the Rawalpindi-division. Even more disturbingly, a proposal to contain them within a certain place and issue them chip-based identity cards was reportedly under consideration.[65] At the same time, reactions like that of ANP leader Asfandyar Wali Khan, who threatened forcible eviction of Punjabis from KP. Khyber Pakhtunkhwa (KP) Chief Minister Pervez Khattak said no one is more Pakistani than the Pakhtuns and any discrimination to them is unlawful act. Speaking to a gathering by the Pakhtoon Welfare Organization, Mr. Khattak said, Pakhtuns were Pakistani and considered Punjabis, Baloch and Sindhis their brothers.

On 03 March 2017, Fawad Ali Shah reported the humiliation of a Pashtun young man by local police: "Amir Khan, a resident of Nowshera district of Khyber-Pakhtunkhwa was sleeping in his apartment when the police knocked at his door. "They told me that my neighbors thought that I was a terrorist." The 35-year-old was living in that apartment for seven years and never faced any issues with his neighbors. "They [the police officials] were in no mood to talk," he said. "As soon as they entered my apartment they started asking questions about my links to terrorists." One of the policemen slapped him.[66] On 21 February 2017, Pakistan Today reported citizens were asked to report any persons of Pashtun descent to the Punjab police as part of an ongoing crackdown launched against terrorists in the province.[67] However, on 28 February 2017, Express Tribune reported the same story, and NADRA allegedly began suspending the Computerized National Identity Cards issued to hundreds of Pashtuns living throughout Lahore in November 2016.[68] Finally, I am highly indebted of my publisher Rohan Vij of VIJ Books India Pvt Ltd for his encouragement and stimulation.

Musa Khan Jalalzai,
April, 2018, London

Summary

The story of Pakistan's nuclear weapons has now become dreamy and oblivious by reason of national and international print media is no longer interested in highlighting its offensiveness, and inoffensiveness, its effectiveness and ineffectiveness.[1] In February 2004, Dr. Abdul Qadeer Khan was forced by military dictator to appear on a state-run television to admit responsibility for operating an international black market in nuclear-weapons materials.[2] General Musharraf saved Miltablishmen.[3] Mr. Musharraf told the Times that he was aware of Abdul Qadeer Khan's secret nuclear business with Iran, North Korea, and Malaysia.[4] Pakistani leaders viewed nuclear weapons as their deterrent against a conventional attack, and Cold Start in particular.[5] Pakistan army also empowered local commanders to launch retaliatory nuclear strikes on the assumption the chain of command is disrupted.[6]

The country's nuclear smuggling and the challenge posed to its nuclear security by terrorist groups like Taliban, and ISIS need a detailed argument in order to elucidate the future prospect of its insecure nuclear weapons. The challenges coexist and often overlap, leading to their reinforcement.[7] For instance, the presence of the terrorist network such as Lashkar-e-Toiba and its affiliates in South Asia and, increasingly, the Middle East, the fragility of many governments, and the existence of Pakistan's insecure nuclear weapons arsenal exacerbated the possibility of nuclear terrorism.[8]

In a provocative statement, India's Army Chief General Bipin Rawat warned that Indian army was ready to call Pakistan's "nuclear bluff" and cross the border to carry out any operation if asked by government. "We will call the [nuclear] bluff of Pakistan. If we will have to really confront the Pakistanis, and a task is given to us, we are not going to say we cannot cross the border because they have nuclear weapons. We will have to call their nuclear bluff," Hindustan Times quoted Gen Rawat as saying.[9] He was responding to a question during a press conference on the possibility of Pakistan using its nuclear weapons in case the situation along the border deteriorates.

However, Pakistan challenged India to test its resolve over a nuclear war in response to Indian Army Chief's recent comments. Foreign Minister Khawaja Asif denounced Indian Army Chief Gen. Bipin Rawat's remarks as "irresponsible" and vowed to expose "Pakistan's nuclear bogey" in the event of a war between the two countries. "Very irresponsible statement by Indian Army Chief, not befitting his office, amounts to invitation for nuclear encounter. If that is what they desire, they are welcome to test our resolve. The general's doubt would swiftly be removed", Insha-Allah," Asif wrote on his Twitter.[10]

Pakistan army has played an important role in the country's nuclear black marketing business as it has been dominant power in decision making process at various times by imposing martial laws. The primary objective of all of Pakistan's four military regimes was to destabilize Afghanistan and India, promote terrorism, nuclear black marketing, and narco-smuggling across South Asia. Miltablishment failed to put forward a long-term nation building strategy that could forge the country into a cohesive and a stable whole.[11]

Spread of nuclear, chemical and biological weapons by the army generals, proliferators have been able to procure and acquire goods for these programmes with relative ease.[12] The country promoted procurement of sensitive goods and technology for illicit WMD programmes across the globe. Individuals were trained to carryout proliferation.[13] Later on, these individuals used networks of middlemen and agents located overseas to procure necessary materials.[14] Furthermore, these proliferators used of several transshipment points before the goods reached their end destination. Trans-shipment points, where goods can be relabeled, are a useful way for proliferators to obscure the logistical path.[15]

Now as Pakistan plays different games against Afghanistan and India, its political and military establishment is struggling to counter the wrath of the United States by dancing to Russian tango in the Middle East and Afghanistan. Pressure on Pakistan from the UK and US to put a cap on the proliferation of terror from its soil in India and Afghanistan has been on the rise in recent years, with numerous commentators pointing towards the need to constrain it regarding this.[16]

Abhay K. Singh in his research paper noted the US standpoint against Pakistan's terrorism sponsorship in South Asia: "The US Department of State, in its reports on terrorism in 2015 and 2016, pointed out that Pakistan-based terrorist organizations have continued to threaten the US interests in Afghanistan. Further, Pakistan has not taken sufficient action against the Afghan Taliban, Lashkar e-Tayyiba (LeT) and Jaish-e-Mohammad (JeM), which have continued to operate, train, organize and fundraise in its territory. The US has been progressively tightening the screws on Pakistan. In July 2017, the US with held $50 million in reimbursements to Pakistan, adding to the $300 million that had been already withheld in light of the above-mentioned US reports, due to insufficient action against the Haqqani Network group. Though Pakistan was expecting a rap on the knuckles, President Trump went further. He said the US would 'further develop its strategic partnership with India' and asks the latter to contribute more to stabilize Afghanistan".[17]

On 11 January 2018, Diplomat Magazine reported the US President Donald Trump's inaugural tweet of 2018, suggesting that recently revamped U.S. South Asia strategy was in jeopardy. The South Asia strategy was in some ways a test run for the National Security Strategy (NSS). President Trump announced the new South Asia strategy on August 21, 2017, and stated that "Pakistan and India are two nuclear-armed states whose tense relations threaten to spiral into conflict. And that could happen.[18]

This narrative of Pakistan's failure in resolving its key security challenge can be found in the book of C. Christine Fair, who closely observed Pakistan miltablishment and its illegal nuclear and military tactics. "Pakistani generals are not fundamentalist Islamists themselves. They drink alcohol all day and in the evening give lectures of how to be a good Muslim. Supporting Islamist groups is the central objective of the Pakistani army to give itself an Islamic identity, a special place in the Islamic world, and save itself from a virtual collapse. Pakistani army supports separatists, funds, and even sends insurgents into Kashmir and other parts of India as they fight against India to create a view that

Muslims and Hindus cannot live in peace in one state. Pakistani army supports Islamist radical elements within its own territory in order to make sure that the secular wind blowing from all directions from Europe and America on the West and from India on the East is put far away from its borders".[19]

Consultant of the Institute for Defence Studies and Analyses (IDSA), New Delhi, PK Upadhyay has also painted an ugly picture of the establishment of terror networks within the army ranks in his research paper: "The integration of "terror" into military concepts of war and strategy and involvement of civilians in a total holy war naturally led to evolution of the idea of non-state players who could be acting in concert with the military as part of their pre-action preparations, including striking "terror" in the hearts of the enemy. The launching of various civilian militant groups during Zia-ul Haq's time could be traced to the evolution of this military doctrine. Sipah-e-Sahaba Pakistan (SSP) and its militant wing the Lashkar-e-Jhangvi were floated to quell Shiite and Christian opposition to pro-Sunni Islamization measures and the promulgation of Blasphemy Law, respectively. Pretty soon this doctrine of "terror" was married to 1976 White Paper on Kashmir, brought out by Z.A. Bhutto regime and Kashmir specific terror groups were launched, beginning with JKLF and then JI floated Hizb-ul Mujahedeen and others.[20]

Trained and funded by military establishment, Lashkar-e-Toiba, Al-Qaeda, Lashkar-e-Omar, Jaish-e-Mohammad, Sipah-e-Sahaba, the Jammu Kashmir Liberation Front, Jamaat-ul-Da-wah, Harkat-ul-Jihad al-Islami, the Haqqani Network, Daesh, Jamaat-ul-Mujahedeen Bangladesh and the Afghan Taliban are being used against neighbouring states as a foreign policy tools by Pakistan.[21] On 05 December 2017, days after declaring himself the greatest supporter of Lashkar-e-Taiba (LeT), former President Pervez Musharraf said that his party can form an alliance with the proscribed Jamaatud Dawa (JuD) and its chief, Hafiz Saeed. "If it is meant to be, it will be," Musharraf told Aaj News.[22] General Musharraf was happy to join the terrorist organization for election purposes: "There have been no talks yet, but if they want to be included in the alliance, by all means, I will welcome them," Musharraf said.[23] International community, including the US and India, consider JuD to be a front for LeT, the militant group blamed for the

2008 Mumbai attacks that left 166 people dead. "I spoke about Hafiz Saeed and I will say it proudly that LeT and JuD are both very good organizations of Pakistan," Musharraf added. "In 2005, I saw that they were the best engineers. They did the best work at the time of the earthquake [in Islamabad]." "They are not in favour of Al Qaeda or the Taliban.[24] Why are we pushing them to the wall? They have religious followers, youngsters who are religious. They are not terrorists and we should tell [this to] America and the world," Musharraf said."[25]

Milli Muslim League (MML), a new militant party controlled by 26/11 Mumbai attacks mastermind Hafiz Saeed, backed a candidate in the September by-election for a seat vacated by ousted Prime Minister Nawaz Sharif in constituency-120 in Lahore.[26] Mr. Saeed is an internationally proscribed terrorist, and the United States has offered a $10 million bounty for his capture.[27] A report released by Reuters stated that MML and other militant groups' foray into politics follows the integration plan.[28] Nawaz Sharif's three confidants and a retired army general had said that the plan had been presented by ISI to Sharif last year. However, the former premier had rejected it.[29]

On 06 October 2017, Pakistan army admitted to associations between terrorist groups and its top intelligence agency, Inter-Services Intelligence (ISI).[30] However; it added that the "links" did not necessarily mean "support" of the terror organizations.[31] Pakistan Army spokesperson Major General Asif Ghafoor, while addressing a press conference said, "There's a difference between support and having links. Name any intelligence agency which does not have links. Links can be positive." Mr. Ghafoor, during his press meet, also said that the Pakistani government was discussing ways to attempt to integrate these militant-linked groups into the mainstream of the country's politics.[32] More than 35 to 40% Army recruitments during Gen Zia-ul-Haq years went to madrassa pass-outs. Despite attempts to weed out or segregate religious hard liners, there were many officers who secretly collaborated with extremist groups.[33]

In his research paper published by Journal of Defence Studies, (Vol. 5 No. 04 October 2011), a retired Special Secretary, Cabinet Secretariat, Government of India, Mr. Rana Banerji has painted a disconcerted picture of fundamentalist approach of the army during the ISI Chief Javed Nasir's tenure:

"As ISI chief, Javed Nasir was keen to find ways of supporting Islamic causes worldwide. He set up arrangements to arm and supports Bosnian Muslims, in collaboration with Iran. He saw opportunities to hurt India, not only in Kashmir but in other regions as well. He is reported to have established contact with Tamil extremists (LTTE) and set up a gun running operation with links to LTTE in Bangkok. He funded Arakenese Muslims (Rohingiyas)-who inhabit the area bordering Myanmar's frontier with Bangladesh, to help them in their struggle for an independent enclave. A strange, almost non-military atmosphere developed at the ISI office during Javed Nasir's tenure. Bearded officers in 'shalwar kameez', many of them hitched up to their ankles (a signature practice of the Tablighi Jamaat) strolling about in office corridors. The 'strong room', which had currency stacked to the roof during the heyday of Afghan operations was now empty as 'adventurist' ISI officers had been allowed to take away suitcases filled with cash to the field, ostensibly for operations even in Central Asian countries".[34]

Experts believe that one of the biggest threats to peace and security in South Asia could be the presence of extremist elements within Pakistan's military establishment.[35] Writer Mr. Saleem Shehzad in his book exposed links of ex-officers of the Armed Forces with Al Qaeda and Taliban. Many junior officers and other ranks still place faith above the country and accordingly many former officers who were earlier involved with Afghan and Kashmiri 'jihad' have joined Al Qaeda.[36] Number of army officers became members of extremist groups during the Afghan jihad in 1980s.[37] Radicalization and sectarian trends were facilitated within the armed forces by radicalized generals and religious groups.[38] On the other hand people like Hafiz Saeed, Mullah Fazlullah and Omar Khalid Khorasani and many mullahs were patronized and perceived as strategic assets to counter enemies, but they actually became Frankensteins and started killing the creators.[39]

Most recently, attack on a Karachi naval facility was likely facilitated by an al Qaeda cell within the Navy itself. Chief of Army Staff Ashfaq Parvez Kayani and other Army brass were worried about the enemy within. However, some Army personnel were arrested for ties with Hizb ut-Tahrir, an outlawed extremist organization in Pakistan.[40] The Pakistani Army has long relied on Islam within the institution, but its un-Islamic characters created misunderstanding. Islam has also served to motivate the Army to fight an enemy that has always been conventionally superior: India.[41] The army supported both Imran Khan and Tahir-ul-Qadri. Mr. Imran Khan and Dr. Tahir-ul-Qadri brought Pakistan to a point where democratic forces were likely to be subdued if the military becomes actively involved.[42] Gen Raheel Sharif met Prime Minister Nawaz Sharif to force him on reconciliation process, but Prime Minister refused. There was a group of five army commanders who felt that the army should have intervened in the crisis.[43]

In November 2017, a scandalous video of Pakistan army emerged that showed a senior Pakistan Army general handing out cash to protesters who held several cities of the country to ransom.[44] The Pakistan government struck a deal with the protesters as part of which the law minister quit and protesters, who were arrested over the weekend, were released.[45] The protesters, belonging to Tehreek-e-Labaik (TLP) Pakistan had staged a sit-in in the capital Islamabad for about three weeks. General Naved was seen giving the money and heard saying, "Please take it.[46] That video exposed conspiracy of military establishment and its nexus with fundamentalists in the country.

The army long ago arrogated the right to step in whenever it felt wanted and repeatedly reminds Pakistanis that civilian leaders are the bane of the nation while the army is the only savoir.[47] Analyst Mr. Shekhar Gupta in his article noted the moral and political weaknesses of the army and argued: "Pakistan's military establishment lost Pakistan's territory, ideology, financial and intellectual capital, ruined its institutions, democracy, the respect for its passport and, like it or not, reduced its status to a globally acknowledged university of jihad, this is the real problem with the Pakistani army. It is delusional. It's tough, efficient, audacious, but its brains sit in the nether and wrong part of its autonomy instead of the head".[48]

However, Pakistan lost a large part of its territory, and a majority of its population, thus knocking its ideological basis of the two-nation theory. An independent Bangladesh is now doing much better than Pakistan.[49] The army has a long history of strategic incompetence.[50] The army has been rewarded by its foreign patrons despite its incompetence and unaccountability.[51] Pakistan army acts virtually as an economic class and in doing so it has no qualms about deploying and using jihadi proxies both at home and across the borders.[52] No less than a former director general of ISI justified the domestic blowback from using the jihadists such as a brutal massacre of 144 schoolchildren in my hometown as mere "collateral damage" or the cost of doing business.[53] The most disheartening saga of the Baloch people's struggle is very much connected to the rising number of "enforced disappearances" which is wreaking havoc across the province.[54] Writer Khursheed Sardar in his recent analysis noted important fact on the development of radicalization in Pakistani society: "The worldwide acceptance of the idea that Pakistan is not only internalizing but mainstreaming militancy and terrorism should not surprise Pakistanis at all. Ours is a country where a convicted terrorist like Hafiz Saeed is not only allowed to run his own "charity" (Jamat-ud-Dawa), he is also allowed to form a political party (Milli Muslim League) as an extension of this charity...... Pakistanis, thus, must ask themselves: whom are we trying to fool when we refuse to accept that our country's armed forces, and we, the people, ourselves, are involved in safeguarding terrorists and terrorist organizations? The country has repeatedly yielded global most wanted criminals, dead or alive. Leaving aside the controversial assassination of Osama bin Laden, the likes of Egyptian terrorists Ahmed Mohammed Hamed Ali and Saeed al-Masri, Saudi terrorist Adnan Gulshair el Shukrijumah, Libyan terrorist Abu Laith al-Libbi and American terrorist Adam Yahiye Gadahn were all reportedly killed on Pakistani soil".[55]

Pakistan's military establishment has long been accused of fostering militant groups as proxy fighters opposing neighbouring arch-enemy India, a charge the army denies. Saeed's religious charity launched the Milli Muslim League party within two weeks after the court ousted Sharif over corruption allegations.[56] On 10 September 2014: "Unfortunately, there are a number of cases where those with links to the armed forces have been involved in attacks targeting the military. For example, former army medic Dr. Usman was said to be one of the main planners in the 2009 militant assault on GHQ. Also, dreaded militant Adnan Rasheed, known for various terrorist exploits, including a failed attempt on Pervez Musharraf's life, was a former air force man before he turned his guns on the state. Even in the navy's case it was reported that information from within the service was provided to those involved in the 2011 Mehran base raid".[57]

The recruitments of Islamic State (ISIS) by Pakistan raised serious question about the army so called operations against terrorist groups, but Foreign and the Interior Ministries of Pakistan have been constantly denying the presence and activities of ISIS in Pakistan.[58] In 2016 and in 2017, Pakistani intelligence arrested the ISIS trained members from Lahore, Islamabad, Karachi and Sialkot. Men were recruited as jihadist or mujahids and women as jihadi wives to provide sexual needs of fighters who are fighting in Syria, Iraq and Afghanistan.[59] This encouragement and sponsorship of terrorist organizations prompted decrepitude and dilapidation in relations between Pakistan and its neighbours.

The threat of nuclear weapons falling into the hands of terrorist organizations exists. The Islamic State (ISIS) and Mujahedeen Hind have already hoped that they will get nuclear material from Pakistan. Close relations between Pakistan army, Lashkar-e-Toiba and sectarian organization is the sign of alarm. The army openly supports these organizations against democratic government, India and Afghanistan. A full threat analysis needs to look specifically at how and where the terrorists could actually get hold of CBRN material. In recent years, perceptive observers in Pakistani media have noted that Pakistan "remains an enigma" "clutching at an identity beset by an ambiguous relation to Islam" and struggling still with a coherent national identity". Moreover, it is perhaps "the only countries in the world, where some of the important opinion makers still ask, 65 years after its founding, why Pakistan was created in the first place" and other similar questions, like, "Does Pakistan Make Sense?"[60]

Chapter 1

Pakistan's Miltablishment, Abdul Qadeer Khan's Nuclear Smuggling Networks and the Threat of Nuclear Terrorism in South Asia

The US President Donald Trump's strategy for South Asia noted that Pakistan's nuclear weapons could fall into the wrong hands. "We are particularly concerned by the development of tactical nuclear weapons that are designed for use in battlefield. We believe that these systems are more susceptible to terrorist theft and increase the likelihood of nuclear exchange in the region," the Trump administration warned.[1] Pakistan tested its nuclear bomb (28 May 1998) in Chaghi Hills of Baluchistan Province. The test ceremony was arranged in a poor and agonized province, where Pakistani intelligence agencies and paramilitary forces kidnapped and disappeared 25,000 Baloch men, women and children in so-called military operations during the last two decades. Both poor and rich Pakistanis do not support miltablishment's illegal nuclear black marketing of GHQ and its associates. They need peace, food, security and justice, they do not need nuclear or truck bomb that prompts fatalities, death and destruction. After the test, military establishment started incapacitating residents of Afghanistan's border provinces by dumping nuclear waste inside the country.[2] Researcher Iram Khalid and Zakia Bano in their research papers highlighted Pakistan's resolve as a nuclear state:

Pakistan exploded nuclear test on 28 May 1998 in the Chaghi Hills which is a long the Western border of the province of Baluchistan, Many personalities and organizations were involved in developing the bomb against a backdrop of political, security and economic constraints, as well as opportunities. Pakistan decided to fulfill almost accurately its promise to "eat grass or go hungry" in its mission for the development of nuclear weapons. Pakistan's nuclear program started under severely complex and challenging security dilemmas and circumstances. Historical experience, a blend of cultural nuances, idiosyncrasies of personalities, and domestic politics existed throughout the nuclear development.[3]

In 1950s, Pakistan started discussion on retrieving nuclear weapons to respond to the Indian efforts of destabilizing the country. India dismembered Pakistan in 1971, and continued to challenge the existence of the country by developing nuclear and biological weapons.[4] Pakistani business firms in Europe and the United States invested in the development of Islamic Bomb. In their Congressional Research Report, Paul K. Kerr and Marry Beth Nikitin (2012) noted important points about Pakistan's nuclear journey through different phases:

Pakistan's nuclear energy program dates back to the 1950s, but it was the loss of East Pakistan (now Bangladesh) in a war with India that probably triggered a January 1972 political decision (just one month later) to begin a secret nuclear program. Deterring India's nuclear weapons and augmenting Pakistan's inferior conventional forces are widely believed to be the primary missions for Islamabad's nuclear arsenal........Highly-enriched Uranium (HEU) is one of two types of fissile materials used in nuclear weapons; the other is plutonium. The country's main enrichment facility is a centrifuge plant located at Kahuta; Pakistan may have other enrichment sites. Islamabad gained enrichment-related technology from many sources..........Pakistan produced fissile material for its nuclear weapons using gas-centrifuge-based uranium enrichment technology, which it mastered by the mid-1980s. Highly-enriched uranium (HEU) is one of two types of fissile material used in nuclear weapons; the other is plutonium. The county's main enrichment facility is a centrifuge plant located at Kahuta; Pakistan may have other enrichment sites. Islamabad gained enrichment-related technology from many sources. This extensive assistance is reported to have included uranium enrichment technology from Europe, blueprints for a small nuclear weapon from China, and missile technology from China". The United States had information during the 1970s that Pakistan was constructing uranium facility. Abdul Qadeer Khan has stated that Pakistan begin enriching uranium in 1979 and produced HEU in 1983. Although Pakistan subsequently told the United Stated that it would produce only low-enriched uranium (Which is not used as fissile material in nuclear weapons).[5]

On 01 May 1983, General Zia-ul-Haq visited Dr. Khan's Laboratory, and directed Engineering Research Laboratories, to pursue a nuclear bomb design for a cold test.[6] After the death of Muhammad Zia-ul-Haq in 1988, cooperation with Iran and North Korea on nuclear missile was expedited but Miltablishment never allowed civilian Prime Ministers a single visit to nuclear plants. Iram Khalid and Zakia Bano spotlighted Pakistan's efforts in developing nuclear weapons:

> Dr. Khan was doing the whole task under General Zia. Mr. Zia encouraged both labs, for if one of them was destroyed by the enemy action or sabotage, then the other would continue to manufacture nuclear weapons. This strategy would save nuclearization from being halted completely. Extraction of national uranium was done at Dera Ghazi Khan. Designing and production of fuel was being done at the PAEC. Pakistan Ordinance Factory (POF) was performing the function of fabrication and the machining of the weapons. KRL was running the task of enriching the uranium.........Benazir Bhutto became the Prime Minister of Pakistan in December 1988. She won the election that was held after Zia's death in an air crash. She demanded a reconsideration of Pakistan's nuclear program. She expressed her views in an interview to the Indian Express; 'we only want nuclear energy for peaceful purposes and we are prepared to set all doubts at rest on this score because it has undermined our relations with other countries and has complicated matters for Pakistan.[7]

Pakistan continued its efforts of developing nuclear weapons program and succeeded to test its bomb in 1998. There was news in international press that Pakistan developed more than 100 to 200 kilograms of Highly Enriched Uranium (HEU) in 1998, but military establishment denied and said Pakistan believe in peace and stability of the region, the fact is the country's nuclear program is both civil and military in nature. Former Defense Minister Mr. Khawaja Muhammad Asif warned that if India use nuclear weapons against Pakistan, his country would also use nuclear weapons against it.[8] This statement raised many questions including Pakistan's intention about the use of nuclear weapons against its neighbours. Press reports identified Pakistan's 15 nuclear sites located in different parts of the country. The Project Alpha (2016), in its recent report highlights evolution of Pakistan nuclear bomb efforts:

> Pakistan's nuclear weapons are fuelled by both weapons-grade uranium and plutonium. Both routes of fissile material production are controlled largely by the PAEC facilities across the nuclear fuel cycle being used for the purposes of producing nuclear weapons. Pakistan's fissile material is mined, converted, and processed in a series of non-safeguarded PAEC facilities, which are described below. Pakistan has at least three operational uranium mines. Pakistan's first uranium mine, built at Baghalchur along with a uranium mill in the 1970s, is now reportedly no longer in operation. [The Baghalchur mine (BC-I) forms the basis of a major nuclear complex at Dera Ghazi Khan, which is described below.] Additional uranium mines have since been built at Qabul Khel, Nangar Nal and Taunsa. All three mines use the in-situ leaching process. Pakistan has also received uranium compounds from abroad. In the late 1970s, it obtained 110-150 tones of yellowcake (uranium oxide) from Niger, which was put under IAEA safeguards; and then purchased 450 tones of Niger-origin yellowcake from Libya, which was not safeguarded and used to produce uranium hexafluoride (UF6).[9]

Between 1970s and 2008, several Arab and non-Arab states contributed into Pakistan's nuclear program on the pretext that they will also receive their share in the Islamic bomb. Military Generals and Dr. Abdul Qadeer Khan shared information with Iran, Libya, North Korea, China and Saudi Arabia, and received billion dollars in cash. Saudi Arabia financially backed Pakistan's Islamic bomb in 1970s, 1980s, and 1990s. In 1999, Prince Sultan visited the country's uranium enrichment facility. In 1993, the New Yorker in its report noted Dr. Abdul Qadeer Khan's remarks:

> Western Countries had never imagined that a poor and backward country like Pakistan would end their (nuclear) monopoly in such a short time......As soon as they realized that Pakistan dashed their dream to the ground, they pounced at Pakistan and me like hungry jackals and began attacking us with all kinds of accusations and falsehoods.......How could they tolerate a Muslim country becoming their equal in this field......All western countries including Israel are not only the enemies of Pakistan but in fact of Islam.[10]

Pakistan nuclear material smugglers were also in the field to collect bomb related information from across the globe. Most of Pakistan's nuclear smuggling networks were comprised of businessmen and middle class smugglers headed by Abdul Qadeer Khan and Miltablishment (GHQ). Before the fall of the Taliban regime in Kabul, Pakistan offered services to al Qaeda for developing its non-conventional capabilities. In 2001, Sultan Bashiruddin Mahmood and Choudhry Abdul Majeed visited Osama bin Laden in Kabul. Over the course of three days of intense conversation, they finally reached a conclusion that Pakistan will help Osama in developing weapons of mass destruction in Afghanistan. Sultan Bashiruddin Mahmood had as a uranium expert served in Pakistan's Atomic Energy Commission for 30 year.[11]

After the fall of Taliban government in Kabul in 2001, Pakistani politicians and miltablishment faced deep crisis when the United States focused its intelligence surveillance on the country's nuclear weapons security. President Mushraf hammered Dr. Abdul Qadeer Khan and forced him to immediately respond to international community concerns, but never asked his warlords on their illegal nuclear black marketing across the globe. Dr. Abdul Qadeer Khan was viewed as the founder of Pakistan nuclear Islamic bomb. He was arrested by General Musharraf in January 2004 for his controversial role in nuclear smuggling, and clandestine relationship with North Korea, Saudi Arabia, Al Qaeda, Libya and Taliban.[12] As a matter of fact, the army was behind all these illegal nuclear black marketing, but General Musharraf tried to protect military generals by making Dr. Khan a scapegoat. Former Army Chief General Mirza Aslam Baig was widely criticized for his alleged involvement with the nuclear program of Iran.[13] As a Chief of Army Staff, General Baig had initiated lectureship programs to have better understanding on nuclear policy matters and policy development.[14] General Baig had calculated that such cooperation with Iran was popular and that, Saudi Arabia and the Persian Gulf were less popular as American clients in the region.[15]

Pakistan's nuclear program, however, was essentially intended to counter its conventional forces inferiority vis-a-vis India.[16] After the Pokhran II test in 1998, and the Kargil episode, the real nature of nuclear weapons was emphasized, and the imperative of military involvement dawned on the establishment.[17] In 1999, during the Kargil war, Pakistan's military establishment readied Islamic bomb to attack India while its forces were defeated by Indian army. After this irresponsible act of intervention, the threat of nuclear terrorism in South Asia became real, because measures to secure these weapons were unprofessional and weak as the news of differences between the democratic government and strategic planning division over the security plan, recruitment of nuclear forces, and policy of good and bad Taliban appeared in some sections of print media.

Pakistani journalist Khaled Ahmad in his article noted General Baig's encouragement of Dr. Abdul Qadeer Khan to proliferate technology to Iran and North Korea. Prime Minister Nawaz Sharif was shocked when enlightened of General Baig secret nuclear deal with Iran.[18] In 1990, Pakistan army contacted Iraqi regime for nuclear business. In 1990, United Nations found a memo with details of Pakistani weapons inspectors meeting with Iraqi secret agents asking price of five million dollars for the network's assistance plus an additional ten percent commission for all procurement.[19] Later on, Dr. Abdul Qadeer Khan expanded his network to Kenya, Mali, Mauritania, Morocco, Niger, Nigeria, Sudan, and Tunisia, which caused deep concern for the CIA and MI6 leadership.[20] Throughout the 1980s and 1990s, Pakistan's military established a network of nuclear weapons in Middle East and South East Asia to establish its political and military influence there. Journalist F.M Shakil reported Dr. Abdul Qadeer Khan's laboratory in Karachi provided foreign states with the designs for Pakistan's older centrifuges, as well as more advanced and efficient models:

Khan and his associates used a factory in Malaysia to manufacture key parts for their centrifuges. The other necessary parts were purchased through network operatives in Europe, Middle East, and Africa. His main beneficiaries were the North Koreans, who were using plutonium as early as the 1980s before Khan started sending them equipment for uranium enrichment, as well as designs and lists of materials for centrifuges. After 11 September, 2001, the world's focus was on Weapons of Mass Destruction in Iraq, but nuclear proliferation was going on in Pakistan, where Khan stood at the heart of an intricate worldwide network. Babar did not divulge the identities of those he believed were involved in the transfer of nuclear technology – but it is well understood he was alluding to Pakistan's army.[21]

Terrorist networks of Taliban, Lashkar-e-Toiba and the Islamic State in Pakistan had put the security of nuclear weapon at spike. In 2009, Gen Pervez Musharraf said his government adopted professional security measures, but from 2009 to 2011, terrorists attempted several times to destroy nuclear weapons or obtain it through their networks. Non-proliferation expert, Mr. Paul K. Kerr and Mary Beth Nikitin (2016) explain these measures in their recent research paper:

Pakistani efforts to improve the security of its nuclear weapons have been ongoing and have included some cooperation with the United States; former Pakistani President Pervez Musharraf told a journalist in 2009 that Islamabad has "given State Department non-proliferation experts insight into the command and control of the Pakistani arsenal and its on-site safety and security procedures." Moreover, following the 2004 revelations of an extensive international nuclear proliferation network run by Pakistani nuclear official Abdul Qadeer Khan, as well as possible connections between Pakistani nuclear scientists and Al Qaeda, Islamabad has made additional efforts to improve export controls and monitor nuclear personnel. The main security challenges for Pakistan's nuclear arsenal are keeping the integrity of the command structure, ensuring physical security, and preventing illicit proliferation from insiders. Some observers are also concerned about the risk of nuclear war between India and Pakistan. The two countries most recently came to the brink of full-scale war in 1999 and 2002, and, realizing the dangers, have developed some risk reduction measures to prevent accidental nuclear war. Nevertheless, Pakistan continues to produce fissile material for weapons and appears to be augmenting its weapons production facilities as well as deploying additional delivery vehicles—steps that will enable both quantitative and qualitative improvements in Islamabad's nuclear arsenal.[22]

The country is now in deep crisis to maintain the security of it military installation in the presence of widespread terrorist networks. As terrorist organizations established their networks within the armed forces, the fear of theft exacerbated, and the army set up screening procedures. Nuclear expert, Mr. Bruno Tertrais has elucidated the screening process in his recent paper:

> Two different programmes exist: a Human Reliability Program for civilian personnel and a Personnel Reliability Program for military personnel. They have been applied to up to 4000 people (although the numbers vary), including about 2000 scientists or engineers working in particularly sensitive areas or who have critical knowledge, and who continue to be monitored after retirement. The Strategic Plans Division (SPD) plans to extend these programmes to 10 000 personnel with access to sensitive information. The screening process can take up to a year and involves four different agencies: the Intelligence Bureau, the Inter-Services Intelligence (ISI), the Military Intelligence and the SPD. There are clearance rechecks every two years. Unsurprisingly, checks are said to focus on finances and religious beliefs. Punjabis (who make up two-thirds of Pakistan's officers) are reportedly privileged over people of other origins. There have been reports of attempts by militant groups to infiltrate the nuclear complex through Pakistani scientists trained abroad. SPD officials estimate that 7000 to 10 000 people out of a total of 70 000 people in the nuclear and missile complex are nuclear scientists and engineers.[23]

In February 2004, Dr. Abdul Qadeer Khan admitted that he had transferred nuclear weapons technology to Iran, Libya, North Korea and other countries in 1990s.[24] Not only Khan, military Generals retrieved millions of dollars from this criminal business. Abdul Qadeer Khan told investigators that he had purveyed nuclear technology to some

Muslim states. According to the NTI report, Mr. Khan purveyed nuclear technology to Iran and Libya through a Malaysian middleman, Buhary Syed Abu Tahir:

> On June 7, 2004, Pakistan introduced a bill in the National Assembly, known as the Export Control on Goods, Technologies, Material and Equipment related to Nuclear and Biological Weapons and their Delivery Systems Act, 2004. The bill was subsequently passed by the Pakistan National Assembly and Senate on September 14 and 19, respectively. The bill stipulated that any violation of the act would result in up to 14 years' imprisonment, forfeiture of all property and assets to the government, and a fine of 5 million rupees (about $86,500). Any individuals attempting to commit or abetting the commission of such offenses would be charged as if they had themselves committed the violation. It is believed that should further evidence against Khan's surface, the conditional pardon he received from President Musharraf could be withdrawn. However, recent statements by the Pakistani Foreign Minister, Khurshid Mahmud Kasuri, indicate that the bill will not be applied retroactively, and will not have any effect on the cases of A.Q. Khan and other scientists involved in the smuggling ring.[25]

After the Dr. Khan's confessions in 2004, the emergence of GHQ nuclear black marketing networks, the fall of Taliban regime in Kabul, and the US war on terrorism, international community influenced nuclear threat perceptions in Pakistan. Terrorist infrastructure in the country adversely affected its relations with the United States and NATO member states. These developments prompted terror attacks in Mumbai, Madrid, London and Karachi. In 2001, and 2008, terrorist groups carry out attacks against civilian and military installations in India and Pakistan. The development of Pakistan's weapons of mass destruction further added to the previous concerns of proliferation and stability, and generated heightened allegations and scrutiny. Nuclear power plants, reactors and laboratories became vulnerable to acts of sabotage and blatant terrorist attacks that could cause the release of dangerous amounts of radioactive materials.

During the last 16 years, Pakistan and India have doubled the number of their nuclear warheads, making them the fastest growing nuclear weapons states in the world. However, India deployed a nuclear triad of bombers, missiles and a submarine capable of firing nuclear weapons.[26] Pakistan also developed a network of nuclear weapons factories, plutonium reactors and nuclear missiles.[27] India invested a lot on spy satellites, aircraft, drones and early warning radar, while Pakistan has developed spy and modern warning systems.[28] At present, both the states hold a massive nuclear stockpile and the size of this stockpile doubled since 1998. Both states have developed cruise missiles and are seeking nuclear submarines.[29]

China's tacit support to Pakistan for boosting the country's nuclear weapons is considered to have strategic implications for India. All these weapons and strategic developments in both the states mean that confidence-building measures remain only on paper with no one wanting to extend the hand of cooperation.[30] In 2008, entered to one of Pakistan's main nuclear weapons assembly sites in Wah, and in 2012, terrorist attacked Kamra nuclear airbase. The government's inability to prevent attacks on its most important institutions deepened existing fears about the security of Pakistan's nuclear weapons.[31]

In 2015 and 2016, Pakistani Taliban and Afghan based extremist organization targeted several places in the country that raised serious questions about the safety and security of Pakistan nuclear assets. The fear and frustration of Pakistani parliamentarians intensified while news of nuclear proliferation business of Gen Musharraf appeared in newspapers.

In 2017, a pair of Pakistani lawmakers demanded a "thorough probe" into the proliferation of "several tons" of nuclear materials to Iran, Libya and North Korea under the country's former military ruler, Pervez Musharraf, who was in power from 1999 to 2008. Pakistan People's Party Senator Farhatullah Babar and Jamiat-e-Ulama-e-Islam's Hafiz Hamdullah said that the father of its nuclear program, Dr Abdul Qadeer Khan, was not a lone actor in the "global spread of nuclear technology" from Pakistan, despite making a confession to that effect in 2004. Several others "characters" played a major role in facilitating the materials' proliferation, they claim, but were spared by the president.[32]

Mr. Babar and Hamdullah were calling for the "entire network" of proliferators to be exposed irrespective of their status and standing. Mr.

Babar stressed that it was inconceivable to think that a single individual could have smuggled out huge centrifuge machines and other nuclear material without collusion from "other players." He did not divulge the identities of those he believed were involved in the transfer of nuclear technology–but it is well understood he was alluding to Pakistan's army.[33]

To protect their underground criminal enterprise, military establishment offered Dr Khan a pardon in return for taking full responsibility. The Washington Post, quoting a friend of Dr Khan's, reported in February 2004 that Pakistan had good reason to try to bury the issue. The scientist had "helped North Korea design and equip facilities for making weapons-grade uranium", the newspaper claimed, "with the full knowledge of senior military commanders, including Gen Musharraf, as an army chief."[34] South Asia is boiling as Pakistan's military establishment continues to retrieve more weapons, finance terrorist groups, and destabilize Afghanistan. Researcher Zainab Aziz (2017) in her recent paper has explained new developments in South Asia:

> Deployment of tactical nukes is for the purpose of creating deterrence against the Cold Start Doctrine of India which is "Exclusively Offensive, Blitzkrieg inspired" military strategy, developed by the Indian Military Command (IMC), precisely for Pakistan to replace the obsolete 'Sundarji Doctrine' which miserably failed during 2001-2002 impasse with Pakistan. The year 2017 was started off in Pakistan by launching two significant test of proliferating programme which includes: Ababeel medium-range ballistic missile with a claimed multiple independently targetable re-entry vehicle (MIRV) and Babur-3 Submarine Launched Cruise Missile. Pakistan and India are also involved in the conventional arms race and it is perceived that if Pakistan kept on with developing MIRV-ready strategic deterrent, India may reassess its no-first-use nuclear doctrine due to the growing political pressure. India's nuclear pursuits are also meant for maintaining a suitable deterrent to China. Just recently at the 2017 Carnegie Nuclear Policy Conference, Professor Vipin Narang, an expert on South Asia Nuclear Security gave remarks that India may abandon its "no first use" nuclear policy, if it assessed that

Pakistan is likely to resort to the nuclear weapons first, has raised a question about the traditional prudence of South Asia's strategic stability situation.[35]

In March 2016, President Obama warned in Nuclear Security Summit that terrorist groups were trying to make access to nuclear material. He expressed deep concern on the weak security of some insecure states. Experts warned that risk of nuclear attacks via theft of weapons, which would likely need the assistance of insider working with a nuclear plant in Pakistan, cannot be ruled out. Weak security measures and unprofessional mechanism prompted several terrorist attacks against the country's nuclear installations in the past.[36] On 14 April 2017, Reuters reported revelations of CIA Chief from Washington, in which he said his organization uncovered Pakistan's secret nuclear weapons programme:

> The CIA helped unravel the nuclear smuggling network used by Pakistani scientist A Q Khan, the spy agency's new director Mike Pompeo said.......CIA has been a crucial player in the global campaign against nuclear proliferation," Pompeo said in his remarks at the Centre for Strategic and International Studies, a top American think-tank. "We've helped unravel the nuclear smuggling network used by A Q Khan, assisted in exposing a covert nuclear facility in Syria, and gathered intelligence—with the help of our liaison partners—that persuaded Libya to abandon its nuclear programme," he said in his first major policy speech after he became the head of the Central Intelligence Agency.[37]

In retrospect, Pakistan's nuclear smuggling businesses were established across Asia and Africa. Military generals and Dr. Khan were maintaining local contacts, and selling dangerous weapons to regional states. This suicide mission of Pakistani Miltablishment and civilian merchants of menace put in danger security of their own state. Pakistan sponsor terrorism in Afghanistan causing fatalities. On 22 June 2017, Pentagon warned that Pakistan was 'the most influential' external actor affecting Afghan stability and the military alliance's mission:

> Pakistan views the outcome of Afghanistan to be in its vital national interest and thus remains driven by its India-centric regional policy objectives," the Pentagon said in its six monthly

reports to the Congress. It said the Afghan-oriented militant groups, including the Taliban and Haqqani Network, retained freedom of action inside Pakistani territory and benefited from support from elements of the Pakistani government. "Although Pakistani military operations have disrupted some militant sanctuaries, certain extremist groups such as the Taliban and the Haqqani Network-were-able to relocate and continue to operate in and from Pakistan." The Pentagon said the United States continued to convey to Pakistan at all levels the importance of taking action against all terrorist and extremist groups.[38]

On 15 June 2017, Dawn reported President Ghani accusations against Pakistan's state-sponsored terrorism in Afghanistan. President Ghani said Pakistan recruited terrorists groups such as Lashkar-e-Toiba, Punjabi Taliban and Haqqani terrorist networks to carry out suicide attacks against the civilian population of Afghanistan. Following the investigation, Afghan's intelligence agency, Afghanistan's National Directorate of Security (NDS) found Taliban-allied Haqqani terrorist network responsible for the attacks in Kabul's diplomatic zones. Founded by Jalaluddin Haqqani, the Haqqani network carries out its activities on both sides of Af-Pak border. According to Afghan intelligence officials, Pakistani intelligence agency ISI enjoys ties with the network.[39]

On 06 August 2017, Dawn reported the US National Security Adviser, Gen H.R. McMaster statement about Pakistan support to terrorist groups inside Afghanistan, and said President Donald Trump wanted Pakistan to change its 'paradoxical' policy of supporting militants who caused the country great losses. In an interview to a conservative radio host, Hugh Hewitt, Mr. McMaster also defended President Trump's strategy on winning the war in Afghanistan by giving unrestricted powers to the US military based in the war-torn country.

The president has also made clear that we need to see a change in behaviour of those in the region, which includes those who are providing safe haven and support bases for the Taliban, Haqqani Network and others," Mr. McMaster said. "This is Pakistan in particular that we wanted to really see a change in and a reduction of their support for these groups. I mean, this is of course, you know, a very paradoxical situation where Pakistan is taking great losses. They have fought very hard against these groups, but they've done so really only selectively, he added.[40]

However, MacMaster commended the performance of Afghan security Afghan forces in the war against Pakistan backed terrorist organizations: "There's a tremendously successful campaign going on with Afghan forces in the lead. It's an unreported campaign in Nangarhar Province of Afghanistan," McMaster said.[41] "We're not goanna talk tactics anymore, right?" he added.[42] "Everything before was, you know, troop levels and very specific details announcing to the enemy years in advance exactly the number of troops you're goanna have, exactly what they're goanna do and what they're not goanna do. And so the president has said, that is not the way to fight a war. It never has been. This is an invention of recent years."[43] McMaster also said the President "absolutely" has confidence in the commander in charge of the U.S. war effort against the Taliban and ISIS in Afghanistan".[44]

Pakistan has been supporting dozens terrorist groups in Afghanistan since 1990s in order to further its national agenda, and force India to stop rebuilding the war torn country. Before his statement, on 28 April, 2017, Hindustan Times reported meeting of the representatives of World Muhajir Congress with members of House Foreign Affairs Committee. They briefed them on alleged strong connection between the ISI and the terrorist groups.

Pakistan's ISI is supporting terrorist organizations inside the country, US lawmakers were told by a newly formed Muhajir (refugee) group, which alleged terror outfits like Taliban and al-Qaeda were trying to take control of the port city of Karachi. "Nowadays, Pakistan has become a safe haven for extremist groups with full support of Pakistani intelligence agency ISI," World Muhajir Congress said in a letter to members of The House Foreign Affairs Committee during a Congressional hearing on Afghanistan here yesterday. "We are afraid as Jihadist outfits are getting stronger with the support of ISI, important port city of Karachi which is the supply line of US and NATO could fall into the hands of these terror groups," the letter said.[45]

On 24 May 2017, ToloNews reported briefing of law makers by US intelligence official about Pakistan's involvement in terrorism in

Afghanistan.[46] However, on 29 may 2017 Dawn reported Gen. Vincent remarks about Pakistan's intentions. "Pakistan views Afghanistan or desires for Afghanistan some of the same things we want: A safe, secure, stable Afghanistan. One addition—one that does not have heavy Indian influence in Afghanistan," Lt Gen Vincent Stewart, Director, Defense Intelligence Agency told members of Senate Armed Services Committee during a Congressional hearing on worldwide threats.[47] "They view all of the challenges through the lens of an Indian threat to the state of Pakistan," ToloNews reported.[48] "So they (Pakistan) hold in reserve terrorist organization we define them as terrorist organizations, they hold them in reserve so that—if Afghanistan leans towards India, they will no longer be supportive of an idea of a stable and secure Afghanistan that could undermine Pakistan interest," Stewart said.[49]

On 14 July 2017, ToloNews reported Pakistan's involvement in Afghanistan and Kashmir. With the help of the United States, and under the pretext of equipping and arming Afghanistan's Mujahedeen, Pakistan equipped its own army.[50] According to official figures by the government of Pakistan (Pakistan's National Security Policy 2014-2018), there were more than 150,000 religious schools (madrassas) in that country. Most of them are training recruits in extremism and violence under the name of Islam. According to the document, 51 terrorist groups are active in Pakistan and recruit from the above-mentioned madrassas". ToloNews reported.[51]

However, the ToloNews analyst shared important documents that manifest Pakistan's involvement in suicide terrorism Afghanistan. These documents were retrieved by Afghan intelligence agency (NDS) to tell the world that Pakistani intelligence agency (ISI) does not want peace and tranquility in Afghanistan. These documents are included in this chapter with the permission of the news channel:

> Document (1): *Rabbani, one of the officials from Office MI-422 of Peshawar, in an official letter to Colonel Sahamim Khalid head of Central office of MI-22 in Rawalpindi disclosed the transfer of the Haqqani network commander to Miranshah to North Waziristan after Operation Zarb-e-Azb: According to the directive dated 18.03.2015, by the Central Office of MI, that was contacted by Hotline & Passcom, the office tasked the following employees to transfer Atta Mohammad and Hafiz Luqmanullah, the commanders of group of Mawlawi Zar Mohammad, a member of Haqqani network, to a*

military camp in Data Khalil area in Miranshah, North Waziristan. The two commanders were transferred in border police uniforms and in army vehicles. In order to get more information, the central office was asked to get information from the head of the MI-7th office in Miranshah.[52]

Document (2): This document spotlights important facts about the Haqqani networks in Pakistan. The central office CTC located in Islamabad sent an official letter dated 16.03.2015 to its office in Nowshera, where it directed the office to brief the central office about the situation of all the personnel and commanders of Haqqani network located in the triangle between Nowshera, Mardan and Sawabi and as well as monitoring their current address, get contact numbers and other relevant information. The document specified that the central office of ISI directed the 945 and 935 offices to send all members and fighters of Haqqani network to Tochi, Mir Ali and Miranshah, under the cover of military troops. It is pertinent to mention that the objective of this move by the ISI was the safety of Haqqani network members, because the recent reports from the organization was to alarm them of the threat to the lives of Haqqani network personnel. In this regard, the central office of ISI directed the Nowshera office to task its relevant department to take security measures for families of Haqqani network members and to ensure their transfer to North Waziristan. The Nowshera office was also directed to send a report about the situation in the areas and districts in four rounds to Colonel Ghulam Abbas, Head of CVC Office in Islamabad.[53]

This document discusses secret relations between Pakistan military intelligence and terrorist commanders. Document (3): The central office of Military Intelligence (MI) in Islamabad directed the MI-422 office in Suba Sarhad in an official letter to arrange a direct meeting with two leaders of the Taliban including Hafiz Gulbahadur and Mawlawi Hamdullah and to arrange their residence in Hayat Abad and Tahkal areas in Peshawar. The two leaders and their supporters escaped to Peshawar because of the military operation in Miranshah in North Waziristan. The letter also directed the MI-422 office to arrange and rent residential houses for the commanders, and give them security guards and special vehicles for their safety and security. Afterwards, the MI-422 office leadership had a direct meeting in its office with the commanders where they discussed security, residence and other issues related to the commanders and at the end the leadership promised Hafiz Gulbahadur and Mawlawi Hamdullah to arrange the needed facilities as soon as possible and they (the Taliban leaders) assured the commanders of their best *efforts to follow the goals that they wanted to achieve in Afghanistan, using the collaboration and facilities on hand.*[54]

Document (4): This document discusses the attack on Kabul Airport, which was carried out during President Hamid Karzai's government. On July 2014, an official letter from central office of ISI in Islamabad was sent to MI-422 office in Swabi, Khyber Pakhtunkhwa, where it directed the office to thank those that successfully plotted the attack on Kabul Airport (now Hamid Karzai International Airport) and gave 2.5 million Pakistani rupees to every one of the following people: Haji Khalil Haqqani, Haji Hakim Woluswal, Qari Zahir Shah and Mawlawi Hakim. Moreover, the office was directed to donate 1.5 million Pakistani rupees to the families of those that were involved in the attack. Meanwhile, the office was directed to talk about details of an attack on the Ministry of Borders and Tribal Affairs in Kabul and that it should be done by the Haqqani network, and present their report about their tasks by 3pm on 23 July.[55]

Document (5): The ISI 945 office in Khyber Pakhtunkhwa in an official note dated April 6, 2015 to the central office in Islamabad wrote that: Officials of 945 office in a meeting with Toryalai, head of the network, and his co-fighters on April 5, 2015 were tasked to kidnapped and kill Afghanistan's Shia leaders in Herat, Kabul and Farah. In addition, they gave 2 million Pakistani rupees to the participants at that meeting. It was also specified that the relevant department of office 945 should prepare the required weapons and other equipment by Toryalai through the COD Akora Khattak and give them the weapons on the mentioned date. Meanwhile, the note mentioned that 23 people from Toryalai's group who were busy in military training in Cherat had completed their training.[56]

Document (6): The central office of ISI located in Quetta in a tentative note to central office of IW in Islamabad and 945 office in Rawalpindi, presented the result of the visit of a number of officers with the Taliban's Quetta Shura as follows: "The members of Taliban's Quetta Shura held a meeting about the peace process with the Afghan government in which key commanders of the Shura attended. They talked about mutual interests and policies already given to them. In addition, the involved officials gave needed directions to members of the council about the process. It is pertinent to mention that the note stated that the advisory board (945, CID) forwarded all those terms and preconditions as directed from GHQ. After that the Shura decided it will be mutual then will be forwarded on a priority basis".[57]

Pakistan's relations with terrorist organizations and its involvement in Afghanistan and Kashmir caused its isolation in international community. The ISI is now in trouble since it lost control of FATA, Waziristan and Baluchistan. Now Pashtuns and Balochs have discerned nefarious designs of Pakistani establishment, and called on international community to help them in librating their soil from the occupation of Pakistan. The penetration of terrorist elements within the ranks of the army is viewed by Afghanistan and India as a dangerous development. Prominent journalist and editor of the News International, Mr. Amir Mir in his Asia Times report uncovered penetration of jihadist groups within Pakistan's army grades:

> "While Pakistan's military had been secular and disciplined, it is now being infiltrated at all levels by jihadists and al-Qaeda and Taliban sympathizers. This obnoxious development has brought into open the conflicting ideologies which seem to have caused fissures in the ranks of the Pakistani armed forces by pitting Islamists against reformists. The death sentence awarded to five officers proves that the fidayeen assault on the naval dockyard could not have been possible without "inside help." Those courts martial and sentenced to death by the Navy tribunal after in-camera trials were Sub-Lieutenant Hammad Ahmed (whose father Saeed Ahmed is a retired Army major), Irfanullah, Hashim Naseer, Mohammad Hammad and Arslan Nazeer. The naval authorities concluded the court martial proceedings on April 12, 2016 and promulgated the judgment on April 14, 2016. Those arrested were tried on charges of inciting mutiny, hatching a conspiracy and carrying weapons in the naval dockyard. The naval court reportedly refused to provide copies of trial proceedings to the family members of the convicted officers who want to challenge their death sentences. All the five officers had links with AQIS led by Commander Asim Umar who is an Indian national from the state of Uttar Pradesh".[58]

On 21 June 2017, Pentagon in its report warned that Afghan-oriented militant groups, including the Taliban and Haqqani Network, benefit from "support" from elements of the Pakistan government. Pentagon's new report identified Pakistan as the most influential external actor affecting Afghanistan's stability and the outcome of the missions in this war-torn country:

Although Pakistani military operations have disrupted some militant sanctuaries, certain extremist groups such as the Taliban and the Haqqani Network were able to relocate and continue to operate in and from Pakistan," the report said. "India is providing significant training opportunities for Afghan officers and enlisted personnel. Approximately 130 Afghans travel to India each year to attend various military academy and commissioning programs," it said in the six- monthly report to the US Congress. "India is Afghanistan's most reliable regional partner and the largest contributor of development assistance in the region, including civil development projects such as the Afghanistan-India Friendship Dam and the Afghan parliament building," the Pentagon added.[59]

Pakistan's military continues to support terrorist groups that attack India to keep it "off balance" and draws international mediation into dispute over Kashmir, according to a report by a group of eminent South Asian experts from 10 major American think tanks.[60] Pakistan's military has often disrupted nascent peace efforts pursued by Indian and Pakistani civilian rulers, most notably in 1999, during the Kargil war: Pakistani military leaders continue to support terrorist groups that attack India in an effort to keep it off balance and to draw international mediation into the dispute with India over Kashmir," said the report.[61]

On 01 June 2017, Afghanistan's intelligence service, the National Directorate of Security (NDS), issued a statement that attributed blame to the Haqqani Network, a Taliban-affiliated group in Pakistan. It alleged the group had received help from ISI, the Pakistani intelligence service. However, Pakistani Foreign Ministry spokesman Mr. Nafees Zakaria rejected what he called "baseless allegations," saying the "accusatory approach is unhelpful towards efforts for peace."

In an exclusive conversation with India Today, Afghanistan government blamed Pakistan's Inter-Services Intelligence (ISI) and the banned terror group - the Haqqani network - for massive bomb explosion in Kabul's diplomatic area which killed at least 90 people and wounded around 450 others. Afghanistan Interior Ministry spokesperson Sediq Siddiqui said, "We have nailed Pakistan's ISI role (in Kabul blast). Afghanistan expects Pakistan to crack down on Haqqani network. The attack will surely impact ties between the two (Afghanistan, Pakistan) countries".[62]

Recently, nuclear security experts warned that nuclear Pakistan is more dangerous than North Korea. Pakistani miltablishment continues to build more weapons and develop tactical nuclear weapons-challenging peaceful security environment in South Asia. Pakistan remains the most volatile, unpredictable and dangerous player in the South Asia nuclear security dilemma.[63] However, the Islamic State (ISIL) Magazine report claimed that the group could purchase a nuclear weapon in Pakistan and smuggle it through Latin American trafficking networks into the United States through its "porous border," the same way "illegal aliens in America" arrive.[64] This "sum of all fears for Western intelligence agencies" scenario is "infinitely more possible today than it was one year ago," claimed the article in Dabiq in 2016.[65] If terrorist groups retrieved nuclear weapons from Pakistan, this would be a dangerous development in South Asia. Pakistan has been deeply involved in nuclear smuggling since 1990s, and sponsored various terrorist organizations in the region to further its nefarious designs. On 16 June 2017, Dawn reported two Pakistani lawmakers called for a thorough investigation into the Dr Abdul Qadeer nuclear black marketing.[66] On 21 July 2017, Dawn reported the United States report —titled "Country Reports on Terrorism, 2016"—recognized Pakistan as "an important counterterrorism partner" but also listed it among countries that provide safe havens to terrorists.

> The State Department sent the report to Congress as part of its annual assessment of terrorism across the world. Before these allegations, Director General (DG) Inter-Services Public Relations (ISPR) Major General Asif Ghafoor announced operation Khyber-4 under Radd-ul-Fasaad (RuF) to "wipe out terrorists" in the Rajgal area of Khyber Agency. "An operation to wipe out terrorists has been launched in Rajgal area in Khyber Agency," Major General Ghafoor said.[67]

Strategic dilemma exist between Pakistan and India as Islamabad specifies that its nuclear weapons are only India-centric while for many in India, Indian centricity even gets larger and at times more ambiguous.[68] Analysts Hannah E. Haegeland and Reema Verma explain the danger of nuclear theft and wave of terrorism in South Asia:

> South Asia is home to expanding and maturing nuclear weapons programs and widespread, frequent, and organized domestic and cross-border terror attacks. Recent incidents include

a September 18 assault by terrorists who crossed the border from Pakistan to attack an Indian Army camp at Uri. This incident was followed by Indian retaliation, in the form of a publicly touted "surgical strike." But this clash is one of many. Past attacks, thefts, transportation accidents, and personnel reliability issues show that while security failures involving sensitive nuclear materials appear to occur infrequently, they do occur—in both countries. Even more concerning: India and Pakistan are primed to expand their nuclear facilities, production of fissile material, and types of delivery systems, multiplying risks. These expansions make for an even more target-rich environment for motivated non-state actors to exploit. Further, the prevalence of terror attacks in districts where sensitive materials and facilities are located demonstrates that violent non-state actors have demonstrated the capacity (that is, the networks, intelligence, and resources) to reach these areas and threaten hardened targets. While the vast majority of attacks lack sophistication, the low probability but extremely high-risk threat of nuclear and radiological terror highlights the need for swift policy shifts to bolster sensitive material security on the subcontinent.[69]

Nuclear proliferation regime in South Asia evolved since the nuclear tests by India and Pakistan in 1998. Presently, there are only nine countries with nuclear weapons, and that number remained the same in the last decade. Several states voluntarily relinquished nuclear weapons (Argentina, Brazil, Egypt); and some were forced to relinquish (Iraq, Libya, South Korea, Syria). Belarus, Kazakhstan, Ukraine willingly relinquished; and one country built a small arsenal before unilaterally eliminating it (South Africa).[70] On 21 April 2017, Analyst Mr. Todd Royal in his Asia Times article noted escalation of military crisis between India and Pakistan:

> Pakistan is racing to catch up in overall military strength, but India is boosting plutonium production to overtake Pakistan's lead in nuclear warheads. The two countries would only have minutes to respond if either launched a missile attack. They have diplomatic ties, but there's no dialogue to counter a nuclear-armed conflict. Experts believe Pakistan has tactical nuclear weapons which could fall into the hands of militants, causing India to rethink its first-strike policy, according to Professor Vipin

Narange of MIT. Further, India has believed it could beat Pakistan in a conventional war without resorting to its nuclear arsenal. If India thought Pakistan would use its tactical weapons first, then India would wipe out Pakistan's strategic arsenal before Pakistan devastates Indian cities. If India thought Pakistan would use its tactical weapons first, then India would wipe out Pakistan's strategic arsenal before Pakistan devastates Indian cities. For that scenario to happen, India needs more nuclear weapons, and Pakistan would need to dramatically increase its nuclear arsenal to survive an Indian first strike. The threat of escalation became more real after an attack last year by a Pakistani militant group—Jaish-e-Mohammad—on an Indian army base near the Pakistani border killed 17 soldiers.[71]

The three states that present precarious threat to world peace are; Pakistan, Iran and North Korea by developing nuclear, chemical and biological weapons. These developments provide opportunity to radicalized and extremist organizations to retrieve nuclear weapons. Researcher Carlotta Gall (06 February, 2016) in her report Afghan President Ashraf Ghani's ruckus on Pakistan's support to terrorism:

How much worse will it get?" Mr. Ghani asked in a recent television interview. "It depends on how much regional cooperation we can secure, and how much international mediation and pressure can be exerted to create rules of the game between states."[72] Meanwhile, in Pakistan, the Haqqani network, the most potent branch of the Taliban, moved from North Waziristan into the adjacent district of Kurram. From there it continues to enjoy safe haven and conduct its insurgency against American, international and Afghan targets. Pakistan regards Afghanistan as its backyard. Determined not to let its archrival, India, gain influence there, and to ensure that Afghanistan remains in the Sunni Islamist camp, Pakistan has used the Taliban selectively, promoting those who further its agenda and cracking down on those who don't. The same goes for Al Qaeda and other foreign fighters.[73]

Chapter 2

Islamic Bomb, Black Marketing, Military Generals and their Cronies

The venturesome and pitfall saga of Pakistan's nuclear smuggling does not end here; military establishment launched a new programme of tactical nuclear weapons to exacerbate its fighting capabilities against India. In previous chapter, I spotlighted the danger of nuclear terrorism emanating from Pakistan, while in this chapter; however, I want to have an iota highlight on nuclear black marketing business of Pakistani Miltablishment on the same streak, but with different perspective. In February 2004, to protect Miltablishment and its clandestine nuclear smuggling networks, General Musharraf forced Dr. Abdul Qadeer Khan to admit the transfer of nuclear weapons technology to Iran, Libya, North Korea and African states in 1990s.[1]

Pakistani Generals retrieved millions of dollars from their nuclear smuggling networks, and forced Dr. Abdul Qadeer Khan on state-run TV Channel to declare he was the sole manager of weapons proliferation.[2] On 30 May 2008, Dawn News reported Dr. Abdul Qadeer Khan's regret over his confession made in 2004, and alleged that he had been 'betrayed by his friends' who had promised that nothing wrong would happen to him and he would live a respectable life.[3] In the first detailed interview since he was put under a virtual house arrest, Dr Khan said he had been made a 'scapegoat' and he had made the confession in the larger interest of the country. "I think the confession was my mistake," Dawn News TV channel reported.[4] In one of his interviews with a local news channel,

GeoNews, Abdul Qadeer Khan expressed his disappointment on the attitude of military establishment and said:

> They are unappreciative, and I regret and feel uneasiness that I should not have served this careless nation, I served this nation for decades, but military dictator General Musharraf threatened to take me to the military court. They view me with scorn and think that I am a Pathan and I am not a Pakistani citizen.[5]

In February 2004, newspapers reported Dr. Khan's business. Investigators discovered that he made millions of dollars from the sale of nuclear-related blueprints and technical assistance to Iran and Libya through a nuclear black market. Abdul Qadeer Khan told investigators unwillingly (forced) that he purveyed nuclear technology to some Muslim states. According to the NTI report, Mr. Khan purveyed nuclear technology to Iran and Libya through a Malaysian middleman, Buhary Syed Abu Tahir:

> On June 7, 2004, the Pakistani government introduced a bill in the National Assembly, known as the Export Control on Goods, Technologies, Material and Equipment related to Nuclear and Biological Weapons and their Delivery Systems Act, 2004. The bill was subsequently passed by the Pakistan National Assembly and Senate on September 14 and 19, respectively. The bill stipulated that any violation of the act would result in up to 14 years' imprisonment, forfeiture of all property and assets to the government, and a fine of 5 million rupees (about $86,500). Any individuals attempting to commit or abetting the commission of such offenses would be charged as if they had themselves committed the violation. It is believed that should further evidence against Khan's surface, the conditional pardon he received from President Musharraf could be withdrawn. However, recent statements by the Pakistani Foreign Minister, Khurshid Mahmud Kasuri, indicate that the bill will not be applied retroactively, and will not have any effect on the cases of A.Q. Khan and other scientists involved in the smuggling ring.[6]

Dr. Khan told his close friends about the threats he received from miltablishment, the ISI and sarcastic generals, and even Gen Musharraf also threatened him of dire consequences. He was forced to confess the selling of nuclear weapons to save the military establishment and its cronies who sold nuclear secrets to North Korea, Iran, Saudi Arabia and Libya. Journalist Ahmad Rashed and Anton La Guardia reported the failure of successive Pakistani governments to control Abdul Qadeer Khan's black marketing business:

> The admission that Abdul Qadeer Khan freely sold nuclear technology to Iran, Libya and North Korea confirms one of America's worst fears-which a close ally in the "war on terrorism" has turned out to be the secret armored of its worst foes. In a briefing to Pakistani journalists, the official admitted that successive governments had failed to control the activities of Mr. Khan. He claimed that the technology sales were made for "personal greed" and did not involve Pakistani governments - something many experts find difficult to believe.[7]

The real miscreants' behind the screen were military generals who had established dozens networks of nuclear black marketing across Asia and Africa. Dr. Qadeer Khan was used as whipping-boy to swindle and mislead international community about their fear marketing. Devjyot Ghoshal in his recent analysis highlighted nuclear and ballistic missiles development cooperation between Pakistan and North Korea:

> Since the 1970s, Pakistan and North Korea have cooperated extensively on the development of ballistic missile and nuclear weapons technologies. Pakistan's strong alliance with China and the legacy of a major scandal linking the Pakistani military to North Korea's nuclear program have prevented Islamabad from joining UN efforts to diplomatically isolate the DPRK. While economic links between Pakistan and North Korea were established during the early 1970s, the foundations of the modern Islamabad-Pyongyang security partnership were forged during Pakistani Prime Minister Zulfikar Ali Bhutto's 1976 visit to North Korea. In particular, Khan's role in dealings with Pyongyang has been under scrutiny.[8]

The United States was in the loop about the nuclear black marketing business of Pakistan in 1980s and 1990s, but tongue-ties willingly due to the miltablishment-led jihad against the Soviet Union. After the fall of Taliban government in 2001, the US administration adopted inconsistent policy towards Pakistan. Congressional Research Service in its report to the US Congress: Pakistan's Nuclear Proliferation Activities and the Recommendations of the 9/11 Commission: *U.S. Policy Constraints and Options* spotlighted Pakistan's nuclear smuggling and black marketing networks in Asia and the Middle East:

> Press reports in late December, 2004, underscore the challenge of addressing the terrorist and nuclear threats simultaneously in U.S. policy towards Pakistan. The New York Times reported on December 26, 2004, that both the Bush Administration and the United Nations' International Atomic Energy Agency (I.A.E.A.) have gathered evidence in the Middle East and Asia indicating that the illicit nuclear supply network set up in the 1990s by Pakistan's most celebrated nuclear scientist, Dr. A. Q. Khan, may be much more extensive than previously assumed. The evidence is said to include the discovery in Libya of plans for an atomic bomb and other elements of a "nuclear starter kit." Reportedly, some U.S. experts strongly suspect that Khan's network, rather than Russia, as had been long assumed, has been the source of most of Iran's nuclear know-how and technology. Underscoring the American dilemma, some contend that concerns about the stability of Pakistan, a key ally in the war against terrorism, have made the Administration reluctant to pressure the military-dominated government of President Pervez Musharraf to gain access to A. Q. Khan.[9]

More than 50 cronies and agents of Dr. Khan and military establishment were actively seeking nuclear information across the globe. His close associates were deeply involved in nuclear smuggling, while Buhary Syed Abu Tahir, a Sri Lankan national was his Chief Operation officer. A German businessman Heinz Mebus was involved in nuclear business with Iran.[10] An India Businessman Mr. S. M. Farouq was also involved with Iran and Libya, and Peter Griffin, was also in the field. Mr. Paul Griffin was based in Dubai.[11] Mr. Urs Tinner, a Swiss national was overseeing the production of centrifuges parts in Malaysia.[12] Mr. Friedrich Tinner was involved in smuggling business with Iran. However, his best friend was Mr. Gotthard Lerch, named as Tahir. Mr. Tahir and Gerhard Wisser were also involved in nuclear business with Iran and Libya.[13] Mr. Muhammad Farooq was in charge of procurement and sales abroad.[14] In 2009, Abdul Qadeer Khan was released from five years of house arrest by a court. After release he told Guardian newspaper:

> It's a nice feeling, the worry is gone. I can lead a normal life now, as a normal citizen. It's a fine feeling........In seven generations, no one [in my family] has ever taken part in any politics. My father was a teacher, a headmaster. We are mostly interested in education," Khan said. "Mostly I'll be dealing now with educational problems, and problems we are facing in the country about agriculture, education and water shortage. I'll concentrate on those.[15]

Nuclear smugglers of miltablishment were managing their different businesses including soldiers for sale in Middle East, Afghanistan, Kashmir, Yemen, Syria, Iraq, (reorganization of their own blackwater (Fuji Foundation), and marketing of fear in 2000s, but never thought their trained hydras would turn their arms back on them. From 2009 to 2011, their trained terrorists attempted several times to destroy nuclear weapons or obtain it through their networks. Non-proliferation expert, Mr. Paul K. Kerr and Mary Beth Nikitin (2016) explains these measures in their recent research paper:

> Pakistani efforts to improve the security of its nuclear weapons have been ongoing and have included some cooperation with the United States; former Pakistani President Pervez Musharraf told a journalist in 2009 that Islamabad has "given State Department nonproliferation experts insight into the command and control of the Pakistani arsenal and its on-site safety and security procedures." Moreover, following the 2004 revelations of an extensive international nuclear proliferation network run by Pakistani nuclear official Abdul Qadeer Khan, as well as possible connections between Pakistani nuclear scientists and Al Qaeda, Islamabad has made additional efforts to improve export controls and monitor nuclear personnel. The main security challenges for Pakistan's nuclear arsenal are keeping the integrity of the command structure, ensuring physical security, and preventing illicit proliferation from insiders. Some observers are also concerned about the risk of nuclear war between India and Pakistan. The two countries most recently came to the brink of

full-scale war in 1999 and 2002, and, realizing the dangers, have developed some risk reduction measures to prevent accidental nuclear war. Nevertheless, Pakistan continues to produce fissile material for weapons and appears to be augmenting its weapons production facilities as well as deploying additional delivery vehicles—steps that will enable both quantitative and qualitative improvements in Islamabad's nuclear arsenal.[16]

Secret nuclear business between North Korean and Pakistani generals was uncovered by letter written by North Korean smuggler Jon Byong Ho. David E. Sanger explains the emergence of a single-page letter written by a North Korean official 13 years ago, became a solid proof of the involvement of Pakistan army generals in secret dealing of nuclear equipments to North Korea. The letter, Davis reported is a solid evidence of the corruption of Gen. Jehangir Karamat, who received $3 million and asked that; "the agreed documents, components, etc." be placed on a North Korean plane returning to Pyongyang after delivering missile parts to Pakistan.[17] On 20 September 2009, Sunday Times reported the arrest of Dr. Khan daughter, Kausar Khan, and recovery of the letter:

> The year was 2004. The raid went unreported but was part of the worldwide sweep against associates of Dr Abdul Qadeer Khan, the Pakistani scientist and father of the Islamic bomb, who had just been accused of selling nuclear secrets to Libya, Iran and North Korea. The house belonged to one of his brothers, a retired Pakistani International Airlines manager, who lived there with his wife and daughter. The two secret agents asked the daughter for a letter she had recently received from abroad. Upstairs in her bedroom, she pulled it from a drawer. It was unopened. The agents grabbed it and told her to put on a coat and come with them.[18]

Police raided her residence and recovered a document confirming Pakistan's nuclear smuggling. Dawn newspaper reported the letter recovered by the police stated: "We put up a centrifuge plant at Hanzhong (250km southwest of Xian).[19] It further explained: "The Chinese gave us drawings of the nuclear weapon, gave us 50kg of enriched uranium, gave us 10 tons of UF6 (natural) and 5 tons of UF6 (3%).[20] The letter revealed about the Iranian consignment: "Probably with the blessings of BB [Benazir Bhutto, who became prime minister in 1988] and [a now-retired general] General Imtiaz [Benazir's defense adviser, now dead] asked me to give a set of drawings and some components to the Iranians. The names and addresses of suppliers were also given to the Iranians.[21]

International Atomic Energy Agency (IAEA) Chairman, Mohamed El Baradi, in his January 2008 statement further conflagrated the issue of nuclear non-proliferation, in which he expressed deep concern about Pakistan's nuclear weapons falling into the hands of Islamist militants. Earlier, experts highlighted the threat of nuclear weapons falling into the hands of terrorists and extremist organizations based in Pakistan. Senior Consultant to the Global Security Program of the East West Institute and International Legal Adviser to the International Crisis Group, Mr. Ken Berry in his research paper (2008) noted important facts about the safety and security of Pakistan's nuclear weapons:

> While security at Pakistani nuclear sites might be adequate in normal circumstances, it could certainly be improved, as the most recent crisis has highlighted. The United States has spent billions in securing its own nuclear assets, and that is ongoing expenditure just to keep one step ahead of the terrorists. Even with high security and stable domestic political and social systems, accidents can happen, as illustrated by an incident in 2007 in which, due to a series of errors and oversights on a number of different levels, nuclear weapons were flown across the whole of the continental United States without any senior officials being aware of it. Nuclear security in Russia also needed considerable boosting after the fall of the Soviet Union, and despite the billions the United States has spent in Russia on improving nuclear while claiming that their security is adequate, there have nonetheless been some hints from Pakistani authorities that they would appreciate some external assistance in this regard. The matter is complicated for Pakistan, however, by the secrecy surrounding its nuclear weapons development as well as the embarrassment it might feel in the Islamic and non-aligned world if it openly sought assistance from the West. For the United States, providing such assistance would be made extremely difficult by the legislative and other measures imposed on Pakistan in the wake of its 1998 nuclear tests and the 2004 revelations on the A.Q. Khan nuclear network. In addition, the United States would not want any

material assistance to Pakistan to adversely affect its growing, but still problematic, relationship with India.[22]

However, speaking in the General Assembly's Disarmament and International Security Committee, Ambassador Tehmina Janjua said the key tools for preventing non-state actors from acquiring; producing or using chemical and biological weapons included national physical protection efforts, international assistance and capacity building.[23] In that regard, Ambassador Janjua, who was Pakistan's permanent representative to the U.N. in Geneva, pointed out that Pakistan had supported the Russian proposal for a Bio-Chemical Terrorism Convention.[24] The Pakistani envoy, who was participating in a debate on weapons of mass destruction, said Pakistan condemns the use of chemical weapons by anyone, anywhere, and welcomed milestones that had been achieved in the destruction of Syrian and Libyan chemical weapons. "We remain committed to the full and effective implementation of the Biological and Toxin Weapons Convention (BTWC),' she said. "We attach high priority to the Convention's provisions relating to international cooperation and assistance as well as peaceful uses of chemical technology." Tahmina said.[25]

On 20 April 2016, Pakistani analyst Dr. Ashraf Ali reported cautioning of Director General of Pakistan's intelligence bureau (IB), Mr. Aftab Sultan about hundreds of fighters from his country were joining ISIS in Syria, generating concerns about their links and activities when they returned home.[26] Zia Ur Rahman Zia, an international politics professor at Qurtaba University in Peshawar warned that the ISIS could make a dirty bomb. They have safe havens in Iraq and Syria where it can set up a laboratory to satisfy its nasty plans," he said. "Pakistan's nuclear weapons might be secure but not safe." An ever growing danger persists of the militants putting their hands on the country's nuclear arsenals.[27]

On 20 April 2017, Reuters reported the threat of chemical weapons in Syria and nuclear arms in North Korea caused the risk of biological weapons drop off the international agenda.[28] A report in 2016 from the Combating Terrorism Center warned that Islamic State (ISIS) too, was keen to acquire biological weapons. That group has already used basic chemical weapons, including in the battle for Mosul. Pakistan has developed biological weapons and used it by warlord General Raheel Sharif against women and children in Waziristan.[29]

In July 2017, experts in India warned that the ISIS plan to use chemical weapons against security forces in Jammu and Kashmir. The revelation came after a terror attack on Amarnath pilgrims that killed seven in Batingoo.[30] Conversations between terrorist groups intercepted in June 2017 by Indian security agencies indicated the resolve of Hizbul Mujahedeen to use chemical weapons to inflict heavy casualties on security forces.[31] Journalist E Jaya Kumar reported to Asia Times the use of chemical weapons against Indian soldiers or civilians.[32] Mr. Kumar revealed that Pakistan's army used chemical weapons internally: against Pashtuns in Waziristan and Baluchs in Baluchistan.[33] Since these weapons have now fallen into the hands of Hizbul terrorists, the consequences may be far more severe on the Indian side. India has limited options to avert such a situation. Asia Times reported.[34]

On 15 January 2017, Sunday Guardian published article of journalist Areeba Falak on the use of biological and chemical weapons by Pakistan army against the residents of North and South Waziristan, in which hundreds innocent women and children lost their lives. The article noted important evidences bout the use of chemical and biological weapons in the agency:

> The Pakistan military has been using its 'war on terror' to bombard its restive regions that are seeking independence. Pashtuns are demanding a free Pashtunistan. For Jamshed (name changed) and his family members, Waziristan is their home that ceased to be their safe haven. After developing severe blisters on their skin, Jamshed, along with his family members, fled to Bannu, a district in Khyber Pakhtunkhwa, as IDPs (Internally Displaced People). It was only when the doctors in Bannu examined the raw wounds and blisters that they realized that these had been caused by chemical weapons used by the Pakistan army on the civilian population of Waziristan. Areeba Falak noted sources that provided the photographs of Jamshed's family members to this newspaper that Pakistan army indiscriminately used chemical weapons in Waziristan and in certain areas of Khyber Pakhtunkhwa, both areas dominated by Pashtuns—apart from Baluchistan. Until recently, Khyber Pakhtunkhwa acted as a rescue point for IDPs escaping the Pakistan army's so-called war on terror in Waziristan and surrounding areas.[35]

Chemical attacks, killings, humiliation, kidnapping, forced disappearances, and raping of their daughters by army officers forced residents of Wana district of South Waziristan to leave their houses. On 26 September 2014, South Asian Tribune reported stories of refugees fleeing WANA in South Waziristan were targeted by Pakistan army. Security forces used poisonous gas or a bio-weapon on a large scale against them. M. A Siddiqui noted some important cases in his article:

> The refugees have sorry tales to tell as they say the death toll of civilians has multiplied since no medical help was available in places where bombing was taking place. All hospitals, schools, shops, markets, transports have been closed by the Army in the area under siege. "Majority of the wounded persons are on their deathbeds in the absence of medical aid," the refugees say. Another horrible facet of the operation is looting by Army troops in the area. "They are taking away all our valuables during search operations. They do not even spare blankets, cots and mattresses", a refugee, Rafiq Mahsud, said. "Taking away of our cattle and livestock without any payment is a routine affair," he said. "We have been living with Frontier Constabulary for the last 54 years and never faced a situation like this. Now, it appears as if we are under siege of the hostile Northern Alliance of Afghanistan," Dawood Khan, and another Mahsud tribesman, bitterly complained.[36]

On 09 June, 2014, when terrorists attacked Karachi airport and killed two military officers, the army stepped up security around nuclear installations. This was a fresh warning from terrorists and radicalized elements and those whose relatives were killed or tortured in the military operations in Baluchistan, FATA and Waziristan. The attacks on Karachi port authenticated and manifested failure of intelligence agencies to protect nuclear installations. This attack also highlighted the military capability of the Taliban and exposed a gap in the country's security apparatus. After this attack, Pakistanis were apprehensive about possible daring attacks against the country's nuclear installations. On 17 May 2017, Mr. Vinayak Bhat in Outlook magazine noted Pakistan's new secret nuclear weapons storage facility:

> Evidences suggested Pakistan would have deployed its nuclear missiles of Shaheen series in the facility, posing a grave threat to the whole of India. The facility, possibly the sixth nuclear

capable missile bases, is located about 320km from Amritsar, 520km from Chandigarh and 720km from New Delhi. Shaheen-III, Pakistan's ballistic missiles capable of delivering a nuclear weapon, can hit targets as far as 2,750 kilometers effectively. The terrorists yet again exposed the failure of the security agencies. This is a clear challenge for the SPD of the armed forces, which has deployed 25,000 nuclear forces around nuclear facilities.[37]

On 11 December, 2014, former Interior Minister of Pakistan, Mr. Rehman Malik told a local news channel that ISIS established recruitment centres in Gujranwala and Bahawalpur districts of Punjab province. The wall-chalking campaign and leaflets prompted fears about the terrorist group making inroads in the country.[38] According to the leaked government circular in Baluchistan and Khyber Pakhtunkhwa provinces, the ISIS recruited more than 10,000 to 12,000 fighters for the next sectarian war in Pakistan.[39] In 2014, the Islamic State of Khorasan approached extremist and sectarian groups of Pakistan for support, and distributed leaflets and other propaganda material in Pashtu, Urdu, and Persian languages to invite young people from different communities. This group also threatened India and Russia, and became a consecutive headache for Afghanistan. The group has established its networks in South and North Waziristan, Jalalabad, Kunar, and Nooristan province, and wants to infiltrate into Chinese Muslim province and parts of Central Asia-challenging the authority of local governments there. Civilian deaths in Afghanistan become a routine as innocent women and girls are kidnapped, raped and tortured in the group's secret prisons in Kunar and Jalalabad provinces. The Islamic State fighters are being facilitated by the corrupt commanders, and parliamentarians. They are sheltered, armed and transported to their destination.[40]

In November 2016, Russian Television (RT) aired interview of Wikileaks founder Mr. Julian Assange with a UK based Australian journalist, Mr. John Pilger. Mr. Assange uncovered important facts about the wealthy officials from Saudi Arabia and Qatar donating money to the Hillary Clinton's Foundation and Islamic State (ISIS) respectively.[41] In 17 August 2014, Mr. Assange made public an email in which Hillary Clinton had urged the then advisor to US President Barak Obama, Mr. John Podesta, to pressure Qatar and Saudi Arabia for funding Islamic State (ISIS).[42] These revelations sparked wide-ranging debates in print and electronic media across the globe, which later on, dilapidated relations between the Qatar and Saudi governments with the Gulf and South Asian states. There are different opinion about the strength and an area of its influence, but recent events proved that Daesh is more powerful than the Taliban terrorist groups.

In January 2015, Islamic State (ISIS) announced formation of another terrorist group named Islamic State of Khorasan (ISKP), which represents a Salafi school of thought and receives financial assistance from secret channels across the Durand Line. The membership of this newly established terrorist group in Afghanistan and Pakistan was more than 20,000, but keeping in view its sphere of influence and operations, experts fear that the group's fast growing cadre can spread across South Asia in a relatively short space of time. The Islamic State of Khorasan also approached extremist sectarian groups of Pakistan for support, and distributed leaflets and other propaganda material in Pashtu, Urdu and Persian languages to invite young people from different communities. The group also threatened India and Russia, and became a consecutive headache for Afghanistan. In Momand Agency, Jamaat Al Ahrar, and TTP are operating in collaboration with ISKP. On 15 November, 2016, expert Khyber Sarban in his Diplomat Magazine article uncovered links of the terrorist organization with Pakistani and Afghan groups and its bases across the Durand Line:

> ISKP in the Afghanistan-Pakistan region is not cut of the same cloth as the Islamic State we have witnessed in Syria and Iraq; therefore it is a mistake to think of them as the same. The regional brand of ISKP in the making is more a consortium of several TTP fragmented groups combined with the already existing LeJ, JuD, Jem, Jundullah, IMU, disgruntled Taliban groups, and a dozen other groups nurtured through the decades in Afghanistan and Pakistan. These terrorist outfits tasked to operate under the banner of ISKP are more like a marriage of convenience than a union based on shared ideology. It is to be noted that these groups have always operated for decades with the blessings of the Pakistani state and its intelligence wing. They are highly dependent on each other for continued existence. This facilitation of the activities of terror groups by Pakistani Intelligence has precedence. For decades, terror outfits have used Pakistan to travel to and from various

conflict zones, often with the connivance of Pakistani intelligence officials as was evident most recently in the case of former Taliban leader Mullah Mohammad Mansour. These terror groups are bargaining chips, as Asad Durrani told Al Jazeera. Despite Pakistan's alliance in the war of terror, specifically targeting al-Qaeda, the group is still active and has now established an al-Qaeda Indian Subcontinent (AQIS) wing. The terror groups active in the region had their own distinct operating principles, but since the emergence of ISIS we have witnessed a systematic attempt to make the outside world believe that they all now operate under Islamic State. For example, previously the LeJ and LeT groups were operating across the Durand Line under the banner of Haqqani Network and since the emergence of ISIS they have been rebranded".[43]

Chapter 3

Nuclear Partnership between Pakistan and Saudi Arabia, and its Investment in Pakistan's Weapons of Mass Destruction

In March 2018, the Saudi Prince Muhammad bin Salman warned that his country has set to develop nuclear weapons if Iran makes the same move in the event of a collapse of the world nuclear deal signed in 2015. This announcement enraged the entire EU, US and Middle East states that Saudi Arabia intentions might provoke other state towards nuclarization.[1] During the last two decades, there has been speculation in print and electronic media that Pakistan would sell or otherwise make available its nuclear warheads to Saudi Arabia, but war in Middle East and the exponentially growing tension between Iran and the country, Pakistan delayed the deal.[2] In August 2016, Muhammad bin Salman visited Islamabad to reinvigorate closer nuclear relations due to Saudi Arabia's concern over Iran's nuclear weapons.[3] Pakistan and Saudi Arabia have been secretly engaged in developing nuclear weapons since the last four decades.[4] The Saudis invested billions dollars in Pakistan nuclear and missile programme in order to become a nuclear power in the Arab world, and counter Shia Iran.[5] Libya, United Arab Emirate, China and wealthy individuals from Pakistan and several other states also supported the development of Islamic bomb. In the past several years, Saudi Arabia has been the subject of speculation regarding nuclear weapons ambitions.[6] International community warned that the country is in possession of undeclared nuclear facilities.[7]

Saudi Arabia denied manufacturing nuclear weapons, but the country allegedly allocated financial funds for its nuclear program, and received scientific assistance from Pakistan. Pakistani scientists and army experts were working with the country's army on various projects. A report of the BBC news exposed the race of nuclear weapons in the Middle East, pitting the Shia Iran against its Sunni- ruled rival, Saudi Arabia, which is allegedly aspiring to become a nuclear power.[8] The BBC News reported that Saudi Arabia invested huge money in Pakistan's Atomic Program.[9] According to a former Pakistani spy agent, "Pakistanis certainly maintain a certain number of warheads on the basis, that if the Saudis were to ask for them at any given time, they would be immediately transferred".[10]

The facilities for nuclear installations, Saudi Arabia has, is sufficient for its nuclear program. The country desperately seeks nuclear weapons as the emergence of Iran as a nuclear state created fear and deep dismal, among the Arab states.[11] Therefore, Saudi generals and Wahabi establishment decided to invest in Pakistan nuclear weapons to counter Shia Iran.[12] In 1994, Muhammad Khilewe, the first secretary of Saudi Mission to the United Nations claimed asylum in the United States, and revealed that his country wanted to obtain nuclear weapons.[13] In 1988, Saudi Arabia also received CSS-2 DF-3 intermediate-range missiles from China. As the security of nuclear installation on its soil was very complicated, the country decided to invest huge money in Pakistan nuclear program. Pakistan received billions of dollars from the Kingdom to prepare nuclear weapons for the country that faced a constant threat from Iran.

In March 2015, Prime Minister Nawaz Sharif visited Saudi Arabia and discussed issues of mutual understanding. The Kingdom's campaign to build a broad Sunni alliance to contain Iran has apparently suffered at least a setback from Pakistan.[14] Pakistani Prime Minister Nawaz Sharif rejected, at least for now, Saudi Arabia's entreaties for Pakistani troops to help guard the Saudi border with Northern Yemen, controlled by Iranian-backed Houthi Shiite forces.[15] After the Iranian Revolution, General Zia ul-Haq deployed an elite Pakistani armoured brigade to the kingdom at King Fahd's request to deter any threats to the country. In all, some 40,000 Pakistanis served in the brigade over most of a decade.[16]

Today Pakistan's military advisers and brigades of armed forces are serving the kingdom. However, the ISIS is projecting itself as a champion of the 'Sunni' cause, putting up a fight against an expansionist, Shia Iran.[17] Moreover, if the Sunni states remain ambiguous about their anti-ISIS policy, Islamists the world over will gravitate towards the extremist group as it continues to play up its anti-Iran and anti-Shia cards.[18] Saudi Arabia link with Pakistan's nuclear and missile program has long been the source of speculation, which Pakistan might either station its nuclear forces on Saudi soil, or provide a nuclear umbrella to the Wahabi state, in return for oil supply; or that Saudi would purchase nuclear weapons from Pakistan.[19]

The Saudi regime always counted on Pakistan to provide the Praetorian Guards of the regime if a need arose.[20] The Iranian reports suggest that there could be Pakistani personnel numbering thousands already serving in the security-related spheres in Saudi Arabia. Saudi Arabia has stationed some brigades of Pakistan military on its soil, and continues to support Islamic State (ISIS), to prevent Iranian invasion.[21] However, thousand soldiers of Pakistan's Blackwater (Fuji Foundation) are fighting in Bahrain, and Yemen, against the Shia population. Pakistan also provided military unites to protect the kingdom. In Bahrain, Pakistani Black water militias are fighting Saudi war against the majority Shia population.[22]

As India Today Magazine reported hundreds of Pakistani militants supporting the ranks of Islamic State in Syria and Iraq, these fighters are believed to be retired army personnel and civilians from militant groups like Lashkar-e-Toiba and the Lashkar-e-Jhangvi.[23] "Hundreds of our Mujahedeen have moved to Syria, and others are preparing to join them soon, "Abu Wahab," commander of a pro-Pakistan militant group claimed.[24] The groups in Iraq are believed to be from the 'pro-government' groups like LeJ, and not the Tahreek-e-Taliban Pakistan that attacked Karachi airport on June 8, 2014, against which the Pakistan army is fighting in North Waziristan.[25]

Pakistan's military contribution in the Islamic State (ISIS) can be judged from the revelations of a former officer of Pakistan army Major Agha Amin; a Lahore-based defense analyst told India Today that Pakistani fighters went to Syria and Iraq with the tacit knowledge of the government. "There is a strong possibility that the Mosul attack was supported by the Pakistani state, both civilian and military, Major Amin said.[26]

In this chapter, I want to concentrate on nuclear relation between Pakistan and Saudi Arabia, and the Saudi demand of its share in Pakistan's Islamic bomb. After some of my articles published in newspapers in 2015, a considerable amount of debate started in international press regarding Pakistan's controversial nuclear program. In my argument, I raised the question of foreign involvement in Pakistan Islamic bomb. Research scholar Reshmi Kazi's analysis of Saudi Arabia's nuclear thinking and Pakistani connection provides my readers with good information in the context of Iranian nuclear threat in the region:

> Saudi Arabia worries that the West will turn its focus away from Iran once the problem over the Iranian nuclear programme is diffused. Riyadh anticipates that in the long run a nuclear Iran will be emboldened in Saudi Arabia's proxy conflict with Iran in states like Palestine, Bahrain, Yemen and most recently Syria. Amidst such concerns, Riyadh's rejection of a coveted seat at the United Nation Security Council in October 2013 followed by the revelation of the BBC news about possible nuclear weapons cooperation between Saudi Arabia and Pakistan in November 2013 has raised questions whether Riyadh aspires to acquire nuclear weapons capability? What has been the level of nuclear cooperation between the two Islamic nations...President Hassan Rouhani emphasized in an interview to the financial Times that Iran will not fully dismantle its nuclear programme as part of a comprehensive agreement.[27]

Pakistani scientists helped Saudi Arabia's National Nuclear Program (NNP). The rise of nuclear Iran in the Persian Gulf and Middle East regions, ISIS and the torment of the Arab world, and their desperately seeking nuclear weapons, have been two interesting issues of debates in international press since years. In the end of 2013, Iran settled its controversial issue and extended hands of friendship to the West. Author Reshmi Kazi highlights the anxiety of Saudi rulers and their encirclement of Iran:

> Riyadh's goal is to encircle Iran in the region, weaken its allies and cap its regional aspirations. However, the nuclear deal

concluded between the global powers led by Washington and Iran seemingly appears to scuttle Riyadh's goal in countering Tehran influence in the region. What bother Riyadh more is the belief that the diffusion of the Iranian nuclear problem, Washington would eventually turn its attention away from the Middle East leading to a deterioration of the US protective umbrella in the region? The Obama administration's abandonment of its long-standing regional ally in Egypt's Hosni Mubarak and its recent diplomatic initiatives in Syria and Iran bears testimony to Iran's apprehensions.[28]

On February 2014, we saw the first visit of Pakistan's Army Chief to Saudi Arabia since he replaced General Kayani in November 2013, after the controversial news reports about the Saudis' investment in the country's Islamic bomb. Pakistani newspapers scrupulously reported his mission, but newspapers in the United Kingdom termed his visit of great importance as both the states faced national security threat from home-grown terrorist groups.[29] In Pakistan, a new Islamic terrorist threat of ISIS is on the rise as Saudi Arabia wants to strengthen its military relations with the country on one hand, and support Taliban insurgents against the ISIS on the other.

On 08 February 2014, Daily Naya Akhbar reported Saudi authorities asking Pakistan to dispatch two more divisions' forces (30,000) to the kingdom as part of bilateral agreement between the two states.[30] Another Pakistani newspaper, Daily Ummat (Urdu) stated that Pakistani troops will train Saudi troops, but military observer feared that these troops might be used in sectarian conflicts in the Middle East, particularly in Yemen against Shia Houties.[31] On 20 January 2014, Saudi Deputy Defense Minister, Prince Salman visited Pakistan to discuss the emergence of nuclear Iran and the emergence of ISIS in the Middle East.[32] Dawn reported on 07 March 2014 that Pakistani government was pursuing plans for a "new era in strategic partnership" with Saudi Arabia, which it desired to be anchored in time-tested defense relationship. Plans were also afoot for expanded defense cooperation with China.[33] Foreign Office spokesperson Tasneem Aslam said at the weekly media briefing that the possibility of collaboration in defense production was discussed during the visit of Saudi Crown Prince Salman bin Abdul-Aziz. "Nothing has yet been finalized... these discussions are continuing," Tasneem said.

Dawn reported impending Pak-Saudi Defense and friendly relations with China. Chinese, Defense Minister visited Pakistan and discussed bilateral cooperation between the two states. "While we do not want to indulge in an arms race and spend our meager resources on buying arms, at the same time, we cannot be completely oblivious to what is happening in the region. We have to keep a level of conventional stability," Foreign Office Spokeswoman said.[34] It is a fact that Saudi Arabia is integrating Pakistan as a key player in its regional strategies. The mystery of the $1.5 billion 'gift' deposited by Saudi Arabia in the State Bank of Pakistan, according to Mr. Bhadrakumar's argument, was falling in place. What emerges was that Saudi Arabia needed Pakistani weapons for equipping the forces, which serve as Riyadh's proxies in various regional theatres.[35] In his Friday Times editorial, Pakistani journalist and scholar Najam Sethi also confirmed the grant of $1.5 billion Saudi help to Prime Minister Nawaz Sharif:

> The Saudi Kingdom has granted $1.5b to the Nawaz Sharif government... A quick fix of $3b is a lot of free money for Pakistan's forex-strapped economy that is struggling to cope with significant international debt payments and a rising trade gap that is putting pressure on the rupee and fuelling inflation. Indeed, the Saudi injection has reversed the rapid fall of the rupee, proving that the finance minister, Ishaq Dar, was not bluffing when he warned exporters six weeks ago not to hoard their dollars.[36]

Mr. Najam Sethi also hinted at the threat of Shiaism arising from Iraq and Syria, which Saudi Arabia wants to counter it effectively. Saudi knows that nuclear Iran is threat to its security and stability, therefore, the country wants to engage Pakistan in the region. On 21 March 2014, in his editorial comment, Mr. Najam Sethi noted:

> The Saudis and the Emirates-Gulfdoms are feeling insecure because of the Shia revival in their heartlands. This is because the restless Shias are sitting on their oil reserves. Iran, too, is unremitting in opposing Saudi influence. Iraq and Qatar, two competitive energy suppliers, are not playing ball either. Egypt and Libya haven't bought into the Saudi Islamist line. Worse, the Americans are seeking negotiated nuclear solutions in Iran instead of succumbing to Saudi pressure for military action. And American self-reliance on shale gas is the first definite step against continued

dependence on Saudi oil. On the heels of the Saudi VVIPs now comes the King of Bahrain to Islamabad. The PMLN government claims that foreign investment deals are in the offing. But the small print betrays the real motive behind "renewed manpower exports."The Bahraini Emir wants well-trained and equipped Pakistani military mercenaries to beef up his police and security forces to repress the rising democratic impulses of the majority Shia populations. It is as simple as that.[37]

Researcher Farhan Bukhari views persisting relationship between Pakistan and Saudi Arabia of great importance. He argued that; "Saudi Arabia's growing engagement with Islamabad means that Riyadh wants Islamabad's support to bolster itself on two fronts; the Southern frontline along the border with Yemen, and to the north to face internal security challenges, as well as tackling any possible spill over from conflict-stricken Syria".[38] On 20 March 2014, journalist Dr. Muhammad Taqi warned in his article that Pakistan's involvement in sectarian conflicts in Middle East can harm internal stability of the country:

> By aligning Pakistan with the Saudis in a conflict that might rip the Middle East along sectarian seams, Nawaz Sharif seems to be making a conscious decision to set this country up to formally becomes a Wahabi confessional state eventually. Mr. Sharif, personally beholden to the Saudis like Ustad Sayyaf, may be signing on to a not just a personal name change but to changing the country's already abysmal confessional outlook for the worse. What are deeply disconcerting are not the small arms that Pakistan has agreed to provide the Saudis, destined for Syrian rebels in all likelihood, but the bigger doctrinal mess that Mr. Sharif might be dragging the country into. It seems like Nawaz Sharif just picked up on doing the Saudi's bidding exactly from where he left off in 1999.[39]

Both traditional Islamic terrorists and the new breed have filled ranks with militants, who receive support from Saudi Arabia. By receiving Saudi financial assistance, extremists in both Pakistan and Afghanistan learned the value of violence, in defeating security forces of the states.[40] They are well funded with an eye on Pakistan nuclear weapons, and developed sophisticated international networks that allow them to successfully attack Pakistani security forces.[41]

Charities from Saudi Arabia and the United Arab Emirates financed terrorist networks in Pakistan that recruited children as young as eight to wage "holy-war."[42] The US diplomatic cable published by WikiLeaks said financial support estimated at $100 million a year was making its way from those Gulf Arab states to an extremist recruitment network in Pakistan's Punjab province.[43] In February 2015, the Saudi embassy issued a statement saying that all its donations to seminaries had government clearance, after a minister accused Riyadh of creating instability across the Muslim world.[44] Pakistani Foreign Ministry responded by saying that funding by private individuals through "informal channels" would also be scrutinized closely to try to choke off funding for terror groups.[45] While the statement avoided mentioning Saudi Arabia specifically, it was widely interpreted as a rebuke.[46] In March 2015, Saudi King Salman Bin Abdul Aziz summoned Prime Minister of Pakistan Nawaz Sharif after unveiling of the covert aid to Wahhabis-allied Deobandis who promote violent extremism and takfiri terrorism in all over Pakistan.[47]

Riaz Hussain Pirzada Minister for Inter-provincial Coordination accused Saudi government of creating instability in Pakistan, through distribution of money for promoting its ideology.[48] Addressing a two-day 'Ideas Conclave' organized by the "Jinnah Institute" think tank in Islamabad, he said, 'the time has come to stop the influx of Saudi money into Pakistan. Mr. Pirzada and the Jinnah Institute were calling for Pakistan to pay careful attention to the consequences of accepting Saudi funds.[49]

Before many young radical Muslims take up arms with jihadist groups such as the Islamic State (ISIS) and al-Qaeda, they receive their first lessons on radical Islam from madrassas, Islamic schools that serve as an alternative to government or expensive private schools.[50] "They create a sensibility among children that later turns into a big support base for extremist and sectarian views," said A. H. Nayyar, a Pakistani physicist and nuclear activist, who has also researched and written on madrassa education.[51] In a country like Pakistan, one difficulty with a high level act of nuclear terrorism is that of credibility; Taliban terrorists have to prove to the government that they are capable of acts that are being threatened. Now they also succeeded in persuading Pakistani government that the settlement of the ongoing conflict is impossible without the cooperation of their forces. Pakistan's nuclear weapons are a constant threat to world peace.[52] If Pakistan provides nuclear bomb to Saudi Arabia, it will create misunderstanding between Iran and Pakistan. Russia's English newspaper, Pravda (2013) reported the Saudi financial aid to Pakistan's nuclear program: "Saudi Arabia's foreign policy is undergoing some significant shifts, as evidenced by the decision not to accept the UN Security Council seat, so the situation has become more unpredictable".[53]

Policy adopted by former Obama administration enraged all Arab rulers. According to American Thinker (2013), there was no more strategic commodity than gulf oil to the entire world economy.[54] Iran is the winner and Arabs are the losers. Arabs and Pakistan will face the consequences of their interventionist policies.[55] Saudi Arabia interfered in Bahrain, Syria, Iraq and Yemen, while Pakistan army is interfering in Kashmir, Waziristan, FATA and Afghanistan. Saudi has also said that it will unleash a pre-emptive war in the Middle East in response to the pro-Iranian policy of the Obama administration.[56]

Experts feared that Saudi may possibly provide these weapons to Pakistani Taliban based in Syria, or it will deploy these weapons on its borders? Because, Saudi's recent diplomatic ruction with the United States has been a demand of stern military action against the Assad regime. The Saudis will not wait more to receive Pakistani nuclear bomb, because they have already paid for it. Libya, Korea and other Muslim states have already received their share.

In 2014, politician Mahmood Khan Achakzai criticized military establishment that it killed more Pashtuns than the remote control drone. Pakistan army continues to kill Pashtuns and Balochs. Recent terror attacks in various cities of Pakistan triggered concerns in international community about the security of the country's nuclear weapons. This perception has wide-ranging strategic, diplomatic, political and economic implications for Pakistan. Today's precarious situation in Pakistan comes in a world where terror groups are actively seeking nuclear weapons. Uyghur Islamic front looks towards Pakistan for its assistance against communist China. Taliban, Al Qaeda and the ISIS group wants nuclear weapons. Syrian rebels need weapons of mass destruction; Haqqani and Mullah Omar also need these weapons to use it in Afghanistan. Can Pakistan meet their demands? Yes, there are speculations and fears in intellectual circles that Pakistan may possibly provide these weapons to Chinese dissidents or Taliban insurgents in near future.

About 1,000 Chinese jihadists received military training in a secret base in Pakistan, while an unclear number of Chinese nationals are already fighting in Syria, Jacques Neriah, a Middle East analyst at the Jerusalem Center for Public Affairs told a high-level delegation from China.[57] The Chinese delegation was made up of 10 representatives, several of them members of the Central Party School, which trains future senior officials.[58] As the country has already warned that in case of Indian military intervention, it would use nuclear weapons against it, we can understand the intentions of Pakistan military establishment, and its secret dealing with CIA and Defence Clandestine Intelligence (DCI).[59]

The continued ties of Deobandi, Barelvi, Ahl Hadeith and Salafi groups and their sympathizers within the army of the country, poses considerable threat to the nuclear installations. According to the recent report of National Crisis Management Cell of Pakistan, more than 400 sectarian and extremist groups operate alongside Punjabi Taliban in Southern Punjab, which receive supports from various civilian and military quarters.[60] Punjabi Taliban control dozens of villages in Southern Punjab and receive funds from the Punjab government. Punjabi Taliban has established a strong network in Army and police forces.

In its report, Weapons of Mass Destruction Commission, initiated by the Swedish Government on a proposal from the United Nations warned that: Acquiring weapons of mass destruction and usable materials directly from a sympathetic government would significantly simplify the requirement for the terrorists, obviating the need to defeat security system protecting such materials.[61] During the civil wars, violence or instability in a country like Pakistan, terror groups can gain control of fissile materials. Insurgent groups, like Taliban or sectarian groups of can make a safe penetration with the cooperation of inside contacts.[62]

Pakistan is the centre of nuclear jihad where Islamic Atom Bomb has received a lot of investment from the Muslim world. Islamic Atom Bomb also inculcates other Muslim states the right and religious obligation to acquire Weapons of Mass Destruction (WMD) and use them against non-Muslim states.[63] Since Gen Musharraf came to power, relations between Pakistan and North Korea further developed, while Pakistan paid for North Korea's missiles and related technology, with dollar and wheat purchased from the US and Australia, and diverted to it.

In October 2017, King Salman and Russian President Vladimir Putin meet in Moscow.[64] Moscow backs the Syrian regime, while Riyadh has supported the government's enemies. According to the Kommersant newspaper report, "agreement between Saudi Arab and Moscow was signed on a $3bn (£2.2bn) deal to supply the Saudis with Russia's most advanced air defense missile system, the S400 Triumph".[65] Independent also reported that, "the deal will be signed off at a WTO meeting at the end of October. Defense is one of few technological sectors where Russia can still claim to be a world leader, with over a fifth of all arms deals in 2016".[66] But with China and India, Russia's biggest markets, looking to move towards military self-sufficiency, Russia is with increasing urgency looking to open new markets. Independent reported on 13 October 2017 that Russia agreed deal to sell Saudi Arabia S-400 air defense missiles. Russia agreed a deal with Saudi Arabia to supply advanced S-400 air defense missiles to Riyadh, Vladimir Putin's aide has announced. The S-400 system comprises a set of four missiles with varying ranges, and is designed to intercept aircraft as well as other missiles. It can respond to threats up to 400km away.[67]

Chapter 4

A New Equation of Pakistan's Nuclear Weaponization

Lieutenant General Gautam Banerjee

Introduction

In 1998, immediately following India's 'Shakti' nuclear tests, Pakistan chose to announce its overt nuclear weaponisation by conducting tests in the Chagai Hills of Baluchistan. Having gained nuclear bomb capability nearly a decade ago with China's active help, all Pakistan needed to do this time was to use weapon components which had already been tested in the Lop Nor test site in the Gobi desert of Xinjiang, China. Subsequently, posing as an 'innocent victim' of India purported propensity to "launch military offensive to overrun Pakistan", it declared the policy of 'first use' of its strategic nuclear arsenal. Pakistan proposes to carry out nuclear strikes against India when its ambiguously (un) defined threshold of nuclear use is considered, by the Pakistan Army, of course, to have been breached by India's 'superior' conventional military forces.[1]

Numbering 130, Pakistan's current nuclear arsenal is reported to be larger than that of India numbering 118. Further, strategic analysts aver that Pakistan is intent on increasing that number to 200 or 250. In a parallel development, in 2011, Pakistan declared its intent to acquire 'Tactical Nuclear Weapons' (TNWs), the purpose being to destroy India's offensive forces even before these can breach its nuclear threshold. Some years down the line, as induction of TNWs in Pakistan's nuclear arsenal takes shape, the pitch of its proxy aggression as well as instigation of misguided elements in Kashmir and elsewhere in India is also seen to be rising. Indeed, these developments are but the escalatory steps of the strategy that Pakistan contrives to tear Kashmir away from India before striking a lethal blow at the very roots of Indian nationhood.

This situation calls for India's strategic community to find ways to break free of a dangerous nuclear imposition by which the ever inimical state of Pakistan seeks to immobilize India while inflicting a 'thousand cuts' on it and bleeding it to disintegration. The debate on India's options in dealing with Pakistan, including the application of its nuclear doctrine, enunciated in 2003, should, therefore, receive a fresh impetus. Accordingly, the discussion in this paper is focused on the implications of Pakistan's inclusion of the TNWs in its nuclear arsenal upon India's security and integrity.

It is intended to discuss the following issues this paper:

> India's objectives, as dictated by its political ideology, in protecting its national security against inimical assaults from external adversaries.

> The *effect of Pakistan's possession* of TNWs on the strategies that India might adopt to secure its objectives.

> The hypotheses and paradigms of *'nuclear-strike-counter-strike'* in the Indo-Pakistan context.

> A revisit of India's nuclear weapon policies, and the advisability or otherwise of *India developing its own* TNWs.

Roots of Indo-Pakistan Strategic Divergence India's Political Ideology

Just as it is with every state, India's political class defers to the exercise of sovereign dispensation in the achievement of the nation's socio-economic progress. But in the application of that ideology, unlike those in most other strategically positioned states, it repudiates a substantive role for its military institution. Picking up the notion that prevailed among the last native Hindu rulers of a politically divided Bharatvarsha before they were decimated by Western invasions a thousand years earlier, the leaders of post-Independence India too believe that 'war solves nothing' (as if 'peace' does!) and go about translating that notion to keep the military institution in a state of comparative emaciation. Post-Independence prejudice or wisdom, whether for good or bad, is not the issue here: the fact is that in democratic India, such convictions prevail across the entire political establishment.

But even if there are noble intents behind keeping military preparedness below par in favour of democratically aspired progress, the hoary lessons of statecraft forbid overdoing that. Conversely, even if unstated but starkly observed, the Indian state, bears the burden of its military institution most reluctantly, and keeps the utility of that institution confined just to resist external aggression – to retard, or, if possible, deny a free run to the aggressors – and nothing more. Resultantly, the military institution in India, notwithstanding the high esteem it is accorded by its citizenry, has been but grudgingly maintained at the *minimalist* scale of operational effectiveness, that scale being decided by such post-aggressive damage suffered at the hands of its instinctively inimical neighbours that even a stoic Indian state is unable to find tolerable. The result is that a passive Indian state emboldens enmity and encourages aggression. Indeed, just as it reflects on the 'hollowed' condition of India's military institution, this political ideology of passive national security also manifests in the country's recessed, even apologetic, nuclear posture.

India's Conventional Power and Nuclear Doctrine

India's nuclear doctrine of 2003 repudiates the military use of nuclear weapons, preferring to depend upon 'recessed deterrence 'to counter any nuclear blackmail which it do two inimical neighbours might thrust on it either singly or in collusion. Thus, consigning nuclear weapons to only political purposes, India's nuclear doctrine subscribes to the policy of 'No First Use' (NFU), leaving the *onus of starting a nuclear war* on its adversaries. Further, to deter the adversary's first use of nuclear weapons, the doctrine declares, *"Nuclear retaliation to a first strike will be massive and designed to inflict unacceptable damage"*. To that end, the doctrine entails the propagation of 'Credible Minimum Deterrence' (CMD) through the possession of a nuclear weapon inventory that would be adequate to inflict 'unacceptable damage' upon the initiator of a nuclear exchange.

For a militarily reticent nation that India opts to be, the reluctance to wield military power may be understandable, particularly when that stance is considered to be helpful in bringing good observations from the global fraternity. The problem, however, arises when in its strategic naiveté; the state is swayed by a simplistic belief that just the passive and reactive modes of a 'minimalist' military response to conventional and sub-conventional aggression would be enough to keep India secure. That absurd belief then goes on to buttress the state's reluctance to invest on maintaining its conventional military power at the requisite level of modernity. Instead, the state finds it expedient to substitute conventional military deterrence with a combination of rightful indignation against aggression, diplomatic rhetoric, light military actions of defensive content, and at the ultimate end, a 'Credible Minimum Deterrence' (CMD) of nuclear-tipped missile stocks.

The contrast and confusion among India's defense decision-makers is palpable; they repudiate the use of nuclear power as well as covert sub- conventional interventions to rely on strong conventional military power to keep habitual aggressors away. And yet, they deliberately keep the nation's conventional military power short-charged – a short period after the 1962 disaster being an exception. Obviously, neither the enemy nor the world powers are impressed. India's purported 'strategic restraint' against constant provocations has, therefore, left open wide opportunities for the habitual intransigent to engage in less intensity, long drawn and highly divisive sub-conventional warfare that strikes not just at Kashmir but at the very roots of Indian nationhood.

Pakistan's Nuclear Posture

Pakistan's all-powerful strategic oligarchy believes, or pretends to believe, that by bolstering its conventional military capabilities with a strategic nuclear posture and then holding out the threat of a nuclear 'first strike' now and then, it has been able to paralyze India's military muscle. Thus, it grants itself unbridled opportunities to pursue its irrepressible urge to strike at the Indian nationhood through armed aggression. After some backtrack in the aftermath of the 2001-02 showdowns (Operation Parakram), Pakistani strategists felt free again to gradually escalate their openly sponsored, aided, abetted and prosecuted sub-conventional aggression of proxy insurgency and crass terrorism against India. Next, as would be seen during the subsequent discussion, by adding TNWs to their nuclear arsenal in 2011, Pakistan's strategists construe to have imposed what they posit as "full spectrum deterrence" upon India. That deterrence, they believe, altogether terminates any option that India has to apply its supposedly superior conventional forces to chastise Pakistan. And that, they smugly aver, leaves India with no option but to suffer at the receiving end of Pakistan's perpetual armed aggression.[2]

Pakistan's aggressive behaviour is further bolstered by the tentative strategy that India's custodians of national defense seem to have adopted. That is so when, adding the poison of Islamist *jihad*, Pakistan has been able to raise the level of aggression to a scale as dangerous as is currently on display in Kashmir, and to a worrying extent, even in the rest of India. In response, all that India is supposedly 'allowed' to do is be confined to defensive measures, which, at best, can only limit the mayhem that Pakistan perpetrates on the Indian soil. Considering that apart from parroting the warnings of 'not tolerating any more' of the mayhem which Pakistan's *jehadi* military 'assets' perpetuate on the Indian soil in the forms of 'proxy war' in Kashmir and terror operations in the rest of the nation, this belief of Pakistan's is apparently vindicated. No doubt, Pakistan's sense of immunity is nurtured by India exercising what is rather pompously described as 'strategic restraint', which has been in demonstration in the wake of such grave provocations like the Kargil, Parliament, Mumbai, Samba, Pathankot, Uri, and Nagrota attacks – the list is rather long. Notably, even earlier, Pakistan believed that its undeclared nuclear possessions had deterred India from taking offensive action in 1990, against its instigation of the Punjab insurgency.

A Situation of Adverse Deterrence

Pakistani strategists have spelt out, albeit informally and as ambiguously as it suits them, the lower 'red-line' for Pakistan to launch its strategic nuclear weapons. According to those indicative pronouncements, Pakistan would resort to the use of nuclear weapons when it perceives its political, territorial, economic or military integrity to be under the threat of collapse. Making the chest-thumping Pakistan state pay when its aggression becomes intolerable—rather far from the notion of triggering the collapse of that intransigent state—being their goal in any case, Indian strategists took note of those messages with due seriousness. Thus, India's offensive strategy against Pakistan was remodeled, the intended depth of offensives curtailed, and the force structure reconfigured – all to prevent offering an excuse for Pakistan to start a nuclear war.

In that process, the Indian state might have gone overboard in buying the theory that even limited objective military retaliation(s) to curb Pakistan's sub-conventional aggression would trigger a conventional war, and then, as India's conventional military superiority starts telling, Pakistan would be provoked to unleash its oft reiterated nuclear 'first strike'. In that case, with the national Endeavour focused on accelerated economic progress, it might be difficult for the Indian state to reconcile with whatever is its share of the consequent destruction. This predicament of India has encouraged Pakistan's strategists to tighten the confinement of the Indian defense decision-makers' minds to just defensive resistance against Pakistan's proxy war, while freezing, if not sequestering, India's conventional military edge to retaliate. It is, thus, in Pakistan's reckoning, that India, many times bigger and stronger, stands deterred from punishing Pakistan in any way for attacking India in its own backyard.

Here is a case of a rapacious state using its nuclear weapons to immunize itself from the consequences of its avarice! Thus, with a bit of overstatement, it may not be out of place to say that here is a case of a weaker enemy adopting a superior strategy to perpetrate overt aggression against a superior power, while immunizing itself against retaliatory retribution.

Appearance of the TNW, Pakistan's TNWs

It was in the backdrop of Pakistan's brash pronouncements of nuclear brinkmanship during the Kargil conflict as well as the 2001-02 standoff (Operation Parakram) that the Indian Army devised its strategy to exploit the 'space' through which limited conventional military retribution could still be meted out against Pakistan's proxy war, without having to breach Pakistan's nuclear threshold. Though anything but 'cold' in its characteristics, the sobriquet of 'Cold Start' has got stuck to this inspiring strategy. The strategy called for the conduct of quick conventional offensives by a number of distinct 'battle groups' across a wide front and limited depth, so to inflict extensive military and political damage to the habitual offender, while remaining short of providing passable excuses for Pakistan to use nuclear weapons, ostensibly to save itself from disintegration.

In response, Pakistani strategists have been intent on devising means to constrict they said 'space 'which, as both the protagonists understand, remains open for India to unleash its conventional forces in the so-called 'Cold Start' mode. Half a decade of efforts later, the addition of TNWs in Pakistan's nuclear arsenal is the fruition of that intent. It is stated that the TNWs would be used to destroy even the shallow penetrations into Pakistan's territory that India's forces might gain across a wide front. In the reckoning of Pakistan's strategists, introduction of TNWs should, thus, close what little options India has to retaliate. India would then have no option left but to resign to being "bled by a thousand cuts", as the rhetoric goes. Pakistani strategists have, thus, devised what they term as 'full spectrum deterrence' to tie India's hands while enjoying 'full spectrum immunity' from retaliation as they go on inflicting those 'cuts' on hapless Indians.

TNWs in the European Theatre

Even if there may be no befitting inference, it may be of interest here to touch upon the advent of TNWs in the post-World War II Europe theatre.

By the 1960s, Soviet Russia had caught up, more or less, with the fission, fusion, thermo-nuclear and neutron bomb arsenal in America's possession. Thus, followed the espousal of various theories of 'first use' and 'follow up' nuclear exchange between the two adversarial parties, 'flexible' or 'proportionate' response to 'first attack', the 'escalatory ladder', the madness of 'mutual assured destruction', and, finally, the nuances of astute 'nuclear signaling', all aimed at saving the civilized world from that madness. At the end, it dawned upon the leaders of both blocs that the state of nuclear deterrence and counter-deterrence had brought them to a permanent stage of stalemate which could be broken only at the prospect of complete mutual devastation. Thus, as the conventionally superior Warsaw Pact Armies hovered over the East-West divide across the then East Germany-Czechoslovakia frontier, the assurance of nuclear 'first use' that had been available to the opposing

North Atlantic Treaty Organization (NATO) Armies to thwart the Communist forces was somewhat neutralized. The favorable asymmetry was, thus, compromised, leaving the Western Alliance vulnerable to the Eastern bloc's overwhelming superiority in conventional military power. The latter's massive military formations could be maintained only in the autocratic regimes; democratic nations, answerable to the people and their immediate needs, could not match that array of conventional forces.[3]

It was at that juncture, when the lunacy of 'assured destruction' had been discarded as unacceptable, unthinkable and abhorrent by both the contestants, that America deployed its TNWs. These weapons were meant to be used under the 'Air-Land Battle' strategy to counter a possible onslaught of successive echelons of massive Warsaw Pact forces which, for the NATO Armies to tackle, would have needed an impractically large conventional order of battle. TNWs were, therefore, introduced to use fewer and smaller yield nuclear warheads to substitute for large conventional formations, and so stop the Communist invasion without having to escalate to a strategic nuclear 'first strike'.

TNWs have been defined in many ways – according to size and weight, mobility, yield, range and usage, but, finally, it all boils down to the actual usage of these against designated targets and ranges of 'counter-force' engagement. Accordingly, TNWs have also been classified under 'battlefield' and 'theatre' weapons. The damage effect and range of 'battlefield weapons' is dictated by targets such as maneuvering or defending forces in field fortifications, force assembly areas, defiles, bridgeheads, communication hubs, logistic echelons, etc., while those of 'theatre weapons' are geared to engage Command, Control, Communications, Intelligence (C3I) nodes, force concentrations, administrative areas, logistic installations, rail, shipping, military-industrial infrastructure, and so on.

Accordingly, battlefield TNWs are likely to be designed for sub-kiloton (below 0.01 to 0.99 kiloton of TNT equivalent) and low-kiloton (1 to 18-40 kiloton of TNT equivalent) yields, to inflict instantaneous 'severe damage' within killing zones of a few hundred and up to some thousand meters radii respectively. However, more than its larger 'killing zone' as compared to conventional bombs, abhorrence of nuclear weapons arises due to the manner in which the target on 'ground zero' is instantaneously 'vaporized', the peripheral areas are subjected to 'total destruction' within a few seconds, and the long-term radiation damage to life and materials that follows. Arguably, there have been claims of turning 'air burst' TNWs harmless in terms of radioactive damage but these claims are to be taken with a pinch of salt.

Apart from higher destruction over a larger killing area as compared to similar weight and volume of conventional weapons, the estimated immediate or primary damage potential of TNWs against deployed military formations is somewhat limited. Thus, a one kiloton weapon might wipe out an Army sub-unit while a 15 kiloton may do that to a full line unit. The overall effects of radioactive fallouts and secondary damage to personnel and hardware would thereafter depend upon weather, terrain, wind, population density and protective measures available to the targeted forces. The point to note is that the ruling factors and variables being many, the figures quoted can only be guess estimates. What is beyond doubt is the intense destruction by nuclear weapons.

By the late 1960s, as the Soviets too caught up with their TNWs, strategists in either camp subsequently realized that the use of TNWs at the extreme height of a conventional war, would, in all probability, start from ones and twos to more and more, till a stage would be reached when escalation to a strategic nuclear strike-counter-strike exchange could not be prevented. That horrendous prospect caused the already prevalent stalemate over strategic nuclear weapon to spill over to the use of TNWs. All nuclear weapons thus, became unusable in war, though these could be retained to find some sadistic joy in taking the enemy along into mutual oblivion. A stage, thus, came when; nixing the TNWs, the 'West' and the 'East' both reinvented the wisdom to stick to conventional deterrence. The scope for massed warfare being rather limited, they now took to satiate their ideological divergence by resorting to sub-conventional, irregular and surrogate warfare, to be engaged on third party lands.[4]

In other words, once the deterrence of strategic nuclear weapons got stalemated, the opposing forces configured TNWs into their conventional military operations. Then, in turn, TNWs too lost their conventional utility, till the end of the Cold War put a stop to that ghastly exercise. Arguably, therefore, *possession of TNWs by both the opposing adversaries puts a valid question mark on the usefulness of these as weapons of war, just as it had been in the case of strategic nuclear weapons.* This lesson could be a term of reference in the Indian context.

Salient Lessons

There are salient lessons to be learnt from the eternal cycles of inflation and deflation of the East-West confrontation that go on even at present in some form or the other. Without going into the case studies, some of the lessons may be recounted as follows:

> ➢ Political leaders do not go to war unless they are certain of strengthening their domestic position. But autocratic rulers, bereft of fair advice, are known to have gone wrong in their assessment of victory. This lesson is exemplified by Pakistan's ventures in 1948-49, 1965, the Western Sector in 1971 and the Kargil conflict. By this token, should India stand firm, *Pakistan's sub-conventional war against India is ultimately bound to fail.*

> ➢ Ruling oligarchies avoid venturing into any act, including warfare that could spell their fall from power and pelf. To that extent, their love for the nation has to be recessed in preference to their personal aggrandizement. This lesson points to the likelihood that notwithstanding its grandiloquence, *Pakistan's ruling clique would not like to invite massive nuclear retaliation, and be reduced from opulence to penury and death.*

> ➢ For an adversary to initiate a nuclear war, it must be such that the war concludes on its terms, i.e. victory. In such an eventuality, the specter of mutual devastation has to be foretold to the people. People do not approve of this, even if they are assured of having to face lesser punishment, of course. *No matter how fanatic they might be, the people of Pakistan would not like to be offered for mass vaporization.*

> ➢ When *there is no escalation control mechanism in place, no party is likely to initiate a nuclear war just in order to de-escalate a conventional war* that is being fought in a defined battle space.

> ➢ A nation with an NFU policy will, of necessity, be required to field a Ballistic Missile Defense (BMD) system to protect

its strategic assets and vital centres. But these have glaring limitations. Conversely, it also provokes the opponent to raise its capability. *The idea that BMD complements nuclear security is, therefore, only partially true.*

➢ Employed at the operational level of war, TNWs could be used with the strategic purpose of *nuclear signaling, to indicate the imminence of escalation, and thereby the necessity of war termination.* Such signals have to be conveyed, and understood in their true sense–when distrust reigns, that is not an easy goal to accomplish.

Inferences drawn from the above lessons suggest that triggering a strategic nuclear exchange could turn unthinkable among Pakistan's ruling feudal elite. Pakistan's adoption of TNWs could be a result of that realization. Therefore, should India offer a counter to this new affliction among the Pakistani strategists, their joy of brandishing TNWs could vanish? Taking a cue from the East-West confrontation, thus, *India's development of counter- TNWs may be desirable.*

Efficacy of Pakistan's TNWs

To evaluate the efficacy of Pakistan's TNWs, the first step would be to examine the technical and tactical efficacy of Pakistan's present TNW capability, as well as of what it could acquire in the coming days. Presently, the Hatf IX (Nasr) Multi-Barrel Rocket Launcher (MBRL) system and ground emplaced Nuclear Demolition Munitions (NDMs) form the inventory of Pakistan's TNWs, though at later stages, induction of more alternate delivery means may be envisaged.

In the context of Pakistan's TNWs, it is reported to be a sub-kiloton warhead set inside a 300 millimeter cylindrical shell weighing around 25 to 35 kg. The shell is launched to a strike range of 60 km from a four or twin-tube multi-barrel rocket launcher mounted on an 8x8 'transport-lay-launch' vehicle of fair mobility. Assuming that 15 kiloton equivalent nuclear shells would have an immediate killing zone of 550 meters radius, and considering the usual distribution pattern as well as the overlap of the killing zones for four launchers, it could be construed that a good part of an Army unit could be wiped out at the first instance by one salvo of the Nasr MBRL system. Since offensive formations are designed to manage with that degree of destruction, Pakistan would have to use many MBRLs and many salvos of TNWs to stop India's offensive thrusts in their tracks. Therefore, unless it is just a warning shot as part of nuclear signaling, Pakistan's use of one or two TNWs may not make sense.

Reports suggest that the Hatf IX (Nasr) system is being improved to get past India's nascent ballistic missile defenses. It is also stated that the system is integrated into Pakistan's centralized defense command-and-control network, for these to be controlled by apex level decision-makers—the Strategic Planning Division (SPD) and National Command Authority (NCA) located at the National Command Centre (NCC), and served by the Strategic Command and Control Support System (SCCSS). Besides, the Pakistan Army Engineers may trigger tactical nuclear demolition devices while the Pakistan Air Force may modify aircraft to drop tactical nuclear bombs. In the coming years, it is expected that Pakistan would be able to mate low-kiloton nuclear warheads with its inventory of longer range ballistic as well as cruise missiles; including the 350 km range air launched 'Ra'ad Hatf VIII' system. The Nasr is then unlikely to be its sole recourse to the use of TNWs.

But whatever are the weapons and the modes of delivery, Pakistan would require a larger number of TNW strikes to blunt any Indian conventional offensive. Even then, for Pakistan's rulers, that would be a contentious decision to make, considering the secondary destruction to life and materials, triggering of international outrage and India's formally pronounced 'massive retaliation to inflict unacceptable damage'.

The 'Surgical Strike': A Strategic Invigoration

As mentioned earlier, Pakistan's script of India's strategic disconcert is revealing. In Kashmir as well as the rest of India, Pakistan and its terrorist minions would perpetuate, with full impunity, a terrible war against the very core of Indian nationhood; and conversely, India would be prevented from using its advantage of conventional military power to deter or defeat that brazen act of aggression. In other words, should Pakistan's strategy succeed, the Indian government, in preserving Kashmir's integrity, would be allowed no option but to resign to long-lasting and bloody preventive and defensive actions at the sub-conventional level. Since such passive response to the hard power of aggression offers little chance of putting an end to it, Pakistani strategists, with the initiative in their hands, seem to be smug in their belief that Jammu, Kashmir and Ladakh would eventually fall into Pakistan's lap.

But a more damaging disconcert comes from the suicidal inferences drawn by some of India's myopic policy-influencers who, psyched into considering conventional power as of little use after the advent of Pakistan's TNWs, are reluctant to invest in military modernization. In their line of thinking, strategic nuclear weapons and various grades of missiles, on one end, and various modestly armed sub-conventional forces, on the other, might be enough to keep India secure, while leaving them to invest on their electoral base. Truly, as many of the past policies indicate, the spell of such strategic naiveté in the Indian state apparatus may not be an exception. Considering that through all wars, insurgencies and catastrophes, conventional military power has provided the fulcrum of the nation's post-independent sovereign strength, that kind of conscious degradation of the military institution defies wisdom. Apparently, many among the custodians of India's defense seem to have lost the battle of the 'mind' thus.

The Indian Army's 'surgical strike' across the Line of Control (LoC) in Kashmir in September 2016 has opened another chapter of the debate over India's officially promulgated nuclear doctrine. Ever since India developed its nuclear weapons as a political tool to deter nuclear arm-twisting by China, an assertive nuclear power, and Pakistan, India's ever-obsessive enemy, it was the first instance of India overtly crossing the LoC The salience of this action is not in its occurrence— such cross-border mini-actions are undertaken now and then without any significant gains apart from keeping the military institution primed. The salience of this instance comes from its multi-point scale, retaliatory purpose and popular effect. One, it was a chain of orchestrated raids across a wide frontage but shallow depth across the LoC, so shallow that even an inveterate falsifier like the Pakistan state could in no way view it as anywhere near its ambiguous nuclear threshold.

Two, it was declared, unapologetically, as an action not targeted at the Pakistani state but to destroy terrorist camps, which, by Pakistan's own admission, had uncontrollable *jehadi* fighters. Three, it belied the political trepidation of the Indian state against crossing the LoC in the face of Pakistan's nuclear rhetoric, into what was asserted this time as

Indian territory. And, four, it rescued, notionally and temporarily, of course, the Indian state from its pusillanimous image in the eyes of its own citizens–they loved and lapped up the military action and adopted the terminology of 'surgical strike' like a national slogan. The net effect was that it has been proved; if indeed there was any need to prove a well tested logic of warfare, that beyond a point, Pakistan's nuclear bluff must fail to work.

Pakistan's reaction to the surgical strike was revealing. For years now, Pakistan had shed the bombast about its purported 'Allah willed' military power and 'tenfold abilities' of its 'Muslim' soldiery when pitched against the 'infidel Hindu' (*sic*). Instead, it had switched over to 'spook' India – and the global watchers – through irrational pronouncements over its nuclear brinkmanship in all its ambiguity. In the instance of the 'surgical strike', however, when the situation came to the crunch, the Pakistan state, recovering from dismay and confused reactions, chose to remain innocent about the operation, and yet, impelled by its wont, attempted, and continues to attempt, to seek retribution for the 'loss of public face'.

By undertaking the surgical strike, therefore, a new facet of passable military retaliation against Pakistan's sub-conventional aggression has been revealed to India's usually nonplussed defense policy-makers, and even to the pacifists among the military leaders. Articulated with strategic wisdom, this could be the first step towards imposition of a credible 'sub-conventional deterrence', something that has so far been missing from India's strategic repertoire.

Paradigms of the Indo-Pakistan Nuclear Posture

Pakistan's Narrative

Pakistan state's narrative is rooted at its extraordinary make-belief that attends to its innate paranoia, that India must be intent on decimating its sovereignty. Having conjured up this notion that state proceeds to devote all its strength to undermine the Indian nationhood in any way that it possibly can. Impelled to satiate that irrepressible urge, it also must find means to insure itself from India's retaliation in response to its hostility. That agenda, as the Pakistan state concedes after it's repeatedly failed conventional aggressions, cannot be furthered in the face of India's military power. It, therefore, seeks to skirt around that hurdle by achieving superior nuclear weapon capability in terms of inventories of strategic as well as tactical nuclear weapons. Pakistan's policy of 'first use', should a stage comes when its vital interests are considered to be under threat from India's conventional military forces, is one key feature of that agenda. Unilateral and ambiguous delineation of that stage, mixed with rhetorical brinkmanship now and then, completes the Pakistan state's nuclear narrative.

Notably, considering the inherent suspicion and hatred of India that envelops the Pakistani strategists' vision, the said stage might not take much to be reached but for the bulwark of India's policy of *massive retaliation* and the unequivocal *credibility* of that policy. The appearance of TNWs in Pakistan's inventory is aimed at freeing Pakistan from that stalemate. The limited destruction that TNWs might inflict, as many strategic analysts consider, cannot justify India's massive retaliation. The resultant dilution of the *unequivocal credibility* of India's policy must be a dangerous situation for the belligerents as well as the regional community.

Hard Realities

To dispassionately examine Pakistan's TNW posture, Indian strategists would do well to be free from hopeful assumptions and consider the following hard realities:

> ➤ Pakistan has, or would soon have, prepared itself for the use of TNWs in tactical battle areas in terms of formalizing the battle procedure, deployment, targeting, hierarchy of command and control, communications, protection of own troops, etc.

> ➤ In tactical terms, the Pakistan Army would give itself the prerogative to decide the stage when it would find itself compelled to hit India's offensive forces with TNWs. That stage might be a specified depth of penetration into Pakistan's own or Pakistan held territories. Pakistan would try to brandish that prerogative to arrest the Indian decision-makers mind.

> ➤ Further, Pakistan's mitigating assurances of using TNWs in its own territory cannot bring any comfort. When national

interests are construed to be at stake, such assurances are liable to be set aside. Therefore, TNWs may be used on either side of the Line of Control (LoC) or the International Border (IB), as influenced by the Pakistan Army's 'forward line of troops' and disposition of Indian forces at the instance of use.

➢ It would be futile to confine Pakistan's TNW capability just by the range, caliber and numbers of the Hatf IX Nasr systems. Given their intent, and as discussed under the previous heading, Pakistani strategists would, as a foregone possibility, find many alternates to configure the use of longer range, higher payload delivery systems – the range of missiles and aircraft in its inventory – by under ranging and under tipping these with TNW warheads.

➢ Similarly, talking points over Pakistan's 'competence' in nuclear weapon miniaturization need not raise complacency. By its well honed dubious methods, Pakistan would certainly find that competence, by hook or crook.

➢ Concerns over leaving TNWs in the hands of 'trigger-sensitive' field commanders are unfounded. The highly professional Pakistan Army would definitely keep the nuclear control at the NCA level through its SCCSS, even if the trigger is to be pulled by local commanders.

➢ There is the talk of TNWs not being effective in mountainous terrain and unusable in the plains due to various factors like ground, wind, existence of value-assets, population, etc. These may be viewed as just 'feel good' notions. Indeed, users of TNWs would see to the effectiveness of these to the extent of their yield wherever battles are to be fought, and as much as the usual 'fog' and 'friction' of war would usually permit.

➢ There is also the talk of 'limited' casualties that a TNW could inflict upon the Indian forces. Actually, however, a TNW strike would be one part of overall conventional fire plans. In such fire plans, the TNWs could be used against troop concentrations and base echelons, while conventional fire power tackles manoeuvre forces, and vice versa. Immediate casualties of the combine, therefore, would be considerable. Besides, the TNWs would prop enough secondary effects to disrupt the command and control set-up and cause physical and psychological damage across the larger radii of the primary, secondary and tertiary killing zones. Thus, even if calculations state that a 15 kiloton nuclear weapon would account for just a part of a military unit, the fact is that it would render the better part of a formation as unfit for continued battle.

> Further, unless the launch is an intended part of nuclear 'signaling', the smaller destruction zone of a TNW would necessitate many more than one TNW to be launched at the first instance itself. Damage from multiple TNW strikes would, therefore, not be limited to just a 'few tanks and some personnel', as is hoped, but would be more widespread and disabling – materially as well as psychologically.

The appearance of TNWs into the nuclear-conventional equation, therefore, needs to be deliberated upon in the light of the above listed hard realities.

Nuances of India's Nuclear Doctrine

India's draft nuclear doctrine was formally adopted in 2003. Most appropriately, this doctrine offers the assurance of 'NFU'. Further, it warns the initiator of the nuclear weapon attack(s) that India's *"nuclear retaliation to a first strike will be 'massive' and designed to inflict 'unacceptable' damage"*. However, after Pakistan introduced TNWs into its conventional warfare arsenal, questions have been raised and suggestions made regarding the purport and sanctity of these three terms. These questions tend to dilute the Indian decision-makers' doctrinal resolve. Well intended or a part of the inimical 'mind game', such questions cannot, therefore, be left unaddressed if the right dividends of India's nuclear weaponisation are to accrue. Indian strategists cannot but ensure that their declared doctrine is taken seriously and scotch the expression of self-doubts regarding its key provisions.

Actually, the three key operative terms–'NFU', 'massive' (retaliation) and 'unacceptable'(damage)—as used in the doctrinal text, need not have any preconceived and fixated definitions, neither may India, while being subjected to nuclear doom, be expected to be bound by such definitions. Truly, a doctrine serves the end of preparation and planning – but it does not, and cannot, override strategically or tactically sensible courses of action-reaction to be adopted in the battlefield. Therefore, academic hair-splitting debates over the text and terminologies of the doctrine should not dictate the courses to be adopted by India to save itself from nuclear destruction.

In the nuclear mind game, it is sometimes desirable to buttress ambiguities in order to seek meanings to unresolved issues. Truly, therefore, the courses of India's actions and reactions would be appropriated by the 'signaling' that Pakistan communicates, and as India interprets those 'signals' at the time of the decision. One meaning to the questions and suggestions over India's nuclear doctrine could, therefore, be in the nuanced *understanding* of these three terms—NFU, 'massive' and 'unacceptable'–and viewing these as *situational variables*, while subscribing to the definitional sanctity of these.

Situational Variables: 'Massive Retaliation' and 'Unacceptable Damage'

Irrespective of Pakistan's level and scale of nuclear attack – that is, even if Pakistan's 'first use' attack is of miniscule proportions, a TNW strike, for example—the professed doctrinal interpretation of India's *massive retaliation* points to the 'annihilation' of the state of Pakistan. Conversely, it is also insinuated that the Indian decision-makers might not be as demonic as to take such a step of extreme inhumanity – curiously, no such sublime idealism is ascribed to Pakistan's decision-makers. Whether genuine or a contrived psy-war to confuse the Indian leadership's resolve, this dichotomy could infect serious misunderstandings in the 'signaling' of the opponent's nuclear postures – here too, India is supposed to bear the onus.[5]

Possibly, appreciation of the extent and scope of India's 'massive' retaliation to inflict damage that would be 'unacceptable' to Pakistan should be linked to variable factors – either term does not have fixed measures, in any case. In practice, therefore, infliction of damage to variously graded clusters of national assets – one, more or most of the industrial, logistic and communication hubs, rail, sea or air infrastructure, military bases and population centres – could fit the variable parameters of 'massive' retaliation to inflict 'unacceptable' damage. Further, even if counter-force strike is preferred, collateral counter-value destruction might still become unavoidable. Therefore, in today's world, even wiping out, say a cantonment or even a large military formation could be unacceptable to all parties. Accordingly, to project varying packages of 'massive retaliation', the extent of targeting may be decided in a manner as to create more than one step on the escalatory nuclear posture.

Situational Variables of NFU

As discussed at the very beginning, the policy of NFU is in tune with India's political ideology. Even otherwise, for India's own good, in a hostile neighbourhood infested with nuclear weapons, it is the right policy which need not be diluted or questioned. However, there are certain conditions to be met for the policy of NFU to make a mark. In this context, the matters to be considered are, firstly, the appropriate interpretation of the term, and, secondly, the underpinning capabilities that are needed to uphold this policy of NFU.

Truly, NFU is a pledge, not a ban from the hoary principle of 'right to defend'. Depending on the situation prevailing, the term 'NFU' may have more than one connotation. The dumbest one of these would be to wait for a nuclear strike to occur before retaliating with whatever weaponry is left usable. Next, Indian decision-makers cannot even be sure if the movement and deployment of delivery systems are meant for conventional or nuclear use, or if the warheads or bombs carried by these are nuclear, non-nuclear or mixed. In the India-Pakistan context, the matrices of the short flight path, limited early warning and targeting capability, and roving launch sites leave virtually no time for the options of 'Launch on Warning' (LOW) or 'Launch on Attack' (LOA) to be exercised within the ambit of NFU.

Consideration of a 'pre-emptive attack' as a facet of NFU – a rather liberal concession, of course—on the other hand, is unthinkable. It would not be difficult to know for certain the Pakistani strategists' intent of initiating a nuclear attack upon India nor there the certainty of being able to destroy all or most of Pakistan's nuclear assets in the pre-emptive mode. With even the best 'Ballistic Missile and Air Defense' (BMAD) unable to guarantee adequate protection, all of the above mentioned connotations would lead to a nuclear exchange and heavy destruction that India wishes to repudiate in the first place. In sum, it appears to be most sensible to let the classical connotation of NFU remain valid and settle with the one described above as the 'dumbest 'one.

The policy of NFU also needs four major props to sustain it. One, the policy must be founded upon telling superiority in conventional military power. It then becomes possible to achieve the politico-military objectives of war by prosecuting through conventional military operations; even in the face of a nuclear strike should the 'first use' party turn undeterred by massive retaliation. Two, the policy entails survival through the enemy's first, and possibly, second, nuclear strikes while retaining the retaliatory CMD. Three, the sanctity of the NFU policy is contingent upon efficient BMAD, surveillance, target acquisition, interception and strike-back capabilities. Four, the NFU policy is best backed up when there is full range of Information Warfare (IW) capabilities in all their diverse facets to disrupt the enemy's war-waging structure. Needless to state, in all the four said aspects, there is much to build before India's policy of NFU can reach its full maturity.

Strategic Nuclear Weapons

India considers strategic nuclear weapons not as weapons of war but just for deterrence against the bullying of the stronger and the blackmail of the intransigent. But should its nuclear deterrence fail to impress, there would be a heavy price to pay. India's credible retaliatory capability, therefore, needs to be built up in terms of both nuclear and IW–Command, Control, Communications, Computers, Intelligence, Information, Surveillance, Reconnaissance (C4I2SR), deception, cyber and space capabilities—to deter the enemy's usage of strategic nuclear weapons to smother India's sovereign interests.

The underlying principle in the matter of India's nuclear posture must be: firstly, there need be no dilution of the doctrinal text or its intended definitions; and, secondly, the implications of doctrinal terms would be for the decision-makers of the time to adopt. It would, thus, be for Indian decision-makers to retain the flexibility to decide as to what would constitute 'massive retaliation to inflict unacceptable damage' at a point in time. In that, they could opt for one or more steps of 'flexible', 'proportionate' or 'annihilatory' responses, and choose the appropriate connotation of NFU as the situation might demand. Academic hair-splitting over the nuclear doctrine may, thus, be rested and Indian strategists left to do what they have to under conditions of war.

In the above perspective, it is possible to see through the haze of factual ambiguities and logical contradictions that are invariably to be built into any nation's nuclear strategy. The indication in that respect is that India's posture in the domain of strategic nuclear deterrence might be working. Pakistan is less exuberant of the utility of its nuclear card to trump India's deep conventional offensive, and that realization has pushed Pakistan into introducing the TNWs to cover up for the limitations of its conventional military capability.

TNW: The Indian Dilemma

India formalized its nuclear doctrine at the strategic level at a time when Pakistan's TNWs had not been in the picture. That equation has changed with the induction of TNWs in Pakistan's nuclear inventory. Propagation of the use of TNWs further curtails India's conventional options, howsoever limited the objectives these might have been, to punish Pakistan for incessant hostile behaviour. Pakistan's nuclear red-line having further lowered as compared to the Cold Start scenario, thus, the new problem with India's strategic nuclear deterrence is that it would encourage Pakistan to feel more safe from India's conventional offensives and so perpetrate warfare at the sub-conventional level–in the form of proxy war, terrorism and societal subversion. India's recent unshackling from strategic inertia to undertake limited offensive action in the form of the 'surgical strike', and Pakistan's deflated, if pragmatic reaction to that event point to certain new inferences in this regard. However, strikes of such shallow depth might not chastise Pakistan's irrepressible aggression. The next course in this context should, therefore, be to preserve India's option to inflict conventional military retribution of sufficient extent and depth in Pakistan's or Pakistan controlled territory that would deter the Pakistan state from continuing its sub-conventional offensive in Kashmir, and yet save it from falling to a stage when it must use the TNWs to rescue itself from the adverse consequences of its wrong doings.

Following this consideration, the intermediate purpose would be to find appropriate responses to Pakistan's use, or threat of use of TNWs to prevent the fruition of India's conventional military strategy.

Unless such responses are found, possession of TNWs would permit the perpetrator to continue to attack India's integrity and sovereignty with impunity. In formulating an appropriate response policy in the Indian context, however, the East-West Cold War 'templates' of the nuclear paradox, the only reference point one has, may be of little help.

It would be sensible for Indian strategists to take the threat of Pakistan's TNWs with extreme seriousness—the purpose being not to allow Pakistan to go berserk but to adopt determined counter-measures and so keep the chronic trouble-maker in check. Therefore, it would be in order to consider certain hypothetical models so as to focus on plausible situations when Pakistan's TNW could be used, and the corresponding Indian reactions, both active and passive. These models are as discussed in the following paragraphs.

Situation Extreme A: Pakistan Irrational, India Restrained

1. **Stage 1**: This stage opens when India launches a conventional offensive into Pakistan or Pakistan held territory either on own initiative or under grave provocation. India announces it as a 'limited objective retaliatory response'. Pakistan does not give credence to that pronouncement and views it as an aggression to decimate its sovereignty. It threatens to use nuclear weapons. The Indian offensive continues.

2. **Stage 2**: Pakistan's nuclear posturing and messaging is followed by India's counter-messaging and posturing. Undeterred, Pakistan announces deployment of TNWs. While international pressure to back-off builds up, as per the past trend latent sympathy and bias is towards the 'underdog 'Pakistan's version. India continues with its offensive operations nonetheless.

3. **Stage 3**: Pakistan launches one or more TNWs either as a warning as much to India as to the world powers, or for effect against the Indian forces. There is moderate destruction.

4. **Stage 4**: The global powers intervene to prevent India from responding by "massive retaliation to inflict unacceptable damage".[6] Concurrently, the disconcerted global powers join together for the immediate 'neutralization' of Pakistan's nuclear arsenal. India agrees not to retaliate but presses on

with its conventional offensives to secure its desired end state. Pakistan is forced to fight a conventional war in which it is likely to come second best.

Result: Pakistan ceases to be a nuclear threat. India gains the moral ground. But for a long time into the future, India loses the credibility of its stated policy of *massive retaliation* and the ability to withstand international pressure. Domestic reaction to India's lack of 'will' is adverse, but it is assuaged by the gains achieved through conventional war.

Verdict: Overall, it is India's gain.[7]

Situation Extreme B: Pakistan and India both Irrational

Take-up after Stage3, Situation A:

> ➤ Stage 4: Ignoring international pressure and de-escalatory suggestions, India sticks to its policy and responds by 'massive retaliation to inflict unacceptable damage'. Pakistan launches its strategic first strike. India's second strike and Pakistan's strategic second strike follow. Both still have a few nuclear weapons left in reserve.

> ➤ Stage 5: International principals intervene by force to stop the carnage. The nuclear assets of both nations are neutralized by IW and then physically taken over by force.

Result: Pakistan ceases to be a state and has to come under an interim administration of the world body. India is crippled.

Verdict: Both nations are devastated.

Situation C: Pakistan Irrational, India Reactive, Pakistan Rational

Take-up after Stage 3, Situation A:

> ➤ Stage 4: Prepared for that eventuality, India treats the warning shots as bluff and continues with its conventional operations. Pakistan then launches more TNWs, this time for more effect.

> ➢ Stage 5: Continuing with conventional operations and accepting casualties from TNW strikes, India launches 'massive'–but not 'annihilatory'–retaliation', in both counter-force and counter-value modes. There are nuclear strikes against the defense industry, logistic and communication hubs, rail, sea or air infrastructure, military bases and by default, some population centres, to a severity that might usually qualify as 'unacceptable damage'.

> ➢ Stage 6: The international community is disconcerted at Pakistan's initiation of a nuclear exchange, and outraged at what they view as India's 'unjustified overreaction'. Both nations suffer international condemnation. Due to self-restraint and the international reaction, Pakistan refrains from launching a strategic nuclear strike and there are no more nuclear exchanges. India continues to seek the objective of its conventional offensive of wreaking retribution upon the ever-intransigent Pakistan, till the global powers issue an ultimatum to enforce a ceasefire.

Result: Pakistan suffers in a conventional as well as nuclear exchange. Pakistan is helped to recover and progress through generous aid and assistance. India is ostracized and singled out for crippling sanctions, to suffer their adverse consequences for many years, if not decades. India's economy goes into a tail-spin. The global powers join up to make the region nuclear weapon free.

Verdict: Pakistan's supposed restraint or otherwise would be determined by its powerful factions which dominate decision-making, viz, either the hate- radical-extremist faction or the mature-astute-state functionaries. Pakistan's record in this aspect has so far been mixed. In any case, Pakistan is devastated but is helped to rise, while India, saved from devastation, stands 'sanctioned' in a crippling way. Overall, Pakistan stands to gain by exercising restraint.

Situation D: Pakistan's TNW Strike is reciprocated (If India too has TNWs)

Take-up after Stage 3, Situation A:

> ➤ Stage 4: Pakistan's warning TNW strike is reciprocated by India's warning launch of TNWs. Pakistan strikes with more TNWs which is reciprocated by India. Conventional operations continue. Global principals administer stern warnings to both sides to desist.

> ➤ Stage 5: Both sides relent from escalating to strategic nuclear strikes. In case both, in their foolishness, choose to persist and escalate, then the 'Situation Extreme B' would arise. In all probability, international intervention would put a stop to the madness well before that stage.

Result: Pakistan's reliance on TNWs, to altogether close the conventional options open to India, is belied.

Verdict: Apparently, India's reflect reaction through TNWs would derail Pakistan's nuclear posturing. Pakistan's fundamental purpose of neutralizing India's conventional power from punishing Pakistan's perpetual sub-conventional war would, thus, be defeated. In this case, India's possession of TNWs is justified as it reinforces the avoidance of a nuclear weapons exchange.

Situation E: Rhetoric Apart, Both Sides Desist from Actually Using TNWs (If India too has TNWs)

Take-up after Stage 2, Situation A:

> ➤ Stage 3: Conventional operations continue till a ceasefire is called under the aegis of a world body.

Result: Behind the chest thumping and bravado, Pakistan is chastised – even if only for the time being.

Verdict: Peace is likely to prevail for some years. India and Pakistan would be wise to use this opportunity to reconcile. India lives with Pakistan's chronic hostility, as it has done so far.

From 'Mad' Logic to Sublime Realization

Pakistan is expected to take India's stated policy of *'massive retaliation to inflict unacceptable damage'* very seriously. In the light of India's past show of resolve in attacking across the International Boundary in 1965, liberating Bangladesh in 1971, going nuclear, refusing to submit to unacceptable nuclear treaties, recovering Kargil, etc., there is no reason for Pakistan not to do so. Accordingly, the point is that having launched its first TNWs, why would Pakistan wait to suffer the inevitable 'massive retaliation' to be inflicted, in the distant hope of getting away lightly, without having to suffer 'unacceptable damage'?

A logical option for Pakistan would be to launch its 'first strike', or maybe even 'full strike' simultaneously with its first firing of TNWs, in the hope that a devastated Indian system would be left in no position to respond with effect. In other words, it would make more sense for Pakistan to trigger all or most of its larger inventory of nuclear weapons to cripple India to an extent that India is either in no position to carry out its first strike, or if it still does, the force of a retaliatory strike is much weakened.

In practice however, that situation is unlikely to occur; howsoever India is devastated, its size and the fire of wounded resolve would not be able to suppress due retribution. Both nations would be devastated, but if it could be viewed as a macabre consolation, India will be crippled while Pakistan would be decapitated. This brings out a similar situation that stupefied the strategists of the Western and Eastern blocs and forced them to sequester their nuclear weaponry from the actual design of warfare. That lesson then led them to work out various nuclear weapon repudiation and non-proliferation treaties, more or less discard the TNWs, and, finally, curtail their nuclear white elephants. Development of a more precise, larger killing zone and more lethal conventional weapons, to compensate for the TNWs, followed.

Arguably, *just as nuclear near-parity at the strategic level led to strategic nuclear weapons being high-shelved with just the deterrence tag, so may be the case with the TNWs* – the caveat being that TNWs have to be backed with strategic nuclear weapons.[8]

Situational Inferences

Hypothetical situations as depicted above point to certain possible inferences. Even if these inferences can be no better than tenuous, these give rise to the following bona fide considerations in the usage of nuclear weapons:

> ➢ Unless the national leadership is autocratic and then seized in madness, *strategic nuclear weapons have no military employment.* These are, however, *useful in deterring a mad opponent from triggering a nuclear war.*

> ➢ The peg of 'unacceptable damage' in the contemporary world could be very, very low. In recessed deterrence, a *race to build up a nuclear weapon stockpile is, therefore, meaningless* beyond a certain point. The arsenal needed to hit that peg dictates the construct of a comparatively modest CMD.

> ➢ Use of TNWs needs to be underwritten by strategic nuclear deterrence. Since the latter is considered unusable, that brings the entire exercise back to the starting point. *Inter alia,* therefore, *TNWs too are of no use in deterring war.*

> ➢ In fact, the damage caused by the use of TNWs can be also being achieved through conventional means, with the added advantage of controlling warfare through limitations of hardware and logistics.

> ➢ All considered, it may be *preferable to possess TNWs rather than not having these.* It would better discourage the enemy from adventuring into the use of TNWs.

> ➢ The situational hypotheses discussed above suggest that *nuclear restraint brings many advantages.* It permits the issues to be settled at conventional battlefields without having to buy total destruction. It also nurtures international relationships and interdependencies.

Whither India's TNW?

Deterring Pakistan's Sub-Conventional War

The situations depicted above are hypothetical. But these only have logical lines which may have many permutations and combinations. Generally, the inferences flowing out of these situations converge at the preference of India developing its own TNWs; *just as India chose to acquire a nuclear arsenal to be freed of nuclear arm-twisting; it could also acquire TNWs to blunt TNW brandishing.* Simply put, India's option to harness its conventional military power to retaliate against Pakistan's so far immunized sub-conventional war would be better served by India having its own TNWs, in some form or the other, rather than not having these at all. That could then add another layer of response mechanism and nuclear signaling, backed up by strategic nuclear weapons, for India to avoid Pakistan's spooking by the TNWs. That would also be in consonance with India's approach to keep pushing Pakistan's nuclear threshold higher. Finally, it would make the use of conventional power more acceptable to the usually passive Indian decision-makers.

Of course, India's acquisition of TNWs could lead to global disconcert and political and economic sanctions that could slow down India's technological and economic progress, particularly in the field of the much needed nuclear power generation. Therefore, the matter of the timing and fallouts are to be addressed with due discretion through political and diplomatic articulations. Here again, there may be scope for defining suitable alternatives to meet the purpose through the tactical configuration of existing nuclear assets.

Configuration of Tactical Use Nuclear Weapons (TUNWs)

What are TNWs after all but low yield and more accurate versions of nuclear bombs meant for counter-force targeting in conjunction with conventional forces. Therefore, configuring sub or low kiloton yield 'Tactical Use Nuclear Weapons' (TUNWs) from India's existing inventory of nuclear weapons, missiles, air platforms and demolition munitions, miniaturized as feasible, could be a low key option for India. To that end, India's cruise and short and medium range ballistic missiles and air platforms could be mounted with low kiloton nuclear devices.

Certain dilution in the Circular Error of Probability (CEP) may be acceptable in that case. The effects of these weapons on the target may be further controlled through variable flight trajectories and height of burst. In similar vein, Nuclear Demolition Munitions (NDMs) could also be prepared for triggering at the intended ground zero at an appropriate juncture. Notably, most of the 'Shakti' nuclear tests had been in the sub or low kiloton ranges. The option of TUNWs might help keep the global disconcert in control.

Dealing with Nuclear Arm-Twisting

Next, as discussed, it is for the Indian strategists to interpret the doctrinal contention of *'massive retaliation to inflict unacceptable damage'* to suit own strategies rather than binding themselves to academic debates. Other provisions of India's nuclear doctrine may also continue to stand thus. But whatever be the situation, *India cannot hope to restrain Pakistan's unending armed assault upon its nationhood unless it counters Pakistan's nuclear bluster, builds up its conventional military power to a superior combat ratio and then puts the onus of conventional provocation as well as nuclear escalation on Pakistan.* In that context, *with the possession of TUNWs, India's political leadership would be more confident in punishing the Pakistani state for its sponsorship of proxy wars in Kashmir and outrageous terrorist assaults elsewhere by undertaking deliberate cross-border strikes, hot-pursuit, deep sanitation attacks and punitive offensives when Pakistan's belligerent acts cross tolerable limits.* Presently, as seen since the 2008 Mumbai attacks, the Indian decision-makers are not so sure of adopting such options, while their counterparts in Pakistan seem to be confident of having their way, with immunity.

May be, India's possession of TUNWs and situational adaptations of its nuclear doctrine would bring relief to the sensible sections in Pakistan from being marginalized by their raving anti-Indian factions.

Conventional Power

That brings to the fore the matter of conventional military power. Needless to state, *India's security from external – and to an extent, even internal – enemies of the state has been, and would remain, completely dependent on conventional military power;* even the purpose of TNWs is construed to be within the higher extremities of conventional warfare. The Indian political preference for distancing from power group alliances, charting own path to progress, and avoidance of military confrontation – genuine as these must be – accentuates that dependency. It is, therefore, incumbent on the Indian leadership to maintain a highly effective conventional military institution.

It is true that India possesses sufficient military capability to deter Pakistan from venturing into conventional military aggression as it had done in the past. Indeed, it is that deterrence that makes Pakistani strategists exercises various means of sub-conventional warfare to bring about India's disintegration. However, maintenance of past superiority in conventional military power cannot be confined to a tally count of men and basic material alone – hardware modernization, organizational upgrade, efficient decision-making system and fruition of the entire range of IW capabilities have to be factored into that assessment. Conversely, due to stagnating, even 'hollowing', since the past quarter of a century, India's military institution has not been allowed to maintain the overwhelming edge that it had possessed earlier. The defocus of the state is best exemplified by the fact that in spite of being an Information Technology (IT) giant, Indian defense planners have failed to harness the advantages of military IW. The deterrence, therefore, has worn thin – Kargil, the Mumbai attack and the current Kashmir fire-fight are the manifestations of that strategic debility.

On the other hand, having reoriented itself according to the current tenets of wide-spectrum warfare, Pakistan's military establishment is well up on its way to expand, modernize and upgrade its capabilities. It must, therefore, be incumbent on the Indian state to invest on re-energizing its conventional military power and so keep India secure from aggression from either of its perpetual adversaries.

China Factor

In the foregone discussion, the China factor has been confined to the background. That is so even when that factor played the key role in India's nuclear weaponisation. Doubtlessly, India's strategizing for nuclear weapons, as discussed in this paper, would have its fallout on the Sino-Indian military equation. In this respect, it may be appropriate to keep the following observations in contention:

➢ Pakistan's nuclearization started as an extension of China's regional strategy. It was aimed at saving Pakistan from being 'overrun', so to say, by India's superior conventional forces, and, thus, keep India's chronic nuisance in business. Over the years, however, that posture has generated its own dynamics. Presently, that posture has morphed into a facilitator for Pakistan's sub-conventional aggression to undermine India's integrity. Consequently, therefore, besides strait-jacketing India into a hapless internal security situation, that dynamics has less to do with China's cause.

➢ With overwhelming superiority in conventional military power, unbridgeable as it indeed is, China has little cause for use of its nuclear weapons against India. Besides, considering the trends of political decision-making, it is not likely to use its nuclear weapons to bail Pakistan out from the latter's misadventure. In any case, Pakistan's burgeoning nuclear arsenal does not need China's backing any more. With Pakistan well propped up with its own nuclear arsenal, apart from 'signaling' for mutual benefit, it may be impractical to think of the collusive use of Sino- Pakistan strategic nuclear assets.

➢ There, however, may be situations when the use of China's TNWs on Indian forces becomes plausible, that is, if China's conventional forces are checkmated by Indian defense and then cornered into a position of collapse. Should India devote more attention to its military institution that indeed could be a reckonable condition? Under such a condition, Pakistan, not repeating what it believes to be a post-1962 'missed opportunity', is likely to join the fray with its conventional forces and TNWs and try to 'liberate' Kashmir. A converse could also be possible; if it comes to it, a serious conventional adversity might entail India's use of TNWs to save the annexation of its northern and eastern provinces. Of course, this matter would experience many seen and unseen nuances over the coming decades, but the probabilities remain alive, if hazy. It would be foolish of India to allow complacency is this regard.

Sino-Indian confrontation would be a long affair. In the overall analysis of Sino-Pak-Indo confrontation, therefore, it remains incumbent upon the Indian state to maintain its conventional power in the best fettle. It may also be inferred that development of its own versions of TUNWs would strengthen India's external security more than not doing so.

Conclusion: Charting a Native Path

Estrangement between Pakistan and India is moored on fundamental ideological differences. Having been primed ever since the call for 'Muslim Pakistan' was raised in the 1940s, every Pakistani is firm in his/her belief that Jammu and Kashmir (J&K) had been unfairly gobbled up by India, so much so that no Pakistani leader would ever dare to go slow on the issue. Indeed, 'liberating' Kashmir into its fold is an issue of Pakistan's national identity and sovereignty, just as not letting that happen must be a factor for India to preserve its secular, democratic dispensation. There is just no common ground, and so there would be no let up in Pakistan's hostility in the foreseeable future – unless the political entity of Pakistan undergoes drastic changes. Meanwhile, Pakistan's armed aggression, in various forms, would go through endless cycles of highs and lows.

Further, even if Kashmir is the currently visible cause of Pakistan's aggression, there are more of the intrusive perceptions and interpretations that foul India's concept of its nationhood. Rooted in the self-appointed role of religious flag-bearer, the subscription to a negative brand of religious practices and a sense of entitlement to re-establish Muslim rule on India, are the absurd perceptions and interpretations that are likely to be in force among the powerful religious-cum-social masters of Pakistan's society in the foreseeable future. Pakistan's rich and feudal ruling elite would not buy peril by daring to overlook those popular masters. India has to remain conscious of that situation.

India's strategic nuclear weapons deter Pakistan from first use of nuclear weapons while India's superior conventional power deters the repetition of Pakistan's past conventional aggressions. However, India has no deterrence against Pakistan's sub-conventional aggression; whatever there was in the form of conventional retaliation is sought to be neutralized by Pakistan's induction of TNWs. That allows Pakistani strategists to brandish "full spectrum deterrence" on India. Resultantly, India's can be rid of Pakistan's relentless animosity only by retaining its conventional power to punish Pakistan's sub-conventional war. The issue of India's strategic nuclear posturing, TUNWs, and, indeed, the mainstay of all safety harness, conventional military power, have to be seen in that light. In that, the cardinal principles to be appreciated are:

> Even if it takes a two or more to fight, one rogue is enough to start it. This adage fits both of India's neighbours who, by innate compulsion, cannot desist from altering the stable status quo, and so are inclined to use politics to impose a military solution, rather than vice versa.

> Even if it takes weeks and months to start a war, it takes decades to prepare for it. This one fits India's placid policies on its defense preparedness.

Notes

1. Most Pakistani and many Indian analysts speak of India's 'superiority' over Pakistan in terms of conventional military forces. That assertion, howsoever pleasing to Indian ears, needs to be taken with some realism of military logic. Indeed, defense analysts point out that India's edge in the comparative 'combat ratio' has reduced from more than two: one to just over one: one, which is well below what is statistically considered to be the factor of success. Besides, in the extent of war zones, state of military hardware, process of mobilization, network of strategic communications, military and political solidarity from co-religious and strategic allies, and, above all, the ranks of the suicidal fifth column, the level of India's conventional superiority may turn out to be disturbingly misconceived.

2. Indians in their bones and blood, the inherently diverse people of Pakistan have had to contrive artificial identities to justify their common nationhood. False cultural and religious identity, repudiation of everything of their roots and innate expressions of the anti-Indian agenda are the manifestations of their 'two nation' theory that provides the very basis of Pakistan's existence. Obviously, the day is far when Pakistan's mission of sabotaging India comes to a stop, unless, of course, India surrenders the state of J&K, and then goes about restoring the

so-called 'Muslim rule' over the entire 'Hindustan'! In simple terms, there would be no let up of the Pakistani state's hostility in the foreseeable future – India would do well to come to terms with that reality.

3. It was in that context that the slogan "better red than dead" gained popularity in Germany, the United States and then in the rest of the Western alliance. Horrors of a nuclear holocaust, depicted in literature and films, made people reject the East-West ideological animosity.

4. Intercontinental and inter-state confrontation is endemic to geopolitics and the core of human nature. Therefore, when there was no compulsion to fight on their own or their ally's lands, the power blocs settled their issues by triggering warfare, of varying shapes and lethality, upon surrogate parties.

5. It is time for the Indian strategists to unequivocally admit and reconcile to the fact that the Churchillan distaste of 'scheming' Indians – the 'native' cultural power that put an end to an empire that never saw the sun set over its realm – continues to pervade the all-powerful Western world. Helped by the 'underdog' pretentions and ruled by subservient dictators who readily offer their strategic situation to buy endorsement, the Pakistani leadership – particularly it's Army –is close to the Western heart. Ignoring of arms-use restrictions, blatant falsification, contractual violations, nuclear proliferation, even anti-West activities etc., and all such minor irritants, are, thus, tolerated, and even acquiesced to. India, with its show of political morality and non-alignment with the Western cause, obviously cannot expect to be treated with comparable camaraderie.

6. The role of 'international pressure' is an oft repeated refrain, almost a diktat that finds ready acceptance among the strategic community. But it is not clear as to why the global powers, in the first place, would not prevent Pakistan from violating the underlying principle of non-use of nuclear weapons in warfare, and wait for India to be hit before waking up to this menace to humanity. It is also not clear as to why the Indian leadership

would defer to the international opinion that otherwise would have failed to clamp down on irresponsible nuclear behaviour. Conversely, it is possible that the global powers would not remain so stoic, and that they may have plans to disable Pakistan's nuclear arsenal through pre-emptive action.

7.   An opportunity to recover POK?

8.   The matter of nuclear weaponisation and its translation into nuclear posturing are played out in the realm of mental perceptions that are laced with partisan prejudices, on the one hand, and scientifically arrived deductions, on the other. Resultantly, inherent ambiguities and contradictions in the interplay of logic, counter-logic and cross-logic have to be accepted -and dynamically articulated. That, as the big nuclear powers would vouch, is a never ending game.

Courtesy: *This research paper "A New Equation of Pakistan's Nuclear Weaponisation, By: Lt Gen Gautam Banerjee", has been added to this book with the special permission of The Centre for Land Warfare Studies (CLAWS). The Centre for Land Warfare Studies (CLAWS), New Delhi, is an autonomous think tank on strategic studies and land warfare in the Indian context. CLAWS is registered under the Societies Registration Act, 1860 and is a membership-based organisation. It is governed by a Board of Governors and an Executive Council.*

Extracts of permission:

"Dear Sir, Permission is hereby granted for the said use of the article as per publication norms". Regards. Dy Dir (04 August 2017), and email dated 23 Apr 2018 reproduced below:

Mr Musa,

The CLAWS has no objection in your including the paper of General Gautam Banerjee in your book. However, kindly ensure that the following as mentioned by you in your email is adhered to in letter and spirit, "I want to humbly request you to allow me to include paper of General Gautam Banerjee (A New Equation of Pakistan's Nuclear Weaponisation, Lieutenant General Gautam Banerjee-2017) as a chapter in my book. I will fully acknowledge your respected research centre (CLAWS), and will give a short introduction of your centre in my book."

Chapter 5

The Islamic State of Khorasan, Lashkar-e-Toiba, Punjabi Taliban, and Afghan and Pakistani Taliban are Seeking Nuclear Weapons

Pakistan is facing international isolation, jihadist threat, and financial turbulence due to its radicalized and Talibanized policy towards India and Afghanistan. Every day hundreds of innocent civilians in FATA, Baluchistan, and Waziristan are being killed by the army and paramilitary forces. The country also faces internal security challenges due to its involvement in Afghanistan, Kashmir, Iraq, Syria and Yemen. Internal security is at stake while the emergence of ISIS and its countrywide terror networks generated new challenges.[1] Experts fear that these groups can make access to nuclear, biological and chemical weapon with the cooperation of their colleagues within state and government institutions.[2] They understand that as the United States has already focused on Pakistan's clandestine efforts to make South Asia and Afghanistan ruin by providing these weapons to terrorist organizations, they can easily make access to these weapons.[3]

There is a blooming possibility of nuclear war in South and Central Asia. Nuclear and biological weapons will be used by terrorist groups based in Pakistan, Afghanistan and Russia. These groups have access to nuclear weapons, while some states will provide the pick and drop facility. Islamic state, Taliban and extremist organizations have restored their old contacts with the Mujahedeen of Chechnya, Tajikistan, Uzbekistan, Chinese Uyghur Muslim movement and Moscow based terrorist groups, and wants to target nuclear and military installation in Russia. These attacks might prompt nuclear war between Russia, Pakistan, US and China. The Islamic State has made dramatic progress in using drones for future warfare. This group is actively seeking to export bombing expertise. Analyst Cahal Milmo, in his recent article has warned that terrorist may use drones to target military and civilian installations:

> In a little-noticed development this summer, Europol, the European Union law enforcement agency, issued its own warning about drones – otherwise known as Unmanned Aerial Vehicles or UAVs – and underlined the "particularly strong security threat" posed by returning fighters who had received "prolonged ideological indoctrination, military training in the use of weapons and explosives or have gained combat experience". In its annual Terrorism Situation and Trend Report, Europol said: "Attack planning against the EU and the West in general continues in Syria and Iraq... Regarding the potential use of alternative and more sophisticated types of [Improvised Explosive Devices], the current trend in using weaponized UAVs in the Syria/Iraq conflict zone might also inspire other jihadist supporters and expand the use of this kind of tactic outside this area of operation.[4]

The Time Magazine in its recent report noted the danger of dirty bomb in near future. Pakistan based terrorist organizations such as Islamic State (ISIS) and Pakistan based Mujahedeen Hind groups are actively seeking nuclear and biological weapons:

> As the number of nuclear-armed countries has grown from at least five to as many as nine since the 1970s, the danger of World War III has been joined by a host of secondary nuclear threats. The possibility that a warhead, or the material to build one, could fall into the hands of a rogue state or terrorist helped drive President Barack Obama's deal to temporarily halt Iran's alleged weapons program. North Korea, which is now believed to have more than a dozen warheads and has been busily testing intercontinental missiles to carry them, has also been the world's

most active seller of nuclear know-how. Pakistan is developing battlefield tactical nuclear weapons, which are smaller and more portable than strategic ones, even as its domestic extremist threat grows. The danger from dirty bombs is spreading even faster. For starters, they pose none of the technical challenges of splitting an atom. Chaduneli's type of uranium was particularly hard to come by, but many hospitals and other industries use highly radioactive materials for medical imaging and other purposes. If these toxic substances are packed around conventional explosives, a device no bigger than a suitcase could contaminate several city blocks—and potentially much more if the wind helps the fallout to spread. The force of the initial blast would be only as deadly as that of a regular bomb, but those nearby could.[5]

The Trump administration is worried that nuclear weapons and materials of dirty bomb in Pakistan could land up in the hands of terror groups while the concerns are aggravated by the development of tactical weapons, a senior US official warned.[6] The South Asian strategy announced by the US President Donald Trump noted that the "nuclear weapons or materials could fall" into the wrong hands, the official said.[7] The danger of nuclear weapons was also mentioned by Trump in his Afghanistan and South Asia policy speech.[8]

However, Washington Times reported nuclear terrorism as a threat to global security. There will be no progress in ensuring global nuclear stability without cooperation between the United States and Russia. This should be a major priority for Presidents Trump and Putin.[9] Washington Time also reported the border security arrangements by some states. Much has been made of states trying to secure their borders against terrorist threats".[10] Former US Chairman of the Joint Chiefs of Staff Admiral Michael Mullen also expressed concern about the existing nuclear threat and said Pakistan's weapons are under threat:

To the best of my ability to understand it—and that is with some ability—the weapons there are secure. And that even in the change of government, the controls of those weapons haven't changed.......And there are limits to what I know. Certainly at a worst-case scenario with respect to Pakistan, I worry a great deal about those weapons falling into the hands of terrorists and either being proliferated or potentially used. And so, control of those, stability, stable control of those weapons is a key concern. And I think certainly the Pakistani leadership that I've spoken with on both the military and civilian side understands that.[11]

Pakistan needs a new strategy and security mechanism to secure its military installations. The country's persisting security measures are so weak and unprofessional. Research analyst Sophie Henderson in her recent comment noted the important routes of nuclear smuggling in Central Asia and warned the drug trafficking in Afghanistan and Tajikistan is the prime source of terrorism in the region:

> Central Asia is geographically positioned to be a transit route between countries that possess weakly guarded fissile material, especially those in the former Soviet Union, and those that seek it, such as groups in Iraq, and Afghanistan. Some reports suggested that state officials are also involved in the drug trade. Thus, the success of Central Asia's drug trade indicates that there are routes through which nuclear material can be smuggled and that the ability or willingness of some states to police them is minimal. Nuclear trafficking in the former USSR was a key concern immediately following its collapse. Alarmist predictions of rampant nuclear trafficking throughout Russia, Central Asia and the Caucasus, were largely proved to be exaggerated, and these fears receded.[12]

The nexus of nuclear terrorism, weapons of mass destruction and biological terrorism poses greatest threat to the nuclear weapons of Pakistan, where Lashkar-e-Toiba, Taliban, Islamic State (ISIL) and sectarian organization have developed military capabilities to detonate dirty bomb. A successful WMD terrorist attack of these organizations could result in the death of hundreds of thousands citizens. It can also produce far-reaching economic and political consequences that would affect all members of the international community. These groups can use weapons of mass destruction In China and Russia, and can obtain these weapons with the cooperation of insiders. Dr. Reshmi Kazi (2013) argued that the possibility of nuclear terrorism in South Asia and the danger of insider attacks is matter of great concern for international community, and all South Asian states:

The danger of insider threats is emerging as the new nuclear threat. This risk is invariably linked with terrorists seeking fissile materials to build a nuclear device. Several experiments have been conducted, which have established that terrorists do not require a sophisticated nuclear weapons building project of a magnitude as that of the Manhattan Project to develop a nuclear device. The probability of atomic terrorism in South Asia is increasingly gaining grounds. The assassination of Pakistan's former Prime Minister, Benazir Bhutto has reinforced apprehensions over the probability of Pakistan's nuclear weapons and materials falling into the hands of the Al Qaida. Pakistan's former President, Musharraf was also subjected to seven known assassination attempts in some of which, Pakistani military and intelligence officials were deeply involved. When such is the state of Pakistan's security system where they cannot accord adequate and effective security to their heads of the state and where political instability is deepening, it is not easy to ignore the probability of penetration by Al Qaida militants to obtain fissile materials, if not weapons, from Pakistan's inventory.[13]

There is concern that TTP, Punjabi Taliban or their allies may possibly attack Pakistan's nuclear facilities by detonating a small, crude nuclear weapon in near future.[14] Nuclear power plants, research reactors and uranium enrichment plants of the country may, at any time come under potential attack from the TTP and its allies. The possibility of a nuclear attack might be of several types—a commando type attack that might cause widespread dispersal of radioactivity, aircraft crash into an atomic reactor and cyber attack.[15] After several incidents of terror attacks on Pakistan nuclear facilities (Wah, Kamra, Dera Ghazi Khan, Karachi, Peshawar Sargodha), it became clear that the TTP and ISIS extremist groups can gain access to nuclear facilities with the help of their radicalized allies in the armed forces.[16] In December 2011, an article in Atlantic Magazine labeled Pakistan as the "ally from hell." The article warned that Pakistan was transferring its nuclear weapons from one place to another in very low security vans to hide them from CIA. The inability of Pakistani armed forces was evident from the fact that instead of transferring nuclear weapons in armoured vehicles, they were shifting them in unsafe vans.[17]

On 22 August 2008, the Nation reported two suicide bombers targeted military installation in Wah Ordinance Factory killing around 70 persons and leaving over 100 injured.[18] Press release of Pakistan Ordnance Factories Board explained the real story of the attacks; "the bomb blasts occurred outside two exit gates of POF Wah Cantt when a large number of workers of POF were coming out at the time of shift change".[19] However, on 16 August 2012, Dawn reported another terrorist attack on the country's largest nuclear site, where terrorists killed several security officials and damaged aircrafts.[20]

Taliban Militants armed with rocket-propelled grenades and automatic weapons carried out a brazen attack under cover of darkness on the Minhas base of the Pakistan Air Force at Kamra.[21] Eight militants and one soldier were killed. "The attack was repelled and only one aircraft was damaged," an air force spokesman told Dawn. That Tehrik-e-Taliban Pakistan claimed responsibility for the assault.[22] Its spokesman Ehsanullah Ehsan told newspapers by telephone that they were proud of this operation. Minhas Airbase in Kamra is Pakistan's Air Force largest base located at Kamra, Attock District of Punjab, Pakistan.[23]

On 22 May 2011, Pakistani newspapers also reported Taliban attacks on nuclear submarine base, PNS Mehran. More than 15 attackers killed 18 military personnel and wounded 16 in a sophisticated terrorist attack. Two American-built P-3C Orion Surveillance Aircraft were destroyed.[24] The US intelligence agencies said this attack was most dangerous and better planned. The News International reported in December 2011 that the TTP-associated Punjabi Taliban had been involved in the attack.[25] Taliban also attacked nuclear base in Sargodha, Khushab and in Peshawar. Commando style attacks of these groups on Pakistan naval base in Karachi, Wah Ordinance Factory in Rawalpindi, Dera Ghazi Khan nuclear base, Sargodha and Aeronautical Complex in Kamra, highlighted once again the poor security infrastructure of the country and the undetected infiltration of extremists into the ranks of armed forces. Indian military experts said these terror attacks were made possible by elements inside the armed forces. Indian military intelligence veteran, Vinayak Bhat expressed the same concern in his recent analysis about the danger of nuclear weapons falling into the hands of terrorist groups in Pakistan:

The possibility exists that individuals who work at a facility will remove weapons or weapons components without proper authorization. The insiders' objectives may be to control these items for their own use, transfer control of the items to a previously identified outsider, or to sell these items to a previously unidentified outsider. In the case of transfer, the insider may be motivated either by profit or ideological affinity with an outside group. The possibility that insiders and outsiders would conspire together to obtain weapons or weapon components is high. Again, the motivation for the theft may be either profit or ideology. Leakage of Sensitive Information — Insiders provide key information about Pakistan's nuclear weapons to outsiders. The information could include classified nuclear weapons data, exact storage locations, security and access control arrangements, or operational details about the weapons.[26]

On 01 April 2016, in the Australian newspaper, Catherine Philip reported fears about the vulnerability of Pakistan's missiles that emerged on the eve of the nuclear security summit in Washington. Islamic State (ISIS) publicly claimed about its nuclear ambitions, citing Pakistan as the most likely potential source of materials. Pakistan has boasted of developing an arsenal of "tiny" nuclear weapons to counter its arch-rivals significantly larger conventional capabilities".[27] However, on 09 August, 2013, The New York Times reported Pakistan's armed forces were abruptly ordered to be on high alert for a possible Taliban attack on the country's military installations. Taliban and their allies had a plan to sabotage the country nuclear facilities and use a dirty bomb.[28]

On 06 September 2012, Pakistan army deployed commando force at one of the country's biggest nuclear site in Dera Ghazi Khan District of Southern Punjab after an intelligence report warned of a possible Taliban attack.[29] A recent report of The Washington Post also warned that extremist groups could seize components of the stockpile or trigger a war with India. There are reports from the US intelligence agencies that during the Kargil war, Pakistan readied its nuclear weapons without the knowledge of Prime Minister Nawaz Sharif. On 01 April 2016, Daily Express reported the vulnerability of Pakistan's nuclear weapons:

Pakistan's nuclear weapons arsenal could fall into the hands of terrorist groups unless the volatile South Asian state bolsters security at strategic military bases, Tom Batchelor reported a high-ranking US official. In 2015, the newspaper reported how ISIS was preparing a new push to seize territory in the province of Baluchistan, which borders Afghanistan and Iran. The area is widely-known to be the centre of Pakistan's nuclear weapons programme, with controversial underground testing of atomic explosive devices in the 1990s. Middle East terror experts warned at the time that the extremist group could be close to obtaining a 'dirty' bomb. Afzal Ashraf, a former senior officer in the RAF, said Pakistan was "the most likely place" for ISIS to obtain a nuclear explosive.[30]

In another report, the same concerns were raised by India. On 02 April 2016, Defense News reported terrorist group's access to Pakistan nuclear weapons. The warning comes as world leaders meet for the Nuclear Security Summit, which for the first time included a simulated nuclear terrorist attack.[31] The same views were expressed by expert Mr. Joseph V. Micallef in his Huffpost article in 07 February 2017. He warned that Pakistan's nuclear weapons are under threat from terrorist organizations like al Qaeda and the Islamic State:

> In recent years the concern over nuclear proliferation has centered on Iran's ongoing effort to develop a nuclear weapons capability. Pakistan's nuclear weapons program, however, may prove to be just as dangerous and just as destabilizing as that of Tehran's. That country is well on its way, within another decade, to amassing the third largest stockpile of nuclear weapons. Moreover, its current focus on deploying theatre nuclear weapons, so called (5 to 10 kiloton) low-yield battlefield weapons, represents a dangerous new strategy that has wide-ranging impact on both the stability of the Indian subcontinent and the threat that a militant organization will obtain a nuclear device.[32]

The availability of nuclear material in South Asia, and the networks of radicalized groups in Pakistan, and their links within the state institutions has raised concern that these groups may possibly gain access to nuclear material to constitute Nuclear Explosive Devices. Terrorist attacks on Pakistan's nuclear installations in the past proved that these groups can retrieve material of dirty bomb with the help of insiders. On 23 May 2015, Express Tribune of Pakistan reproduced the Independent article that warned the Islamic State (ISIL) resolve to obtain Pakistan's nuclear weapons within a year.[33] In its propaganda magazine, Dabiq, the Islamic State suggested that the terrorist group was expanding so rapidly that it could buy its first nuclear weapon from Pakistan within a year. The article claimed this arrangement of groups had happened at the same time as ISIL militants seized "tanks, rocket launchers, missile systems, anti-aircraft systems," from the US and Iran before turning to the subject of more extreme weapons the group is not in possession of – such as nuclear weapons.[34] On 30 January 2017, in his Small War Journal research paper, Sajid Farid Shapoo warned that nuclear assets of Pakistan can any time come under attack by terrorist organizations:

> The possible catastrophic scenario of the acquisition of a nuclear weapon by a terrorist organization with the active help of rogue insiders nearly played out when a group of navy officers attempted to high-jack a sophisticated Pakistan navy frigate. In Sept 2014, an audacious attack was led by serving and former Pak navy officers to take over the Pakistani Navy frigate PNS Zulfiqar. The alleged plan was to gain control of the vessel, steer it to open sea and then turn its guns on a U.S. naval vessel. The attack was thwarted by Pakistan navy commandos. Four persons were killed which included two serving officers and an ex-navy officer. All four were associated with Al Qaeda in Indian Subcontinent (AQIS). It appears the officers on-board were to be joined by other militants who were to arrive by boat and stow away onboard. The plan was to get close to U.S. ships on the high seas and then turn the shipboard weapon systems on the Americans. Among those killed was former Pakistan Navy Lt. Owais Jakhrani. He had been recently dismissed from the Navy for harboring extremist views. He was the son of a serving senior police official in Karachi and he reportedly played the key role in recruiting naval officers for Al Qaeda. The group was led by a 'senior officer' who was even saluted by a navy guard before other guards became suspicious of their presence in the dockyard and alerted commandos.[35]

Pakistan is facing the wrath of international community for its application of unprofessional security measures in protecting nuclear assets, and its consistent support to terrorist and sectarian organizations fighting inside Afghanistan and Kashmir. The nature and course of Taliban attacks in Afghanistan can be interpreted in a number of ways, but the fact is that they cannot carry out a single attack without the financial and military assistance of their masters. Taliban and the ISIL want to make multiple deaths a central element in the planning of their attacks. In this way, the old 'rule' of terrorism research, which maintains that terrorists are interested in creating large numbers of spectators but not victims of their attacks, is challenged. Terrorist and extremist organizations can transfer nuclear materials by land, by drones and by sea.

During the last two decades, terrorist groups carried out attacks against the country's nuclear installations times and again to obtain material for a dirty bomb, but Pakistan's military establishment never mentioned this in official and unofficial statements the nature of these attacks. The threat of retrieving material for constituting nuclear explosive device still exist as these groups now infiltrated into the ranks of armed forces. The danger of Pakistan's nuclear, biological, radiological and chemical weapons is real. On 28 October 2015, General Pervez Musharraf said terrorists like Osama bin Laden and the Taliban were heroes for Pakistan. Mr. Musharraf admitted that Pakistan supported and trained groups like Lashkar-e-Toiba (LeT) in 1990s to carry out militancy in Kashmir.

In 1990s the freedom struggle began in Kashmir...At that time Lashkar-e-Toiba and 11 or 12 other organizations were formed. We supported them and trained them as they were fighting in Kashmir at the cost of their lives," Musharraf said. The former army chief was responding to a question about action against LeT's Hafiz Saeed and Zakiur Rehman Lakhvi. He said Saeed and Lakhvi type people enjoyed the status of heroes at that time.[36] The Kashmiri freedom fighters including Hafiz Saeed and Lakhvi were our heroes at that time. Later on the religious militancy turned into terrorism. Now they (referring to terrorism in Pakistan) are killing their own people here and this should be controlled and stopped, we trained Taliban and sent them to fight against Russia.

Taliban, Haqqani, Osama Bin Laden and Zawahiri were our heroes then. Later they became villains," he said, adding that people need to understand the whole environment at that time.[37]

On 17 September 2017, Ariana News reported Afghan President hammered Pakistan for its undeclared war against Afghanistan. During his visit to India, Afghan President warned that the undeclared war between Afghanistan and Pakistan is intensifying and almost taking the shape of a declared war. President Ghani speaking in an exclusive interview with Indian NDTV said. Pointing to his approach to Pakistani political and military officials he said that his dialogue with Pakistan was 'conditional'. "I have said that there is a window, the window can become a corridor, a pathway, a highway etc. But it can also shut down.[38]

Before the statement of Afghan President, on 16 July 2016, Reuters reported former Afghan spy Chief; Rahmatullah Nabil criticism on Pakistan's financial help to terrorist organizations inside Afghanistan. Mr. Rahmatullah Nabil exhibited two letters explaining how Pakistani intelligence services helped leaders of the Taliban and the Haqqani network in 2014 and 2015.[39] Mr. Nabil told journalists in Kabul to whom he released the letters that he wanted to provide concrete evidence of Pakistan's collusion with the Taliban and the Haqqani network, which has been blamed for a series of kidnappings and high-profile suicide bombings in the capital. "For the past 14 years, no one has disclosed documents of this kind. Here, I'm proving it," Mr. Nabil said. "They kill us every day and commit all kinds of atrocities, we have to show them.".[40]

One letter, Reuters reported, addressed from a section of Pakistan's military intelligence service in Peshawar, was headed "Arrangements of Secure Houses and Protection to Afghan Taliban and Their Leadership".[41] In the letter, dated August 2014, Mr. Nabil claimed that official arranges for safe houses and vehicles were provided for Afghan Taliban commanders forced out of a remote area of northern Pakistan while an army operation is conducted.[42] Another letter, dated March 2015, Reuter reported requested an update on Haqqani network personnel in Nowshera, Mardan and Swabi, in the Pakistani border province of Khyber Pakhtunkhwa.[43] On 23 February 2017, Journalist Anders Corr noted in his article that Pakistan sought to turn Afghanistan into its backyard and put the government under its sphere of influence.

It seeks "strategic depth" in Afghanistan for Pakistan's competition with India. It seeks to influence, through political, military, and economic measures, the government of Afghanistan in order to limit Iranian influence in the country. Pakistan is doing this with military strikes, state-sponsored terrorism, economic inducements, and economic punishments such as border closings.[44]

Pakistan's support to terrorist organization in Afghanistan and India badly affected its relations with neighbours. The country has been supporting Afghan Taliban and Kashmiri Mujahedeen to further its political agenda in South Asia since the last two decades. On 05 April 2017, JK Verma also noted some aspects of Pakistan's way of tackling insurgency and terrorism on its own soil.

Pakistan which produces and train terrorists to carry out terrorist activities in neighbouring countries could not control all the terrorist outfits and few terrorist groups flouted the dictates of ISI and involved in terrorist activities in the country. According to reports in first three months of 2017 there were about 16 terrorist attacks in which 184 persons were killed and more than 683 were maimed. These terrorist activities included bomb blasts at Sehwan Sharif in Sindh in which 89 persons were killed and 350 were injured and explosions at Mall Road Lahore in which 15 persons lost lives and 85 were injured. Punjabi controlled Pakistan was shaken as the bomb blasts occurred in Punjab hence both military and civilian government took urgent actions and on one hand they launched Operation Radd-ul-Fassad an anti-terrorist operation all over the country especially in Punjab and on the other hand they blamed Afghanistan for sponsoring terrorism in the country.[45]

For more than two decades, the threat of nuclear and biological terrorism has been at the forefront of the international security agenda. Nuclear experts warned that terrorists and extremist organizations operating in South Asia must be prevented from gaining access to weapons of mass destruction, and from perpetrating atrocious acts of nuclear terrorism.[46] Pakistan have applied unprofessional measures on protecting its nuclear weapons sites but nuclear proliferation still poses a grave threat to the national security of all South Asian states. Military experts and policymakers have also expressed deep concerns that if the two nuclear capable states purvey explosives to their favourite terror groups, it might cause huge destruction and fatalities.[47]

Both India and Pakistan have sea-based second strike capabilities. India can launch General Area Weapons of higher yields from longer distances while Pakistan can launch lower-yield missiles from shorter distances due to constraints on weapon ranges. But even this asymmetric triad capability is potent and precise enough to knock-off important nerve centres, which are crucial for war.[48] Ahmad Jawad in his article Express Tribune, 08 April 2017 noted some facts about the Indian cold start strategy:

> Adoption of a first use, or first strike, nuclear policy is highly unlikely for three reasons. Firstly, India's nuclear policy has always been aimed at China. India has always argued for a position of Credible Minimum Deterrence towards any potential Chinese aggression. India has maintained that any acts of aggression from Pakistan would be met by massive conventional retaliation, a concept truly captured by India's Cold Start doctrine. This makes the Indo-Pak security relationship completely asymmetric, as Pakistan's nuclear arsenal solely serves the purpose of "existential deterrence" towards India but India's deterrence towards Pakistan is based upon its superior conventional capability. The threat of a potentially more aggressive Indian nuclear posture has put an additional strain on an already rocky India-Pakistan relationship. However, it must be understood that these talks are mere signaling and the odds are that they will not amount to any concrete policy shifts.[49]

In Baluchistan and FATA regions, Pakistani armed forces pursue the kill and dump policy, used chemical and biological weapons, killed women and children in night, bombed their houses and kidnapped tribal elders. The way Pakistan army counter insurgency in Baluchistan enraged neighbouring states as the country's armed forces continue to use chemical weapons against civilian population. In his India Today article Anil Kumar quoted allegations of Baloch nationalists leveled against Pakistan army:

> The Pakistan Army has intensified their military operations against Baloch nationalists and freedom fighters. According to Baluchistan's activist ground report, the Pakistan Army has resorted to snatch, kill and dump tactics for Baloch freedom fighters and civilians. The activists are alleging that the Army

is also using certain chemicals to poison their water supply and punish them. Baloch activists told India Today that the Pakistan Army intensified their operations after Prime Minister Modi's Independence Day speech from the ramparts of the Red Fort. Army's brutality in Baluchistan is nothing new but its scale is said to have gone up after PM Modi's speech from the Red Fort in New Delhi. Large number of men were said to have been abducted from Kachchi Bolan, Quetta, Dera Bugti, Mastang, Awaran and other areas of Baluchistan.[50]

Pakistan lives in a complicated neighbourhood sandwiched between Iran and Afghanistan. Its support to terrorist groups fighting in Afghanistan prompted its isolation.[51] The army runs illegal and criminal enterprise without sharing its revenue with the state and government, and purveys military and financial support to these organizations to secure its strategic depth in Afghanistan. In March 2016, the US President warned that the ISIL access to nuclear weapons was matter of great concern. On 01 April 2016, the Times published an article on Pakistan's nuclear weapons vulnerability, which Catherine Philip noted the threat to the country's nuclear weapons:

> Small battlefield nuclear weapons developed by Pakistan could fall into the hands of terrorists if the country does not do more to secure its arsenal, leading western powers have warned. Fears about the vulnerability of Pakistan's missiles emerged on the eve of the nuclear security summit in Washington, which will discuss the threat of Islamic State acquiring nuclear materials. For the first time, the summit will include a simulation of a nuclear terrorist attack. Islamic State has spoken publicly of its nuclear ambitions, citing Pakistan as the most likely potential source of materials........In 2014 Pakistani naval officers recruited by al-Qaeda tried to hijack a Pakistan navy frigate and use it to attack US navy vessels on patrol in the Indian Ocean. The attempt was foiled only after a gunfight and a suicide bombing that killed 10 militants and one petty officer.[52]

Violent escalation of religious and ethnic conflict in Baluchistan province became more irksome as Sunni militant groups and the army targeted Shia Muslims. The 62-page report of the Human Rights Watch revealed heartbreaking stories about the killings of innocent Shias in

Pakistan. A Baloch journalist, Mr. Ali Baloch, criticized the killing policy of Pakistan army in Baluchistan. He also raised the issue of extra-judicial killing in the province. These insiders have time and again allied with various jihadi organizations to strike at the state itself. The ISIL and Taliban have demonstrated intent to use chemical weapons, while there is also evidence that Islamists trained foreign fighters to manufacture and use chemical weapons.

Pakistan's nuclear smuggling network was able to offer and provide wide-scale nuclear assistance to foreign countries during the last two decades. The notion of promoting strategic objectives through third parties or proxies is incorporated in Pakistan's national security thinking. Pakistan's agenda was heavily influenced by the military and particularly by the Army which is the most dominant organization in Pakistan's defense establishment. Development of more than 75 terrorist networks in Punjab province, and their links within the armed forces raised many questions including the possibility of insider attacks in a nuclear facility in the country, which may prompt huge destruction and lose of human life.

The ISIL seeks the allegiance of either the Tehreek-e-Taliban Pakistan or the Afghan Taliban. If the ISIL obtains nuclear explosives or biological weapons in Pakistan, this would be a new chapter in its war against civilians. But with presence of all but 25,000-30,000 nuclear personnel in the country's army, how could they possibly attain nuclear weapons from Pakistan?[53] The answer is simple-insider can facilitate the group in obtaining nuclear and biological weapons. The UK's fears can be justified amidst these speculations and looming threats of nuclear terrorism.[54] On June 6, 2015, Pajhwok News reported that dozens of schoolgirls were targeted by unknown terrorists using biological agents in Panj Aab district of Bamyan province.[55] This could also happen in Punjab, Baluchistan, Sindh and Khyber Pakhtunkhwa or Delhi and Mumbai unless the export control regime is tightened.[56]

Chapter 6

Monkeys, Jihadists and the Sleepwalking to Hell

The threat of nuclear terrorism in Pakistan is real. Measures to secure these weapons have become ineffective in the presence of ISIS and Extremist sectarian groups in the country. Ethnic and sectarian confrontations in GHQ over the frail of kill and burn strategy in FATA and Waziristan regions, and some controversial political appointment on important posts within the army exacerbated the fear of nuclear weapons theft. Strategic Planning Division and arm Control Department also face greater challenge where some elements are making things worse. In view of this rift, international print and electronic media, forums and researcher focused on the threat of insider attacks in Pakistan's nuclear facilities. Military experts in Europe and the United States fear that these insiders can inflict huge fatalities on civilian population.

From Strategic Planning Division (SPD), to Arms Control Department, and Joint Chief of Staff Office, many things are not going in right direction. There are several stakeholders with miltablishment, while Department of Arms Control is also under threat from these stakeholders. Media war between ISI and IB further added fuel to the fire and twisted the knife. This war might cause the leak of nuclear secrets to terrorist organizations. Earlier, during the conduct of a probe against former Prime Minister Nawaz Sharif, an interim report submitted to the apex court by the Joint Investigation Team (JIT) had hinted that military-led intelligence agencies were not on good terms with IB, and alleged that the bureau was hampering their investigation.[1] Senior fellow of the IDSA-India, Dr. Bidanda M. Chengappa in his intelligence analysis spotlighted important factors of the ISI involvement in politics, and noted the role of military intelligence in politics before the formation of a political desk for Inter Services Intelligence:

> The rationale for the ISI involvement in domestic politics could be attributed to three reasons (a) the need for the military to manipulate politics and indirectly rule the country (b) to marginalize the civilian intelligence agency which could become powerful with patronage from an elected government (c) the absence of a genuine external threat to national security. Whenever the ISI was controlled by a civilian government the MI reoriented itself to political intelligence activity to keep the generals informed about the relevant developments around the country. In the process the IB by design and not default has been relegated to a 'runners up' or second slot in the intelligence community with the first place reserved for the ISI. Also the MI appears to be peripherally involved with an internal role, especially counter-insurgency duties in Sind, which by its very nature would imply an element of an involvement in provincial politics. The theoretical framework conceived three models of intelligence agencies namely (a) bureau of domestic intelligence (b) political police (c) independent security state. The ISI would fall under the category of an independent security state with the following characteristics. It lacks external controls and differs from the political police because its goals are determined by agency officials and are likely to differ from that of the political elite. Importantly, agency officials rather than elected officials direct its operations.[2]

As the threat of insider intensified, the nature of intelligence war between agencies, and their sectarian affiliations exacerbated. Strategic Planning Division (SPD) started screening to spotlight rogue elements working inside the bomb factories. With the culmination of the screening process, and multifaceted investigation within the Strategic Planning Division and all nuclear sites, dozens suspected experts, engineers and scientists were removed from their services due to their sectarian and ethnic affiliation. It means ethnic, sectarian and political radiation is existed within and around nuclear weapons sites, and, however, an abrupt blaze and inferno can inflict huge fatalities.

Moreover, strong, fortified and invigorated nests of sectarian, ethnic and extremist brigades around big cities can be more dangerous as these groups are desperately seeking conflagration. On 13 October 2016, India's former National Security Advisor, Shivshankar Memon told Indian Express that increasing risk to Pakistan nuclear weapons was from army not terrorists. Noting that terrorists had easier and cheaper ways of wrecking havoc, Mr. Menon said:

> Nuclear weapons are complex devises that are difficult to manage, use and deliver and require very high level of skills".[3] The newspaper reported. "To my mind, the real threat (to Pak nukes) is from insiders, from a Pakistani pilot or a brigadier who decides to wage nuclear jihad, with or without orders, the risk increases as Pakistan builds tactical nuclear weapons for battlefield use, control of which will necessarily be delegated down the command chain, Mr. Memon said.[4]

With Pakistan going nuclear, India's superiority in conventional strength got blunted and the more balanced equation gave further impetus to protracted sub-conventional warfare with India.[5] The emergence of a wide spectral vacuum allowed Pakistan to escalate tensions, yet discouraged New Delhi to engage conventionally.[6] Nuclear assets of Pakistan have always been identified as a precarious threat to regional security while the infiltration of the members of the ISIL, Taliban and other extremist groups into the ranks of armed forces is matter of great concern as these groups have been striving to obtain nuclear, biological and chemical weapon since 2008. During the last ten years, terrorists carried out several attacks against nuclear installations from Baluchistan to Karachi, Peshawar and Khushab, in which several nuclear commandos were also killed.

Terrorist attacks in Lahore, Quetta, Karachi and the strength of Islamic State across Pakistan raised many questions that how could armed forces manage the safety and security of the country's nuclear weapons while Taliban and other religious extremist organizations have established their sectarian brigades within the armed forces. When terrorist target civilian or military installations in Pakistan, agencies accuse Afghan and Indian intelligence of harboring and sponsoring terrorist and extremist networks, but in reality, they understand who sponsor these attacks. On 17 April 2017 Dawn reported Director General of Inter-Services Public Relations (ISPR), Maj Gen Asif Ghafoor, announced that Mr. Ehsanullah Ehsan, former spokesperson of the Tehreek-e-Taliban Pakistan (TTP) and a senior leader of the Jamaat-ul-Ahrar, had turned himself into Pakistan's security agencies.

> The people, the state and the institutions of Pakistan have made considerable progress in the betterment of the country's security situation. We have progressed to the point that the people who've been planning attacks on Pakistan's soil from across the border have started to see that the situation has changed".[7] However, during his media briefing, Maj Gen Ghafoor also showed recorded confessional statement of Naureen Leghari, a medical student from Hyderabad who allegedly fled home to join the militant Islamic State (IS) in Syria. Leghari was arrested after her husband, whom she had married after leaving her home and joining the militants, was killed in an encounter in Punjab Housing Society.[8]

Renowned terrorist and spokesperson of the Jamaat-ul-Ahrar Pakistan abruptly surrendered to the armed forces in April 2017. He was an important commander of the terrorist group that carried out attacks against military and civilian installations. Major General Ghafoor announced that Mr. Ehsanullah Ehsan, a former spokesperson and one of the top leaders of the Jamaat-ul-Ahrar terror faction of the Tehrik-e-Taliban Pakistan (TTP), had turned himself in to Pakistan Army. His real name is Liaqat Ali. Mr. Ehsanullah Ehsan was the spokesperson of Jamaat-ul-Ahrar, a terrorist group operating inside Afghanistan. His group has been involved in suicide attacks against Pakistan's security forces and civilian installations since 2008. In Pakistani press, various newspapers, journals, and electronic media highlighted the activities of the groups in different perspectives, but Afghan media never discussed operational and political motive of the group. On 30 April 2017, Azaz Syed in his article briefly highlighted some aspects of his life.

> Liaqat Ali alias Ehsanullah Ehsan would not face any terrorism or criminal case against him in any court of law including the military court, as he returned after getting assurances from security establishment and promise to share secrets of Taliban...... Asmatullah Moavia, another former militant commander who once headed Punjabi Taliban, played a key role in bringing back

Ehsanullah Ehsan, former spokesman of Tehreek-e-Taliban Pakistan (TTP) and Jamaatul Ahrar (JA). "Moavia connected Ehsanullah with a security agency which resulted in the return of former TTP-JA spokesman. Asmatullah Moavia was the first top militant commander who left TTP from North Waziristan and returned to settled areas of Pakistan in July 2014 after securing amnesty from the security and intelligence officials. A source who is privy to the details of surrender revealed that Moavia is a close friend of Ehsan, who first initiated a debate with former in 2015. Moavia successfully convinced Ehsan following.........After the formal announcement of his surrender by the DG ISPR the TTP-JA spokesman Asad Mansor responded by his statement on very day, claiming that Ehsan along with two others were arrested from Paktika province of Afghanistan. However he did not share who were the other two who got arrested. Actually Ehsan was accompanying his wife and son when he surrendered.[9]

Some Pakistani newspapers reported the arrest of Mr. Ehsanullah from Afghanistan, while Afghan sources also confirmed to this author that he was arrested from Paktika province of Afghanistan, where he and his colleagues were being protected by Afghan government. In his statement before the military authorities, Mr. Ehsanullah Ehsan revealed important facts about his organization operating inside Afghanistan:

My name is Liaquat Ali, aka Ehsanullah Ehsan, and I belong to the Mohmand Agency. I joined the TTP in 2008, when I was a college student. I have been a spokesperson for TTP Mohmand, TTP's central division, and the Jamaat-ul-Ahrar," he says. "I have seen a lot in my nine years with these organizations. These people have misled people in the name of Islam, especially the youth, for their own ends. They themselves do not hold themselves to the same standards they champion for others. A particular group [within them] is responsible for misleading people, kidnapping them and extorting them for money, and murdering innocent. These people have been behind bombing attacks in public spaces and attacking schools, colleges and universities. This is not what Islam teaches us. When the operation in Waziristan kicked off, these people started fighting within themselves for more power and leadership. After Hakimullah was killed, a new succession struggle kicked off.[10]

Dawn reported Mr. Ehsanullah Ehsan's explanation about the internal turmoil of the Taliban leadership, and its links with Indian intelligence agencies. How India used TTP and how NDS and RAW provided training and financial assistance to their operatives, Mr. Ehsanullah gave all these details in his statement before military authorities:

> Separate campaigns were kicked off in support of Omar Khalid Khorasani, [Khan Said] Sajna and Mullah Fazlullah. Everyone wanted power, so a shura decided that there would be a draw of names for who would be leader. This is how Mullah Fazlullah was elected leader of the TTP. What can you expect from a leader who was nominated through a lucky draw? And what can you expect from Fazlullah, who married his mentor's daughter by force and took her away. People like him are not fit to serve Islam. After the operation in North Waziristan, we fled to Afghanistan. Over there, we established and developed contacts with India and RAW. They [the TTP leadership] got their [Indian] support, their funding and took money for every activity they did. They pushed the TTP soldiers to the frontlines to fight against the Pakistan Army and went into hiding themselves. When they started taking help from India and RAW, I told Khorasani that we're supporting the kuffar [non-believers] and helping them kill our own people in our own country. He (Khorasani) said: 'Even if Israel wants to fund me to destabilize Pakistan, I will not hesitate in taking their help. At that point, I had figured out that the TTP was functioning according to some sort of agenda that served the self-interest of its leaders. "These [terrorist] organizations have established committees in Afghanistan through which they communicate and coordinate with RAW. The Indians had given them special documents to help them move around Afghanistan with ease. In Afghanistan, these documents function like Pakistani ID cards. Without these documents, it is very difficult for terrorists to move around Afghanistan considering the security situation in that country", Dawn reported.[11]

Mr. Ehsanullah Ehsan also explained the links between his organization and Afghan security forces, and told military investigators how they received support from Afghanistan. His revelations and allegation was not given importance in Afghanistan due some unknown reasons but Afghan media termed his arrest an important development.

These [terrorists] used to keep in contact with Afghan and Indian security forces before they moved anywhere in the country. They used to grant them passage and guide their infiltration attempts into Pakistan. Since Pakistan Army destroyed several Jamaat-ul-Ahrar camps in Parcha and Lalpura and killed many of their commandos in its ongoing operation, they've had to flee the area and abandon their stronghold. Due to this, the morale of their commanders and their senior leadership has been shaken. There are people in those camps who have had enough—who want to quit. I want to send out a message to them. Stop what you are doing and adopt the path of peace, and come back to a life of tranquility. When these people stopped getting airtime and coverage in media to the ongoing operations, they turned to social media to rope in young people who do not know better. They started misleading them and provoking those using wrong interpretations of Islam. They spread propaganda and statements that could turn young people onto their side. I have a message for young people too: these people are fighting only for their selfish designs and are being used by external forces. The reasons I have discussed here turned me away from these organizations and motivated me to turn myself over voluntarily to Pakistan Army," concludes his statement.[12]

There were speculations that either he was arrested during military operation, or he himself surrendered to authorities, but some experts viewed his arrest as a complicated saga. Left politicians said Mr., Ehsan was barking for Pakistan army inside the Taliban groups. On 20 April 2017, prominent Pakistani journalist Marvi Sirmad in her Daily Times article revealed important fact about his surrender.

Only three names-Akbar Gul, and Siraj-were revealed while no other details were shared. Some skeptics believe that Ehsan might have been one of those eight. While many others believe that Ehsan might have been captured during the special operations carried out by Pakistan security forces across the Pak-Afghan border. According to Afghan media, Pak forces had 'transgressed' on March 21 at least 3 km inside Afghan territory and attacked specific locations at the havens of TTP-Jamaat-ul-Ahrar. Although, he had stopped replying to the queries of media persons sometime around 14 March. He had been, previously, quite active in reaching out to the national and international media.[13]

He was one of the naughty children of Pakistan army involved in the killing of innocent civilians. Why he surrendered and why he made unconfirmed revelations about India and Afghanistan is still remains a conundrum. Marvi Sirmad described his acts of terrorism with different aspects:

> Among the major attacks claimed by JuA through Ehsan as spokesperson are, IED blast in Quetta, Gulshan-e-Iqbal Park Lahore, killing of Punjab's Home Minister Col. (R) Shuja Khanzada; killing of nine foreign tourists in Gilgit-Baltistan; shooting in the head of Malala Yousafzai (calling her work an "obscenity" that needed to be stopped); suicide bombings on Shiites in Rawalpindi and Karachi; rocket attack on Bacha Khan International Airport; suicide attack on Wagah border; twin blasts in Mohmand agency (his home town in Safi tehsil), to name but few.[14]

The issue of terrorism has changed into a bone of contention between Kabul and Islamabad and mutual relations hit rock bottom following the deadly attack in the southern Sindh province for which the self-styled Islamic State (ISIL) group claimed responsibility. It is an undisputable fact that terrorist have sanctuaries both in Afghanistan and Pakistan, as many leaders of terrorist groups were killed in Pakistan's soil. For a long time, Pakistani state dithered over definitions of good Taliban and bad Taliban but now realized that how they pose precarious threat to the country's national security. In 2015, International Crisis Group (ICG) hammered Pakistan's counter-terrorism measures in its recent report.

> Revisiting Counter-Terrorism Strategies in Pakistan: Opportunities and Pitfalls." One of the major concerns in the document is related to the Pakistani military's continued dominance over the civilian administration. The militarization of counter-terrorism policy puts at risk Pakistan's evolution toward greater civilian rule, which is itself a necessary but not sufficient condition to stabilize the democratic transition.[15]

Not only Najam Sethi, several important journalists of various newspapers criticized Pakistan's Afghan policy. Pakistan is trying to keep Afghanistan weak and conflagrated. The country trains terrorists, and send them to Afghanistan to carry out suicide attacks against civilians and armed forces. On 07 July 2017, prominent analyst and editor Friday Times, Najam Sethi in his editorial portion spotlighted important policy foreboding of military establishment towards Afghanistan:

> The Establishment's policy towards Afghanistan is also shaped by its India policy. Originally, it was packaged as a quest for "strategic depth". This meant support for jihad by Pakhtun Islamic Mujahedeen in the 1990s. When that project didn't succeed, the Taliban were muscled into Kabul. But when that project also failed, they were provided safe havens in Pakistan's borderlands to bide their time. Unfortunately, the unintended consequences of that reprieve led to the creation of the Pakistan Taliban and their transfiguration into the Islamic State in recent times that threatens both Afghanistan and Pakistan. The strategic doctrine also changed marginally. Instead of "strategic depth" in a client state, the Establishment now furthered the cause of a "friendly state" in an independent Afghanistan. When this too didn't happen, the doctrine was further adjusted to accept a "neutral" Afghanistan with power sharing among the various Afghan protagonists, especially Pakistan-backed Afghan Taliban. But the inability of the Establishment to nudge the Afghan Taliban into such an agreement, coupled with the inability of the US backed Kabul regime to coerce them into submission, has put paid to such efforts too. This failure in Afghanistan is now impinging critically on the Establishment's relations with America. That leads into the second development.[16]

On 06 January 2015, Dawn reported Pakistani Parliament passed the 21st Amendment to the Constitution that allowed military courts to try civilians accused of religious or sectarian terrorism. "This authorization and dispensation further complicated counter-terrorism policy that put at risk Pakistan's evolution towards greater civilian rule in the second phase of a fragile democratic transition. Recent terrorist attacks in which hundreds lost their lives shaken the nation".[17]

During the last two decades, hundreds chemical and radiological devices have been used across the world, but recent attacks on Pakistan's nuclear installation are matter of great concern. In South Asia, the threat matrix became more complex when the ISIS claimed that its leadership had approached Pakistan army for delivering nuclear explosive to the group. On 04, September 2013, one of Pakistan's leading newspapers, the News International reported a 178-page summary of the United States intelligence community, about the US intelligence surveillance of Pakistan's nuclear weapons. Pentagon and CIA focused on Pakistan's nuclear facilities that might come under attack by TTP or ISIS terrorist group.[18]

Pakistan's nuclear doctrine means that, in case of any attack from the Indian side, the government in power would be left with no other option except to retaliate with nuclear weapons. By using nuclear weapons, Pakistan wants to prevent India from disintegrating the country. If Indian armed forces are entered Pakistan in large numbers, and Pakistani security forces are unable to intercept their advance towards Islamabad, the only option they might have is to use nuclear weapons against India, or retreat inside Afghanistan, reorganize and resort to attack on Indian installations.[19] Pakistan's military establishment understands that, as India once dismembered the country in 1971, and continues to challenge it by various means, therefore, a nuclear bomb is the only umbrella to protect the country from its military might. The Nawaz Sharif government tried to bring India and Pakistan to a close, and ease the political and military tension between the two states. In his General Assembly speech (2014), Prime Minister Muhammad Nawaz Sharif said:

> As a responsible nuclear weapon state, we will continue to pursue the goals of disarmament and non-proliferation and adhere to the policy of Credible Minimum Deterrence, without entering into an arms race. We would not, however, remain oblivious to the evolving security dynamics in South Asia, nor would we agree to arrangement that is detrimental to our security and strategic interests. Our position on the proposed Fissile Material Treaty is determined by our national security interests and the objective of strategic stability in South Asia. Safe, secure and peaceful use of nuclear energy is essential for economic development. Pakistan qualifies for full access to civil nuclear technology for peaceful purposes, to meet its growing energy needs, for continued economic growth. By the same token, as a mainstream partner

in the global non-proliferation regime, Pakistan has impeccable credentials to join the multilateral export control regime, including the Nuclear Suppliers Group. Pakistan will continue to participate constructively in the Nuclear Security Summit process, which is a laudable initiative.[20]

The deployment of Pakistan's tactical weapons, according to nuclear experts, meant to use them against India, if it attacks Pakistan's territory in an effort to disintegrate it. Pakistan's Nasr missile is a ballistic missile launched from a mobile twin-canister launcher.[21] The test of this missile on 05, November 2013 and 2017, prompted deep concern in South Asia, while Afghan government was more anxious about the possible use of this missile by Pakistan based Taliban against its military installations.[22] Pakistan has two major strategic assets; its nuclear weapons and The Afghan Taliban. Both are controlled by the army, and more specifically by its intelligence agencies. The army, which gives itself the right of the guardian of the country's "ideological frontiers," still sees India as its main enemy, and views Afghanistan as part of its fifth province.[23] Pakistan continues to create threatening environment in South Asia by developing different types of Tactical Nuclear Weapons. Author Arun Sahgal suggests that these military developments and the modernization of Chinese army and its military influence in South Asia raised serious questions:

> The military modernization of Chinese government, its capabilities, and capacity-building, infrastructure development in Tibet, and moves into the Indian Ocean pose serious challenges to India's security. China's growing footprint in South Asia and attempts to bring peripheral states into its circle of influence only add to these concerns. There is a duality in approaches to dealing with these challenges: while broader political discourse underscores cooperation and downplays competition, there is nonetheless a growing realization that India needs to develop credible hard power as a dissuasive strategy against China. India's strategic dilemma thus lies in shaping its political response to external balancing. Although there is the understanding of a strategic convergence between India and the U.S., there is little consensus on how to shape this relationship to further India's strategic interests. New Delhi continues to face a policy dilemma

on whether to be a regional balancer, a swing state, or a strategic hedge.[24]

China has been the main supporter of Pakistan's controversial nuclear programme. China used the country against India and the United States in Afghanistan to further its national interests in the region. Military confrontations between India and Pakistan and between China and India can also be judged from the recent analysis of Ashley J. Tellis and Travis Tanner, which describes Chinese interests in South Asia.

> At the geopolitical level, the United States is confronted with a challenge that it never faced in its rivalry with the Soviet Union: the growing dependence of its own allies and key neutrals in Asia on China for markets, capital, goods, and in many cases even technology. China's enormous size and its huge economy have made it the centre of a highly integrated Asian economic system, where the growth of every country on its periphery increasingly depends on the extent and density of the linkages enjoyed with China. Such intermeshing inevitably produces geopolitical effects insofar as it makes the littoral nations, even when formally allied with the United States, more sensitive to Chinese interests than they would otherwise be in the absence of regional integration. Even if this process does not lead eventually to the creation of a hermetic trading bloc that excludes the United States—an unlikely prospect for now—it creates an expanded Chinese sphere of influence that, enveloping the United States' allies and important neutrals, complicates their decision-making as they attempt to juggle competing demands pertaining to security and prosperity.[25]

Pakistan has adopted a very negative approach to nuclear race and war in Afghanistan in South Asia, and continued to create more opportunities to terrorist groups' retrieving materials of dirty bomb. The 2008 Mumbai attacks and the Line of Control incidents prompted deep distrust between the two states. In June 2014, Prime Minister Narendra Modi issued a stern warning to Pakistan; "I had told you on television that this is not Manmohan Singh's government; it is Narendra Modi's government. If you do something, we will also do but we cannot sit quiet".[26]

Indian Law Minister, Ravi Shankar Prasad criticized Pakistan and its support to extremist groups across the border. Mr. Ravi Shankar demanded the resignation of Prime Minister Nawaz Sharif. However, Pakistan-based terrorist groups used the same language against Mr. Modi's government. In its video message, Ansar-ul-Tawheed fi Belad Hind group (Brotherhood for Monotheism in India) warned Prime Minister Modi of retaliation for the Gujarat massacre. Given the fast growth of militant organizations within Pakistan in collaboration with foreign terrorists, encouraged by the Pakistan army to achieve their foreign policy objectives. Prime Minister Modi warned Pakistan consecutive support to proxy war against India can push the country to the brink of war. Moreover, various politicians in India issued different statements against Pakistan, creating a hostile environment in the region. In military circles, India's former Army Chief, Dalbir Singh Suhag, warned Pakistan and said that the country is unable to intercept cross-border infiltration.

The exponentially growing terrorist networks of sectarian and extremist organization in Pakistan are a real threat to the country's national security. These groups desperately seek nuclear materials to prepare nuclear explosive devices and use it against foreign forces in Afghanistan. Nuclear installations, research reactors and uranium enrichment plants, might, at any time, come under potential attack from these organizations, and their allies within the armed forces. There are speculations that TTP or the Islamic State (ISIS) might steal fissile material from a military or civilian facility, to construct an improvised nuclear device, and use it against civilian population. Pakistani generals had established a strong network of nuclear smuggling in 1980s and 1990s, and smuggled weapons in large quantity. Taliban and the ISIS networks in all provinces have challenged the authority of the state. Pakistan army is fighting on different fronts but failed to protect civilians. Author Samuel Kane (2012) noted the threat posed by Pakistan's nuclear weapons, and warned that terrorist groups can at any times attack nuclear plants:

> In Pakistan, the threat of nuclear materials falling into terrorist hands is a multi-faceted danger, composed of several different scenarios, such as (1) insiders within the Pakistani nuclear program proliferating nuclear assets and knowledge to

terrorist groups; (2) a terrorist group stealing nuclear materials from a Pakistani facility; and (3) a radical Islamist group seizing control of the Pakistani government and nuclear arsenal, through a coup or democratic elections.... The threat of an individual inside the Pakistani nuclear program transferring nuclear materials or know-how to a terrorist organization is a serious one, and is indeed one that Pakistan has already been forced to confront in various forms.[27]

In June 2014, after the Karachi Attack, there were concerns in Afghanistan, Russia, India, and Europe, that the country's nuclear weapons are not in safe hands. Pakistani nuclear analysts warned that the safety of systems can fail catastrophically. An important lesson of Fukushima, they noted, is that nuclear establishments underestimated the likelihood and severity of possible accidents. Another important lesson they noted, is that Pakistani establishment also overestimates its ability to cope with a real nuclear disaster. The involvement of Pakistani generals in nuclear smuggling put the country in ordeal. There is plenty material on Pakistan's involvement in the smuggling of nuclear weapons to Korea, Iran, Libya and some Arab states, which caused harassment and fear in South Asia, and the Middle East. Terrorists seeking to unleash massive violence and destruction may climb the escalation ladder to the highest rungs: nuclear weapons. Writer Farooq Tariq criticized the government policies on extremism and militant groups, and warned that a large number of religious schools are causing sectarian violence and jihadism:

> In Pakistan the main tool for the growth of Islamic religious fundamentalism is the madressah. According to conservative estimates, there are approximately 20,000 madressahs (USCIRF 2011). There are five main types, which are divided along sectarian and political lines: Deobandi, Barelvi, Shia, Ale-Hadith, Salafi and Jamaat-e-Islami. Eighty-two percent of those belonging to Deobandi madressahs view the Taliban as their model (Ali, 2010). They have been an alternative to public schools in a country where less than two percent of the total government budget is spent on education. Almost all donations to religious charities end up in the coffers of this madressahs.[28]

Chapter 7

Biological Weapons, the ISIL, Kashmiri Extremist Groups and the use of Nuclear Explosives Devices in South Asia

Pakistan has been rubbing eyeballs and experiencing worse political and economic crisis since 2000s. The army maintains criminal enterprise, brings home groceries in case of billion dollars cash, and does not share it with the state budget. This criminal enterprise is being elevated and boosted by narco-smuggling networks, and business of soldiers for sale in Asia and Middle East. The money is being spent in recruiting proxies, and maintaining criminal private militias in order to create instability in South Asia. The miltablishment and its warlords receive huge amount from the United States for its illegal marketing of fear and consternation through its blackwater.

As the clouds of nuclear war are spreading over South Asia, India and Pakistan have entered an undeclared war on the Line of Control. Every day, Pakistan fires missile into Afghanistan and India, and kills innocent civilians. Pakistan's nuclear black marketing is a bigger threat. With the Chinese support, its nuclear and military technology threatened the stability of South Asia. Pakistan has already warned that if India attacked the country, its armed forces will use nuclear weapons against its military targets. Talking to a local TV Channel, GeoNews Defense Minister Khawaja Asif said:

I don't think there is any such threat but as Allah has said in the Quran, 'The horses must be prepared', so we should always be completely prepared. There is also a famous English proverb, "The price of freedom is eternal vigilance"... We are always pressurized time and again... that we have more tactical weapons than we need. It is internationally recognized that we have superiority, and if there is a threat to our security, or if anyone steps on our soil and if someone's designs are a threat to our security, we will not hesitate to use those weapons for our defense, Khawaja said.[1]

Expert views his emotional statement as a true jingoism and false patriotism. Miltablishment times and again delivered such emotional statements, and warned that they can destroy Indian missiles and nuclear systems. However, in June 2016, speaking at a book-launching ceremony in Islamabad, the Defense Minister severely criticized a series of hostile statements from Indian politicians. By issuing provocative statements, Indian politicians want to distract Pakistan's attention from the war on terror," he said, adding that India had been "promoting terrorism in Pakistan." Pakistan has threatened to use tactical nuclear weapons against Indian conventional forces if there is a war.[2]

In 1999, the Kargil war was a test case for the two nuclear states, in which hundreds Pakistani soldiers were killed, but the motive behind that war is still remains unclear. Pakistan readied its nuclear weapons while India mobilized international community against the irresponsible act in Kargil. There were speculations in Pakistan press that Pakistan just wanted to weaken the resolve of Indian forces by issuing irresponsible statements. The greatest threat to the national security of Pakistan and India stems from nuclear smuggling and terror groups operating in Punjab, Baluchistan, Assam and Kashmir.[3] Increasingly sophisticated chemical and biological weapons are accessible to organizations like ISIL, Mujahedeen-e-Hind (MH), and the Taliban and their allies.[4]

These groups can use more sophisticated conventional weapons as well as chemical and biological agents in India and Pakistan in near future, while they have already experimented in Iraq and Syria.[5] They can disperse chemical, biological and radiological material as well as industrial agents via water or land to target schools, colleges, civilian and military personnel.[6] The crisis is going to get worse as the exponentially growing network of ISIL and its popularity in Afghanistan created deep security challenges for Pakistan and its Taliban allies. This group could use chemical and biological weapons once it gains footing in Afghanistan.[7] The fact is that Pakistan is trying to push the Afghan Taliban towards a political settlement in Afghanistan to prevent ISIL from gaining control of the country. The ISIL and the Taliban are not the only security challenges for Pakistan; the country is also facing many social and economic problems, including electricity shortages, ethnic and sectarian divide.

The gradual radicalization of Pakistan army and its links with worldwide terrorist organizations over the last 70 years, poses a grave danger to the country's nuclear installations in terms of insider attacks. The spectrum of rogue and radicalized elements ranges from military officers to employees of Strategic Planning Division, or officers of nuclear force. The Islamic State, Kashmiri organizations, al Qaeda and Taliban are still waiting to receive their share. The US representative for Afghanistan and Pakistan on 16 December 2015 told Committee of Foreign Affairs that the United States was concerned about Pakistan's missiles program. Islamabad retrieved nuclear design information technology from China, while North Korea and China also supplied missile technology to the country. At present, the US government spend $100m dollar on maintain the security of Pakistan's nuclear warheads. On 01 August 2016, The US Congressional Research Service in its paper reported Pakistan's three civilian power reactors:

> Pakistan operates three civilian power reactors under International Atomic Energy Agency (IAEA) safeguards at two sites: a Canadian supplied 100 Mme heavy-water moderated in Karachi (Karachi Nuclear Power Plant-1 (KANUPP), which began operating in 1971, and two Chinese-built 325 Mme pressurized water reactor (PWRs) at Chashma site. Chashma-1 started operation in 2000 and Chashma-2 in 2011. The China National Nuclear Corporation (CNNC) is building two additional reactors at KANUPP. There are plans for forth reactor at KANUPP.[8]

India and Pakistan, with little experience and less contact, have virtually nothing to guide them in a crisis but mistrust and paranoia. If weapons proliferate in the Middle East, as Iran and then Saudi Arabia and possibly Egypt join Israel in the ranks of nuclear powers, each will have to manage a bewildering four-dimensional stand-off.[9] In March

2015, Prime Minister Nawaz Sharif visited Saudi Arabia and discussed military cooperation with the King.[10] The U.S. government says they remained skeptical that Pakistan would directly sell or transfer atomic weapons to Saudi Arabia in response to the perceived threat from Iran. But they said they couldn't discount Islamabad deploying some of its weapons in the kingdom, or establishing a nuclear-defense umbrella.[11]

Mr. Charles D. Ferguson and William C Potter noted the use of fissile material and other explosive devices: "Two types of fissile material could be used for this purpose, highly enriched uranium (HEU) or plutonium, but the former would be far easier to make into a successful IND, as explained in detail, below".[12] According to the conservative figures used by the International Atomic Energy Agency, only 25 kilograms of HEU or 8 kilograms of plutonium would be needed to manufacture a weapon. These materials have been produced in great quantity in nuclear weapon and civilian nuclear energy programs around the world.[13]

There were speculations that on 10 June 2014, terrorists were facilitated by their colleagues within the army to enter Karachi airport. Once again, law enforcement and intelligence apparatus were shown to be inadequate. And even the most secure sites were penetrated. Pakistanis reminded of just how vulnerable everyone was. And yet again, the government was nowhere in sight. Former Taliban spokesman Shahidullah Shahid claimed that the attack was a revenge for the killings of Hakeemullah Mehsud and others in airstrikes.[14]

In 1980s, Pakistani state encouraged Afghan Mujahedeen to fight a proxy war against the Soviet forces in Afghanistan. Most of the Mujahedeen were never disarmed after war ended in Afghanistan, and some of these groups were later activated at the behest of Pakistan in the form of Lashkar-e-Toiba, the Harkat-ul-Mujahedeen and others like the Tehrik-i-Taliban Pakistan (TTP). Rajesh M. Basrur and Prof. Friedrich Steinhäusler argued that once terrorists obtained radioactive material, and classified, they will need more knowledge about the use of such a weapon:

> Once terrorists have obtained radioactive material, they still have to fulfill several logistical requirements before they actually carry out an act of radiological terrorism, such as: knowledge

about the targeted facility; provision of adequate manpower and vehicles to transport the source; access to tools for dismantling the source. These kinds of attacks would result in a wide range of radiation doses to the victims and First Responders (police, paramedics, and fire-fighters), though in most cases unlikely to be life-threatening. However, it is questionable whether initially Indian authorities would even be aware of the fact that a terror act involving radioactive materials has occurred, since most first responders are neither trained, nor technically equipped to detect the presence of radiation at the site of a terror attack. It is safe to presume that terrorists in India would have to inform the media first about the deployment of radioactive material in order to achieve the desired level of panic among the general public.[15]

The authors also mentioned security risk and warned that several kinds of attacks can be carried out by extremist and terrorist organizations in India. India is no doubt, the most vulnerable country where several insurgencies are in operation across the country. These groups would also try to retrieve Weapons of Mass Destruction (WMD) or Nuclear Weapon. In these circumstances, India's nuclear weapons are also under threat from several terrorist and extremist groups based in Pakistan. A small team of trained saboteurs gains access to an NPP, possibly with an insider's assistance, and detonates explosives at sensitive points to cause a release of radioactivity.[16] Islamabad continues to expand nuclear technology and delivery systems. The country wants to placate more states for investing money in its controversial program. James E. Doyle also raised the issue of nuclear terrorism and possibility of nuclear war in the future:

> A chain of events leading to nuclear war can emerge even when no political leader believes it is in the interest of the state to initiate war, and both sides act in a manner intended to avoid it. This long list of nuclear accidents, malfunction, mishap, false alarms and close calls, often initiated by mechanical and human error, continues to grow. Such incidents include crashes of nuclear armed aircraft and submarines, warning system mistaking flocks of geese or reflection of sunlight for enemy missiles launches, maintenance crews dropping tools and blowing up missile silos, and the temporary loss or misplacement of nuclear weapons.[17]

The future relationship between Pakistan army and jihadist groups, and the use of Weapons of Mass Destruction (WMD) may cause huge destruction in South Asia. Pakistani merchants of fear are selling these jihadists in Middle East and Afghanistan to further their national agenda. Authors Gary Ackerman and Jeremy Tamsett warn that terrorists may use WMD in future:

> The future nexus of jihadists and WMD is a topic of some controversy. On the one side, are those who view the use by al Qaeda and other jihadist of WMD as all but "inevitable"? These observers generally point to jihadist's demonstrated capacity for mass casualties' attacks, their evolving capabilities, eroding technical constraints, and the increased availability of the raw materials with which to produce WMD. On the other side are those who take a more skeptical approach, highlighting the persisting technical obstacles to the efficient weaponization of CBRN agents, as well as the lack of sufficient incentives (based on both "pragmatic and jurisprudential reasons"), for jihadists to expand serious efforts on attaining WMD relative to more conventional weapons.[18]

The issue of Pakistan's nuclear danger received considerable attention from international community as the TTP and ISIS seek nuclear weapons to use it either in Afghanistan or in Pakistan. Some Kashmiri militant groups are trying to retrieve these weapons and use it against the Indian army. Over the last ten years, there have emerged renewed concerns over the future direction of the country's nuclear program. Some see it as a worrisome possibility; some believe it is an exaggerated danger. Sadia Tasleem supports Pakistan's stance on the safety of its nuclear weapons:

> Islamabad appears confident in its ability to prevent any such eventuality. This, combined with the confidence that Pakistan draws from its close cooperation with the United States, prevents Pakistanis from perceiving US nuclear deterrence policy as a threat. Pakistan's threat perceptions continue to focus elsewhere. Nonetheless, disenchantment with the United States is heavily reflected in Pakistan's popular discourse. The disenchantment mainly centres on drone attacks and the implications of the Indo-US strategic partnership.[19]

As the CIA already highlighted al Qaeda's general interest in weapons of mass destruction, including nuclear weapons, the Islamic State (ISIS) already retrieved these weapons from Iraq. Nuclear terrorism remains a discrete possibility, hence it should be designated a low probability high consequence event. Writer Vladimir Dvorkin warns about the fatalities of nuclear terrorism:

> Severe consequences can be caused by sabotaging nuclear power plants, research reactors, and radioactive materials storage facilities. Large cities are especially vulnerable to such attacks. A large city may host dozens of research reactors with a nuclear power plant or a couple of spent nuclear fuel storage facilities and dozens of large radioactive materials storage facilities located nearby. The past few years have seen significant efforts made to enhance organizational and physical aspects of security at facilities, especially at nuclear power plants. Efforts have also been made to improve security culture. But these efforts do not preclude the possibility that well-trained terrorists may be able to penetrate nuclear facilities.[20]

Pakistan often engaged in discussion with the United States on its controversial nuclear weapon program at various levels, and in different circumstances for more than 30 years, but, according to some research reports, the U.S and international community is not satisfied with Pakistan's nuclear safety measures. Pakistan's supply of nuclear materials to some Arab and African states including Saudi Arabia, created more suspicion about its Islamic nuclear bomb. Pakistan's envoy to UN, Mr. Munir Akram expressed deep concern about the increasing US-Pakistan tension and emerging differences regarding it supply of nuclear weapons to Saudi Arabia:

> Clearly, Pakistan and the US need to address their nuclear differences urgently and constructively, The US in concert in other major powers, are also well placed to promote a more stable nuclear security environment between Pakistan and India. Absent some measures of mutual assurance, accommodation and cooperation on the nuclear issue, the continuing US military presence in Afghanistan is likely to further intensify Islamabad's concerns and Pakistan-US tensions and affect their positions on other issues, such as counterterrorism and Afghanistan's stability, where their objectives appear to be increasingly convergent.[21]

The threat of terrorist networks acquiring chemical, biological and nuclear weapons (CBRN) to develop and use it is real. In intellectual circles, there is a general perception that as the Islamic State (ISIS) already used some dangerous gases in Iraq; it could use biological weapons against civilian populations in Pakistan. If control over these weapons is weak, or if it is available in open market, there would be a huge destruction in the region. In July 2014, government of Iraq notified that nuclear material was seized by the ISIS army from Mosul University.[22]

In his Criterion paper, Mr. Mushfiq Murshed has warned that religiously motivated groups in Pakistan can retrieve nuclear weapons: "This is accomplished by obtaining clerical sanctions through religious edicts that are primarily based on de-contextualized quotations from the sacred text. The edicts that al Qaeda has pursued and propagated clearly are an indication of what strategy they intend to pursue."[23]As the country is a failing state and the infrastructure of terrorist organization is well established, there are possibilities that these groups can gain access to nuclear materials. Research scholars, Rajesh M. Basrur and Friedrich Steinhausler also noted some atomic sites of Pakistan and their vulnerabilities:

> Though its overall nuclear infrastructure is relatively small, the possibility of leakage is widely feared because of the general sense of the country as a failing state. Pakistan's main uranium enrichment facility is at Kahuta (Khan Research Laboratories). Smaller uranium enrichment facilities exist at Sihala and Golra, and possibly at Gadwal. Plutonium extraction work is done at the New Lab, Nilhore, and at Khushab in central Punjab. Pakistan has two nuclear power plants. One is located at Karachi, the other at Chasma. Its nuclear weapons are believed to be in an unassembled state, with the fissile core kept separate from the bomb assembly. The bomb components and the wider infrastructure are under military control. In February 2000, a National Command Authority was established. In January 2001, the Pakistan Nuclear Regulatory Authority was created to regulate the civilian nuclear infrastructure.[24]

In his research article, Indian scholar, the late B. Raman (2004) noted Russian President Vladimir Putin's concern about the safety of

Pakistan's nuclear weapons during his India visit: When President Vladimir Putin of Russia visited India a year ago, he stated in an interview that Musharraf had repeatedly assured him that Pakistan's nuclear and missile assets were in the safe hands of the Army and that there was no question of their leakage to Al Qaeda or other jihadist terrorists. Putin added that while he had no reasons to distrust Musharraf, he continued to be concerned over the dangers of individual members of the Pakistani scientific community helping the jihadist terrorists to develop a WMD capability.[25]

The threat of Pakistani jihadists using WMD might cause uncontrollable situation, since the threat lies at the nexus of two subjects—jihadist terrorism and weapons of mass destruction—that are both characterized by high level of dynamism.[26] Terrorist groups in Pakistan are trying to retrieve bio-weapons and use it against civilian population in Afghanistan. Dr. Agha Inamullah Khan describes diseases caused by the use of biological weapons in Pakistan.

We had Dengue, Measles and now again alarming figures of Polio. The first incidence of dengue fever was reported in 2003 in Lahore with an earlier outbreak in Karachi almost a decade ago. The disease reappeared in 2006, hitting on alternate years until 2010 and returning with even greater fury following year. Also many Pakistanis, especially in rural areas, view vaccination campaigns with suspicion as a western plot to sterilize Muslims.[27]

In 2013, Global Policy, a journal published by the London School of Economics, warned about the prospect of Ebola being used as a terrorist weapon. Amanda M. Teckman also warned that the Islamic State might possibly use Ebola as a weapon against civilian population. It remains to be seen if a terrorist group like ISIS—which has demonstrated a willingness to engage in large scale mass murder, including the uninhibited murder of civilians—has the capability to produce a weaponized version of Ebola.[28] Author of Bioterrorism, Mr. Daniel M. Gerstein noted that terrorist might not carry out large scale attacks which negatively influence their support. His book contains details of bioterrorism and its impacts on human life:

Terrorists will act in ways they consider rational, even if this rationality is not obvious to outsiders. They will maintain a core raison d'être that will propel their actions and modulate their behavior to positively influence their constituencies. This will be very important as in the case of moderating behavior. Terrorists will be disinclined to engage in large-scale attacks with large number of civilian casualties (i.e., death, disease and morbidity greater than one thousand people) because this would tend to negatively influence their support base.[29]

The threat of nuclear and biological terrorist still persisted in South Asia as Pakistani leaders in their statements often warned that they will use these weapons against India. Therefore, the possibilities of nuclear terrorism cannot be ruled out. Writer Ramtanu Maitra argues that the links between Pakistan army and Kashmir based terrorist groups as a dangerous development. These groups, Mr. Ramtanu suggests were flourishing and harboring by US and Pakistan:

> What are disturbing are the direct ties between the Pakistani military and the terrorists, particularly the anti-India terrorist such as a Kashmiri fighter, who was a commando in Pakistan's Special Services Group (SSG), and was once rewarded by Gen. Pervez Musharraf as a hero for a terror attack in Indian Kashmir. Moreover, a slew of terrorists, who were recruited from the Mideast, North Africa, and Asia, and funded, trained, and harbored by the Americans, British, Saudis, and Pakistanis, continue to flourish inside the vast, virtually ungoverned areas of Pakistan.[30]

Political instability in Pakistan and the fear of nuclear arsenals falling into wrong hands has attracted international attention. In analyzing the likelihood of nuclear and bioterrorism in Pakistan, we have a lot of material indicating the possible collaboration of jihadists and military officers in carrying out attacks against civilian population in Afghanistan and Pakistan. Nuclear experts understand that bioterrorism in the country is a disastrous threat. Michael Krepon has raised the same questions about the vulnerability of Pakistan nuclear weapons. In his policy analysis paper, Mr. Subhodh Atal noted that Mr. Musharraf investigated some of the country's nuclear scientists for their links with al Qaeda. He also noted that Pakistan shared its nuclear technology with North Korea, and possibly with Myanmar and Saudi Arabia:

Even worse, Pakistani nuclear experts are under investigation for links with al-Qaeda...Pakistan is reported to have shared its nuclear technology with North Korea, and possibly with Myanmar and Saudi Arabia, thus contributing to the problem of nuclear proliferation. A nation that is penetrated by Islamic radicals and that possesses dozens of nuclear weapons and proliferate them to other dictatorial countries poses a tangible and immediate problem. But U.S. policy toward Pakistan does not reflect that reality. In the absence of pressure from the United States, Pakistan has not found it necessary to take serious action against Islamic extremists or to end its proliferation activities.[31]

Chapter 8

Is Pakistan Cognizant of the Value of Human Life?

On 20 July 2017, the United States incriminated Pakistani government of not taking significant action against the terrorist organizations operating from their safe havens inside the country. The US State Department, in its annual "Country Reports on Terrorism 2016" said Islamabad failed to take significant action to constrain the ability of the Afghan Taliban and Haqqani Network to operate from "Pakistan-based safe havens".[1] The report accused that the government did not take any significant action against Jaish-e-Muhammad (JM) or Lashkar-e-Toiba (LT), "other than implementing an ongoing ban against media coverage of their activities".[2] Pakistan army has been supporting terrorist and extremist organizations to further it nefarious designs in South Asia.[3]

The threat of nuclear war and the intensity of mutual distrust between India and Pakistan have varied, and escalation of tension between them prompted mounting dark clouds over the region. "The existence of complex security trilemma (Pakistan, India and China) has threatened the strategic stability of South Asia".[4] India and Pakistan have embroiled in a deep security crisis as extremist elements have threatened security and stability of both states. These groups have their own agendas; some wants to further Indian interests and some receive military training and financial assistance from Pakistan to engage India in unending civil war in Kashmir. These groups have often expressed their desire to obtain nuclear, chemical and biological weapons to use it either against Pakistan or against India. They want to bring the two states to the brink. Pakistani scientists Mr. Zia Mian and Dr. Pervez Hoodbhoy have painted the same picture in their recent analysis:

> Pakistan has long been explicit about its plans to use nuclear weapons to counter Indian conventional forces. Pakistan has developed "a variety of short range, low yield nuclear weapons," claimed retired General Khalid Kidwai in March 2015. Kidwai is the founder—and from 2000 until 2014 ran—Pakistan's Strategic Plans Division, which is responsible for managing the country's nuclear weapons production complex and arsenal. These weapons, Kidwai said, have closed the "space for conventional war." Echoing this message, Pakistani Foreign Secretary Aizaz Ahmad Chaudhry declared in October 2015 that his country might use these tactical nuclear weapons in a conflict with India. There already have been four wars between the two countries—in 1947, 1965, 1971, and 1999—as well as many war scares.[5]

In 2016, India and Pakistan came perilously close to all-out war, after India declared the suspension of its policy to restraint. In 2017, every day Indian and Pakistani forces exchange gunfire across the Line of Control. On 28 February 2017, Sampath Perera in his article has elucidated the mood of India vis-a-vis Pakistan:

> India's Hindu supremacist Bharatiya Janata Party (BJP) government has effectively frozen all ties with Islamabad since the mid-September attack that Islamist Kashmiri separatists carried out on the Indian Army base at Uri—an attack the BJP, with the full support of India's political establishment, blamed on Pakistan. In a statement to the Indian parliament earlier this month, External Affairs Minister Sushma Swaraj said India's policy is "no dialogue until peace," i.e., no resumption even of India's normally frosty relations with Pakistan until Islamabad demonstratively curtails support for the Kashmiri insurgency from its territory.[6]

On 11 February 2017, India conducted the successful test of High Altitude Inceptor Missile, Prithvi Defense Vehicle (PDV), which caused Pakistan's torment and warned that this act of India would increase instability in the region.[7] China played Pakistan's card against India and suggested the country to turn Gilgit and Baltistan into a province or allow the country to deploy its army along the Indian border. India rejected this move and warned that the entire state of Jammu and Kashmir, including Gilgit and Baltistan is part of India.[8]

The threat of nuclear weapons theft and bioterrorism in South Asia has become the centre of discussion in the international press that terrorist organizations in Pakistan and India were trying to retrieve biotechnology and nuclear weapons in the past, and wanted to use it against civilian's population and security forces. Recent border skirmishes between Pakistan and India, the intensification of civil war in Afghanistan, and the emergence of Islamic State (ISIS) in Pakistan and Afghanistan, further justified the possibilities of the complex threat of chemical and biological terrorism in the region. As Pakistan and Afghanistan have been the victims of terrorism and Talibanization during the last three decades, the establishment of Islamic State (ISIS) in South Asia may possibly change the traditional concept of terrorism and insurgency in the region.[9]

There is a general perception that forces of the Islamic State (ISIS) can use biotechnologies against neighbouring states if the control on those weapons is weak, the possibilities increased.[10] The nucleation is that the problem of nuclear and biological terrorism deserves special attention from all South Asian states including Afghanistan.[11] Nuclear weapons and missile technologies, and bio-weapons might fall into the hands of TTP or Islamic State (ISIS), Indian and Afghani extremist groups, which might cause destruction and disease.[12]

On 26 September 2014, Dawn reported the outgoing Peshawar corps commander Gen Khalid Rabbani expressed deep concern about the militancy problem in Pakistan. Squarely indicating that regions outside his operational command of FATA and Khyber Pakhtunkhwa had a potent and varied mix of militancy that needed to be tackled urgently, the newspaper reported. By citing militant hotbeds in other provinces, the commander of the ongoing operation Zarb-i-Azb in North Waziristan Agency should not be seen as trying to deflect responsibility, but should be applauded for attempting to put the fight against militancy in its proper context—which means regarding Zarb-i-Azb as an important, but by no means final, step in the right direction.[13]

India's First Secretary to the UN Mission, in 29 December 2014 told the General Assembly that the threat of nuclear terrorism was one of the pressing challenges facing the international community.[14] There were more than 100 incidents of theft or misuse of nuclear material each year in the past. At present, there are 25 states possessing nuclear weapons and nuclear facilities, and continue to expand into dangerous neighbourhoods around the globe.[15] Now, the most challenging problem for the Islamic State (ISIS) in Pakistan would be to obtain fissile material necessary to construct a Nuclear Explosive Device, and use it against civilian or military installations. Pakistan faces a greater threat from Islamic extremists seeking nuclear weapons than any other nuclear stockpile on earth. As the potential spread of nuclear weapons in South Asia is a major threat to regional and global peace, the Islamic State (ISIS) and extremist groups in the country are struggling to retrieve nuclear material.[16]

Washington Post in one of its reports warned that Pakistani extremist groups could seize components of the stockpile or trigger a war with India. Known Pakistani scientist, Dr. Parvez Hoodbhoy warned that his country's nuclear weapons could be hijacked by extremists, as a result of increasing radicalization within the army barracks. "If Pakistan did not have nuclear weapons, Kargil would not have happened. My intention is that it was the first instance that nuclear weapons actually caused a war".[17]

Some Pakistani clerics, army generals and politicians suggest that jihad against India is mandatory on every Muslim. Thus, the fear of India became genuine. On 16 May, 2009, an Israeli website, Debka reported former Indian Prime Minister Manmohan Singh warned President Barak Obama, that nuclear sites in Pakistan's Khyber Pakhtunkhwa province are "already partly" in the hands of Islamic extremists.[18] Before this statement, in 2005, Mr. Singh told CNN that his government was worried about the security of Pakistan nuclear assets after general Musharraf. In July 2012, the EU non-proliferation consortium published a non- proliferation paper No: 19, in which author Bruno Tertrais painted a balanced picture of Pakistan nuclear weapons.[19] Mr. Bruno analyzed the mixed consequences of India and Pakistan nuclear weapons and established the fact that a single incident can lead to a full-scale war in the region:

> The induction of nuclear weapons in South Asia has had mixed consequences. Since 1998 there has been no major

conventional war in the region, but the propensity for risk taking remains high: Pakistan risked war in 1999 by sending armed militants across the Line of Control, wrongly believing that India would be deterred from reacting; both countries went to the brink of war in the winter of 2001–2002; and India was close to retaliating against Pakistan after the 2008 Mumbai terrorist attacks. India has attempted to checkmate Pakistan and block the avenues that it thinks Pakistan might open with its nuclear capability. The 1999 incident led to India stating that it would not hesitate to wage a limited war. The 2001–2002 crises led to India's adoption in 2004 of the Cold Start doctrine: a fast campaign with limited objectives, capturing territory up to 50–80 km inside Pakistan, but without months of mobilization—leaving no time for Pakistan or the international community to react.[20]

Nuclear weapon materials could fall in the hands of terrorists during a period of political turmoil, Cyber attacks, and civil war. Research scholar, Reshmi Kazi warns that Pakistani extremist groups can acquire nuclear weapons by stealing or purchasing assembled nuclear weapons from their friends within the armed forces:

> The situation in Pakistan has further taken a turn for the worse which increasing political instability prevailing in the country giving rise to international concerns on the potential threat of Islamabad's nuclear weapon falling into the hands of terrorists. It is feared that Pakistan might lose control over it national 'crown jewels' to radical elements like Tehrik-i-Taliban Pakistan (TTP) and Lashkar-e-Toiba (LeT) many of who keep close ties with al Qaeda.[21]

In May 2014, Prime Minister Nawaz Sharif visited National Command and Control Center, which oversees Pakistan's nuclear facilities. After his visit, he said that his country wanted peace in the region, and would not be part of an arms race". Amid growing violence across the country and terror threat, the country is steadily expanding its nuclear weapons stockpile. In her research paper, Reshmi Kazi noted Pakistani extremist groups and their possible access to nuclear weapons:

The volatile situation in Pakistan has become further unstable with the existence of terrorist groups like Jaish-e-Muhammad and Harakatul Jehad al Islami who is being influence by the al Qaeda led pan-global jihadist ideology and is intensely active in the Indian sub-continent. The degree of the crisis merits solemn deliberation since the al Qaeda has articulated its aspiration to attain nuclear/ radiological material and weapons, and have touched base with diverse individuals and militant groups to obtain these sensitive nuclear technology and material for purpose of weaponization. Investigations into the recent Mumbai blasts of November 26 2008 have provided credible information of the involvement of the leT operating from Pakistan soil. It is alleged that the LeT had the backing of the ISI which shared intelligence with the Lashkar and provided it protection in the Mumbai terror attacks.[22]

Extremist infrastructure and widespread terror networks of militant groups, corruption in army quarters, along with poor governance in Pakistan, created a climate of fear across the country. Powerful militant networks in Southern Punjab have established training centres for extremist forces. Punjab is home to 80 million people and a web of 85 networks of Punjabi Taliban. Pakistan army supports Punjabi Taliban, provides arms, and specific budget every year. Terrorists are being trained in police and army centres and in jails. On 13 November 2012, James Martin Centre for Non-proliferation studies published an article of Phil Lai on its website, which mainly focused on the threat of nuclear terrorism in South Asia:

> Nuclear terrorism is traditionally understood to take one of the four forms: direct acquisition and deployment of a nuclear device, independent fabrication of a device using stolen materials, release of radiation by attacking nuclear facilities, or release of radiation through other means of dispersal. But the particular circumstances of the South Asian security situation raise the troubling possibility of a fifth scenario: a nuclear exchange intentionally provoked by terrorist activity that is not itself inherently nuclear.[23]

Nevertheless, terrorists planning a nuclear attack would face considerable difficulties in acquiring a nuclear weapon or stealing fissile material for the production of a weapon. On 03, March, 2014, Daily Dawn reported a London based scholar's remarks about Pakistan's nuclear danger. The author voiced alarm about Pakistan's nuclear arsenal, the world's fastest growing, which he said would likely expand until at least 2020. Fitzpatrick said no solution was ideal, but he called for Western nations to offer Pakistan a deal along the lines of a 2005 accord with India, which allowed normal access to commercial nuclear markets despite its refusal to sign the Non-Proliferation Treaty.[24]

"The time has come to offer Pakistan a nuclear cooperation deal akin to India's," Fitzpatrick said as he launched a new book, "Overcoming Pakistan's Nuclear Dangers," in Washington. "Providing a formula for nuclear normalization is the most powerful tool that Western countries can wield in positively shaping Pakistan's nuclear posture," Fitzpatrick said. In his book, Mr. Fitzpatrick expressed concern over an arms race, and said Pakistan was constrained by its lack of uranium ore. Fitzpatrick said Pakistan's production may end in 2020, by which time it would have some 200 nuclear weapons, about double the current estimate.[25]

Chapter 9

Keep the Monkey Mind from Running off into all Kinds of Thoughts

When a bomb falls into the hands of a violent Monkey, everyone manages to escape the scene; neither can they shot the monkey, nor can defuse the bomb.[1] The monkey is free to fling off and hurl the bomb for all that how many people are killed. Pakistani miltablishment is like a violent monkey that threatens everyone with the bomb in its hands.[2] Now, international community has decided to tackle the Monkey due to its violent nature, or impose sanction on its fear marketing.[3] Having tackled the nuclear threat, international community has often asked democratic governments in Pakistan to apply professional and technical measures in securing the bomb, but everyone knows who is responsible for the protection of nuclear weapons but the army never allowed civilian leadership to visit nuclear sites.[4]

The military regimes of Pervez Musharraf, Raheel Sharif, and Strategic Planning Division failed to secure nuclear sites of Pakistan before Taliban carried out several successful attacks against it.[5] The failure of Nuclear Command and Control Authority (NCCA), Strategic Planning Division (SPD), democratic government, miltablishment, ISI, MI, and the IB is evident from that fact that all these institutions failed to intercept Taliban and their associates' from successful attacks against nuclear installations.

In December 2011, another chucklesome security step was exposed in an article in Atlantic Magazine that Pakistan was transferring its nuclear weapons from one place to another in very low security vans to hide them from CIA.[6] Wow, song of praise for the expertise they exercised in securing nuclear weapon. This was an identical and much the same move normally monkeys do. This report created altercation between the GHQ and civilian government that the way army manages security of the bomb was perilous, hazardous and treacherous. Pakistan army lost the confidence of civil society due to its unprofessional nuclear security measures, counterinsurgency, and war strategies.[7] International media also criticized the flawed security approach of the army and its civilian partners, and warned that this kind of security measures were inadequate to secure the bomb. Some military officers already warned that extremist and terrorist organizations in Pakistan can make dirty bomb if they succeeded in kidnapping nuclear scientists, or infiltrated into nuclear sites with help of insiders.[8]

Terrorist attacks on Wah Ordinance Factory, Aeronautical Complex in Kamra, nuclear site in Khushab, Mehran in Karachi, and Peshawar Airport were indicative of the fact that application of flawed security measure of Pakistan army and its civilian partners couldn't secure the country's nuclear installations.[9] Experts warned that this way of securing nuclear weapon can further endanger these weapons.[10]

On 31 March 2018, Dawn reported National Coordinator of the National Counterterrorism Authority (NACTA), Ihsan Ghani expressed deep concerns that the Islamic State in Afghanistan posed a real threat to Pakistan. The presence of Islamic State (ISIL) in Pakistan is also poses a bigger threat to the country's nuclear installations.[11] In 2016, Chief of Pakistan's Intelligence Bureau (IB), Mr. Aftab Sultan warned that Pakistani extremists were joining Islamic State in Syria. His statement prompted countrywide debates about the possibility of the use of a "dirty" nuclear bomb. "There are a possibility of making dirty bomb if the militant abducted some nuclear scientists, metallurgists with some fissile materials and uranium from Iraq and Syria", said Brigadier Nazir.[12]

The lack of effective security system for weapons-useable-nuclear-materials in Pakistan is a major challenge. Notwithstanding several reforms were introduced in security systems in 2012, there is still no effective global system for how nuclear materials should be secured.[13] In

2012, seven states; Austria, Czech Republic, Hungary, Mexico, Sweden, Ukraine, and Vietnam removed all or most of their weapons usable nuclear materials, while 13 other countries promised to decrease their quantity of materials.[14] Despite all these efforts, 5 states increased their stocks of nuclear materials (Pakistan, Japan, The United Kingdom, India and North Korea).[15] The availability of biological and chemical materials in Pakistan and Afghanistan generated a climate of fear. In FATA and other agencies and in parts of Northern Afghanistan the smuggling of these weapons will empower Taliban and the ISIL to inflict huge fatalities on the region.[16]

The use of illicit trade of nuclear materials in South Asia by non state actors and terrorists may further jeopardize the security of the region.[17] The problem of this trade appears to be growing worse as technologies proliferate. On 26 March 2018, the United States added seven more Pakistani companies to the list of foreign entities allegedly engaging in nuclear trade. The move undermined Pakistan's ambition of joining the Nuclear Suppliers Group (NSG), an elite club of countries that can trade fissile materials and nuclear technologies. The move declared that all these seven companies were involved in activities contrary to the national security or foreign policy interests of the United States.[18]

With the global spread of technologies and rapid illegal sale of uranium and plutonium, traffickers could find it easier to flourish their dangerous trade.[19] Pakistan's nuclear security faces critical challenge from its own insiders.[20] The fear of nuclear weapons and materials escaping the protective custody of Pakistan's army is well founded. Former ambassador of the United States to Pakistan, Anne W Patterson expressed concerned that someone working in Pakistan's nuclear facilities might smuggle enough nuclear materials out to make a weapon.[21] The main threat to Pakistan's nuclear installation might also come from the virus or worm activated within the computer.[22]

Terrorists and extremist organizations want to expand the business of fear, terrorism and harassment across the region.[23] Though the United States assisted Pakistan in improving nuclear security, but there are speculations, that the Strategic Planning Division might be subjected to pressure by the ruling party to appoint its favourite individuals within the SPD security infrastructure, as the tussle between civilian and military leaders on the control of nuclear weapons has already intensified.[24]

At present, India and Pakistan hold a lot of nuclear stockpile which have doubled since 1998. They developed cruise missiles, and are seeking nuclear submarines. More worrisome is that India and Pakistan have developed military doctrines that increase the prospects of nuclear use.[25] Although India has pledged not to use nuclear weapons first; it has increased its readiness to launch shallow "Cold Start" conventional military strikes against Pakistan calibrated to deter Pakistani military or terrorist incursions. Meanwhile, Pakistan military planners insist that Pakistan will use nuclear weapons immediately if India attacks.[26] Journalist and expert Ramesh Thakur argued that jihadist provocation, minor incident and misinformation can cause extreme tension between the two nuclear states. He also spotlighted some aspects of India's campaign to isolate Pakistan:

> There are several Pathways through miscalculation, rogue launches, misinformation and jihadi provocations. The backdrop to these unintended and unwanted pathways to a nuclear war is the state of extreme tension in their relations where minor incident can quickly spin out of the ability of either government to control. On Sept 29, Lt. Gen Ranbir Singh announced that Special Forces had attacked and destroyed seven "launch pads" in Pakistan-occupied Kashmir, killing over 30 militants with no loss of Indian life. The action, although officially justified in the language of pre-emption of an imminent attack, was in reality reprisal for an attack by Pakistan-based infiltrators on an Indian base in Uri in Indian-administered Kashmir that killed 18 soldiers. In exceptionally sharp language at the United Nations, Indian officials painted Pakistan as the host of the Ivy League of terrorism. India succeeded also in getting the planned South Asian regional summit meeting in Islamabad cancelled.[27]

India has succeeded to some extent to isolate Pakistan in international community, but China and Russia are backing the country to strengthen their political and military influence in South Asia. India has established strategic relationship with the United States, which caused irksome for Russia and China. However, there are speculations that India has established a commando force to disrupt CPEC and counter Chinese and Pakistani influence in Afghanistan and Central Asia, but no evidence of such move has been identified so for. Expert Ramesh Thakur has criticized Pakistan army that exploited and miscalculated India's strategic restraints:

> India's policy of "strategic restraint" was misread by Pakistan's generals as a successful Pakistani policy of nuclear neutering of the arch enemy. While nuclear rivalry induces extra caution, it does not confer immunity against targeted military retaliation. Yet Pakistan's military establishment seems to have convinced itself to the contrary. Pakistan had exploited the nuclear overhang to nurture jihadi and terrorist proxies to inflict serial attacks across the border. The risk of nuclear escalation was also used to try to blackmail other countries into putting pressure on India to solve the Kashmir dispute or risk a nuclear war. India has effectively called Pakistan's nuclear bluff.[28]

India and Pakistan have deployed armed forces along the Line of Control to defend their territories, intercept terrorists' infiltration, and make secure their military installations. In May 2017, US intelligence warned that a minor incident can cause nuclear war between the two states. Zainab Aziz in her recent analysis is of the opinion that border skirmishes between India and Pakistan can lead to an inevitable all-out nuclear war:

> The nuclear arms race between Pakistan and India is turning into a terrifying state. This insecurity has emerged from the decision of Islamabad of deterring the credible aggression initiated from the tank-led invading Indian Armed Forces by deploying law-yield tactical nuclear weapons (thus, lowering the threshold of nuclear first use) on the entire region surrounding India at it forward military bases designed for carrying out tactical operations. Deployment of tactical nukes is for the purpose of creating deterrence against the Cold Start Doctrine of India which is "Exclusively Offensive, Blitzkrieg inspired" military strategy, developed by the Indian Military Command (IMC), precisely for Pakistan to replace the obsolete 'Sundarji Doctrine' which miserably failed during 2001-2002 impasse with Pakistan. The year 2017 was started off by Pakistan by launching two significant test of proliferating programme which includes: Ababeel medium-

range ballistic missile with a claimed multiple independently targetable re-entry vehicle (MIRV) and Babur-3 Submarine Launched Cruise Missile.[29]

On 29 September 2014, Dawn reported the 69th session of General Assembly of the United Nations observed the first ever annual day for the total elimination of nuclear weapons. In a message released by his office, UN Secretary General Ban Ki Moon urged member states that "the time has come for the total elimination of nuclear weapons stockpiles."[30] While most active members of one group lobbied for a complete, ban on all nuclear arms, others quietly tried to put the spotlight on Pakistan.[31] As Prime Minister Modi said that the time has changed, and the killing of innocent men and women cannot be tolerated in Kashmir, it means, perhaps, the people of India and Pakistan need peace, prosperity and stability not military confrontation. Pakistani Prime Minister called for a resolution of the Kashmir dispute by saying the UN was not the appropriate forum to raise the issue and that his country was prepared for a bilateral engagement "in a peaceful atmosphere, without the shadow of terrorism," a reference to the unresolved investigation of the 2008 Mumbai attacks.[32]

He was correct, of course; General Assembly is no longer a platform for serious discussion, and it is a way for heads of state to build an image for their country and themselves.[33] In this regard, Prime Minister Modi's speech, with its references to Indian spiritual traditions was written for the US public to consume, while Mr. Sharif's bland, narrow focus was everything that western publics feel is wrong with Pakistan—an obsession with India, desire for territory and a total lack of charisma and likeability.[34] India and Pakistan need to puncture the tires of their unaffordable and sarcastic armies, which consumed the two nations for a long time. Pakistan's army adventurism in Afghanistan and Kashmir, through extremists and non- state actors, jeopardized the geographical existence of the country. India's diplomatic presence in Afghanistan also enraged Pakistanis that India has encircled the country from all sides. Now Pakistan army considers this adventurism as the war of survival and strategic interests.[35]

The consecutive firing from both sides shows that relationship remained tense, but Mr. Nawaz Sharif is still optimistic in his efforts. Mr. Sharif assured India that his country wants peace in the region.[36]

But cauldron is still there. Some newspapers in both the states reported more than 63 violations of the ceasefire in October 2014 alone, and during the last 10 months, there have been as many as 209 violations. Now Prime Minister Modi understood that Mr. Nawaz Sharif was not sincere with India, he warned Pakistan that the time has changed.[37] The Indian Express noted that remarks were in response to political opponents who charged the Prime Minister with not speaking directly about the fresh clashes—the worst in a decade. Mr. Modi took a different view. "When there is a challenge at the border, it is soldiers who answer with fingers on the trigger; it is not for politicians to respond."[38] India's Defense Minister also warned Pakistan to stop shelling in Kashmir, after the worst cross-border violence to hit the disputed region in years. "If Pakistan persists with this adventurism, our forces will make cost of this adventurism unaffordable for it,"[39]

Arun Jaitley told journalists in New Delhi that Pakistan must stop unprovoked firing and shelling if it wants peace on the border.[40] The nuclear-armed neighbors have traded blame for the cross-border violence that has killed at least 12 civilians. In October 2014, Pakistan responded to India's warning against any "adventurism" on the borders in Jammu and Kashmir by saying it is capable of responding to Indian aggression. Pakistan has the ability to reply to Indian aggression.[41]

We do not want the situation on the borders of two nuclear neighbours to escalate into confrontation; Pakistan Defense Minister Khawaja Asif was quoted as saying by the media.[42] "India must demonstrate caution and behave with responsibility," Asif said soon after his Indian counterpart Arun Jaitley warned that the cost of any adventurism by Pakistan on the borders of Jammu and Kashmir would be "unaffordable".[43] Meanwhile, Pakistani military planners insisted that Pakistan can use nuclear weapons immediately if India attacks. Prime Minister Nawaz Sharif said that Pakistan plans to build six more nuclear energy plants in coming decades.[44]

These nuclear plants would be built in partnership with China. Islamabad's turn toward more nuclear power also raises questions over the safety of the nation's nuclear reactors. India also needs nuclear weapons to establish strategic parity with China, and secondly, to deter Pakistan's intransigence.[45] China, however, has been willing to provide Pakistan with assistance for nuclear power projects.[46] The two countries have a historically close relationship. China's tactics to violate their international obligations were evident during the immediate period after the end of the cold war, with Chinese cold war, firms acting as fronts for transferring European technology to Pakistan.[47]

In fact, China's relations with the military establishment in Pakistan have never been strained during the last sex decades. China still helps Pakistan in many ways, while rivalry between India and China intensified, Beijing has measured itself alongside superpowers; similarly, Pakistan's rivalry with India is noticed in Delhi only for its use of asymmetric warfare from behind a nuclear shield.[48] China has been bolstering Pakistan's nuclear capabilities for the past five decades in an attempt to maintain parity between India and Pakistan.[49] Not only has China played a crucial role in the North Korean and Iranian nuclear programs, its nuclear engagement with Pakistan potentially remains the most destabilizing factor in the global Management of nuclear technology.[50]

Recent report of Harvard Kennedy School revealed that nuclear theft in Pakistan was high. "The trend seems to be toward increasing risk, as Pakistan's nuclear arsenal expands and shifts toward tactical nuclear weapons, while adversary capabilities remain extremely high".[51] On May 2015, an article in the official magazine of ISIS claimed that the terror army has the financial power to purchase a nuclear weapon, possibly from corrupt officials in Pakistan.[52] The surreptitious and cloak-and-dagger nuclear technology cooperation between Pakistan army and the armed forces of North Korea caused deep consternation in South Asia as the two scoundrel states want to jostle the region towards cataclysm by their sponsorship of terrorism in neighbouring states. Expert Madhav Nalapat in his recent article uncovered secret nuclear cooperation between Pakistan and North Korea:

> Both the nuclear explosions that took place in North Korea this year are "made in Pakistan", according to those silently, and in total secrecy, tracking the nuclear trajectory of the East Asian country. "By end-2005, it was clear that testing of nuclear devices through computer modeling was not yielding operationally significant results", a key analyst based mainly in Hong Kong claimed, adding that from then onwards, a hyper secretive programme of cooperation between the DPRK military and the

Pakistan army was begun. In both countries, the men in uniform control the development and production of nuclear devices. The October 2006 and May 2009 North Korean tests took place with regular participation of scientists from a secret nuclear weapons development facility near Hyderabad (Sindh) in Pakistan, the sources asserted. The sources warn that the covert collaboration between North Korea and Pakistan is geared on the Pakistan side towards developing a tactical nuclear weapon and on the North Korean side towards producing a nuclear device that could be married to a North Korean missile capable of entering the airspace of the continental United States.[53]

In the past, North Korea received help from Pakistan in developing nuclear weapons has been well-publicized. In his article (2005) The US. Air Force Col. Charles D. Lutes revealed the role Islamabad played in spreading nuclear technology to North Korea and Iran. On 28 February 2017, NTD TV News reported indirect Chinese nuclear technology cooperation with Pakistan. The report noted that China supplied technology indirectly to Pakistan through North Korea:

> Now, insider sources in China have indicated it was Beijing that indirectly supplied North Korea by aiding Pakistan's development of nuclear technology and gifting it critical raw materials. According to Huang Huiping, a former researcher at the China Institute of Atomic Energy, "In the 1980s, one of the CIAE's tasks was to transfer our nuclear technologies to other countries, including Pakistan.........Because China and India don't get along, China assists Pakistan [in its nuclear weapons program] to oppose India," Huang Huiping revealed to NTD Television.[54]

The nature of the China-Pakistan military and nuclear alliance makes it beneficial for China to extend its nuclear proliferation tentacles worldwide. In his article, published in Japan Times, Prof. Harsh V. Pant argued that military and nuclear relationship between Pakistan and China is in the interest of both the states by presenting India as a common rival:

> The China–Pakistan partnership serves the interests of both by presenting India with a potential two-front theatre in the event of war with either country. Not surprisingly, one of the

central pillars of Pakistan's strategic policies for more than four decades has been its steady and ever-growing military relationship with China. And preventing India's dominance of South Asia by strengthening Pakistan has been a strategic priority for China. But with India's ascent in global hierarchy and American attempts to carve out a strong partnership with India; China's need for Pakistan is only likely to grow. A rising India makes Pakistan all the more important for Chinese strategy for the subcontinent.[55]

China's fundamental motive behind military assistance to Pakistan is to counter India and establish its military influence in South and Central Asia, but some policy expert recently uncovered trained ties between the two states due to Pakistan's recruitment of Chinese dissidents, and slow move of the CPEC project. In an Asia Program paper, Rosheen Kabraji viewed Pak–China relations in the context of Chinese military influence in South Asia to counter US–Indian influence in the region:

> As Pakistan and China strengthen their relations, questions have arisen around the changing nature of this alliance, the rhetoric that sustains it and the implications of greater Chinese influence in Pakistan for the region....China's strategic relationship with Pakistan and its approach to Indo-Pakistani disputes in the first decade after the Cold War reflected its desire for better relations with India to advance its economic agenda."[56]

Pakistan's nuclear program, however, is essentially intended to counter its conventional forces inferiority vis-a-vis India.[57] After the Pokhran-II in 1998, and the Kargil episode, the real nature of nuclear weapons was emphasized and the imperative of military involvement dawned on the establishment. Analyst Syed Fazl-e-Haider views Chinese cooperation in the context of India-US nuclear and military cooperation:

> China has deepened co-operation largely in response to the civil nuclear energy deal signed between the US and India in 2008. That deal opened up a US$150 billion market for US nuclear trade with India, which was controversially granted an exemption from the Nuclear Suppliers Group. Neither India nor Pakistan, arch-rivals in many aspects, has joined the nuclear Non-Proliferation

Treaty, yet both possess nuclear arsenals. The US denied Pakistan a civilian nuclear deal, saying that it first had to improve its nuclear proliferation record. Pakistan's nuclear arsenal has been a sensitive topic for the US as it tries to improve relations with its frontline ally in the campaign against Islamist extremists. The US has restricted nuclear-related exports to Pakistan since it conducted its nuclear tests in 2008.[58]

The role of nuclear weapons in the India-Pakistan rivalry is disturbing and illuminating. The two sides haven't used their weapons, but their arsenals have changed their military and political strategies in ways that make the region more explosive and crisis-prone.[59] What has caused this situation is the fixation with achieving military parity with India, and the precarious cocktail that the establishment has brewed in nurturing fundamentalist and terrorist organizations as instruments of their policies in Afghanistan and Kashmir.[60] All these weapons and strategic developments in both the states means that confidence building measure remained only on paper, and no one desired to extend the hand of cooperation. Following the deal between the US and India, Pakistan ramped up its production of uranium and plutonium and, it seems, its nuclear weapons arsenal.[61]

The Diplomat Magazine noted that both nations have already come close to nuclear blows–the two countries nearly engaged in a war over Kashmir, which has been described as one of the tensest nuclear standoffs between India and Pakistan since independence in 1947.[62] According to reports, Pakistan currently has the world's fastest-growing nuclear arsenal, with enough fissile material to build 120 bombs and the potential to build at least 80 more by 2020. India has the ability to build 110 nuclear devices, but is also reported to have ramped up its production capacity.[63]

After former US President Barack Obama and Prime Minister Narendra Modi met in New Delhi on 25 January 2015, four key deliverables from the summit meeting were identified to be in the areas of nuclear energy, defense, climate change and the economy.[64] Nonetheless, Obama and Indian PM Narendra Modi announced a break of the nuclear deal deadlock. "I am pleased those six years after we signed our bilateral agreement, we are moving towards commercial cooperation, consistent with our laws [and] international legal obligations," Modi said.[65]

President Obama, in turn, spoke of a "breakthrough understanding on two issues that were holding up Indian ability to advance its civil nuclear cooperation.[66]" "Noting that the contact group set up in September 2014 to advance implementation of bilateral civil nuclear cooperation has met three times in December and January, the leaders welcomed the understandings reached on the issues of civil nuclear liability and administrative arrangements for civil nuclear cooperation, and looked forward to U.S.-built nuclear reactors contributing to India's energy security at the earliest," the two countries said in a joint statement.[67]

This exacerbating militarization of conflict mechanism, the withdrawal of NATO and US forces from Afghanistan, and civil wars in the Middle East, intensified the war of interests between the two states. In the presence of all these weapons, the danger of nuclear terrorism, the potential spread of nuclear materials in black market, and the recent control of nuclear materials by Sunni terrorist groups, Islamic State (ISIS), raised serious questions about the safety and security of nuclear weapons in South Asia.[68] Pakistan faces a series of threats to its national security. These threats come from ISIS and the likely potential use of chemical, biological, radiological, and nuclear (CBRN) devices by domestic terrorist groups.[69]

International Task Force on the Prevention of Nuclear Terrorism once warned that the "possibility of nuclear terrorism is increasing" because of a number of factors including "the conventional forms of terrorism,"[70] and the vulnerability of nuclear power and research reactors to sabotage and of weapons usable nuclear materials to theft. Recently the Islamic State uncovered a complex with stockpiles of WMD in Iraq.[71] "We do not believe that the complex contains CW materials of military value," the U.S. State Department said on the IS matter of WMD discovery.[72]

The danger is that either states might support or back terrorist groups, in case of materials and funds, to prepare Improvise Nuclear Explosive Device and use it against each other.[73] Another development that has also worried nuclear scientists is the cyber attacks during the nuclear crisis management. Cyber warfare has the potential to attack or to disrupt a successful nuclear crisis management.[74] India and Pakistan have developed strong networks of cyber armies, and often attacked each other's sensitive computers in the past.[75]

Cyber attack can make muddy signals being sent from one side to the other side during the nuclear crisis. Cyber warriors can disrupt and destroy communication channels for successful crisis management.[76] Pakistan's nuclear weapons are under threat from violent cyber terrorists operating across the border.[77] Pakistan set death penalty for cyber terrorism in 2008.[78] This was an unprecedented step of making cyber terrorism a crime punishable by death, according to a decree issued by former President Asif Ali Zardari.[79] Cyber terrorism is described as the accessing of a computer network or electronic system by someone who then "knowingly engages in or attempts to engage in a terroristic act."[80] "Whoever commits the offence of cyber terrorism and causes death of any person shall be punishable with death or imprisonment for life," according to the ordinance published by the state-run APP news agency.[81]

The Prevention of Electronic Crimes law became applicable to anyone who commits a crime detrimental to national security through the use of a computer or any other electronic device, the government said in the ordinance.[82] The ordinance also set out punishments for other offences, including electronic fraud, electronic forgery, system damage, unauthorized access to codes and misuse of encryption. Punishments for those crimes ranged from three to 10 years in prison.[83] Terrorist attack on Karachi airport showed that Pakistan's intelligence had badly failed to provide true information about the terrorist's networks in Karachi. That attack also highlighted the military capability of the Taliban and exposed the gap in the country's security apparatus. After the attack, and the killing of Shia Muslims in Taftan, every Pakistani citizen was referring to the previous daring attacks against the country's nuclear installations.[84]

The way in which Pakistan has developed its nuclear policies and strategic forces is directly related to the nature of the security threat, and the structural power imbalance and widening conventional force asymmetry with India. Pakistan believes that the use of TNW would bring about such a material and psychological shift in hostilities as to stun India into a halt. Therefore, in Pakistani perception, the TNW is a deterrent at best, and a war termination weapon at worst.[85]

Writer Michael Krepon highlighted the situation in India-Pakistan context and argued that after testing nuclear devices in 1998, Indian and Pakistani spokespersons downplayed the value of short-range weapons. Instead, Pakistani military officers stressed that any use of a nuclear weapon would have strategic consequences.[86] Mr. Michael Krepon argued that Pakistan was moving very slowly to gain the capabilities needed for successful, limited war options against well-defended territory. While India's Army continues to face many shortfalls, its Air Force is being qualitatively upgraded.[87]

Amit Gupta warned that an Indian attack on Lahore, Islamabad, and Karachi would essentially leave Pakistan with an economy and society that was in the 19th century.[88] A similar Pakistani attack on Mumbai or New Delhi, Mr. Gupta noted would put back India's developmental efforts by a couple of decades as not only would the nation struggle to recover but foreign investors would flee the country.[89] One may argue, therefore, that nuclear deterrence has been achieved by both sides and neither has to worry about feeling vulnerable in this spectrum of conflict. So what do TNW give either side? The answer is a higher level of instability and a much lower level of deterrence. Missiles tests in India and Pakistan prompted deep reaction in both the states. Brigadier Gurmeet Kanwal and Monika also highlighted the missile race in their recent paper:

> Pakistan believes that the successful testing of the 60-km nuclear-capable short-range missile Hatf-9 (Nasr) "adds deterrence value to Pakistan's strategic weapons development program at shorter ranges." In paradox, the fact remains that this step has further lowered Pakistan's nuclear threshold through the likely use of TNWs. The introduction of TNWs into the tactical battle area further exacerbates credibility of their control. Pakistan has not formally declared a nuclear doctrine, but it is well known that nuclear weapons are its first line of Defense.[90]

When India and Pakistan conducted their nuclear weapon tests in 1998, foreign experts repeatedly told them that with weak economies and state institutions, they could not be entrusted with such awesome weaponry. Over a decade on, and multiple crises later—Kargil in 1999, a military standoff in 2001-2, and the Mumbai attacks of 2008—India and Pakistan experienced nothing quite as perilous as the Cuban scare.[91] Pakistan is developing a new generation of tactical nuclear weapons

(TNWs) that target not Indian cities, but Indian military formations on the battlefield. Mr. Hans M. Kristensen and Robert S. Norris in their research paper warned that Pakistan continues to develop more weapons, while concerns about Pakistan's nuclear weapons have deepened:

> Despite its political instability, Pakistan continues to steadily expand its nuclear capabilities and competencies; in fact, it has the world's fastest-growing nuclear stockpile. In the aftermath of the US raid that killed Osama bin Laden, who had made his hideout in an Islamabad suburb, concerns about the security of Pakistan's nuclear weapons are likely to keep pace with the growth of Pakistan's arsenal. Pakistan is building two new plutonium production reactors and a new reprocessing facility with which it will be able to fabricate more nuclear weapons fuel. It is also developing new delivery systems. Enhancements to Pakistan's nuclear forces include a new nuclear- capable medium-range ballistic missile (MRBM), the development of two new nuclear-capable short-range ballistic missiles, and the two other new nuclear capable cruise missiles.[92]

On 12 September 2013, Reuter reported think tank at the International Institute for Strategic Studies, in which experts panel expressed deep concern on the safety and security of nuclear weapons in South Asia: "An arms race in South Asia and Pakistan's development of tactical "battlefield" nuclear weapons are increasing the risk of any conflict there becoming a nuclear war, experts warned."[93] The think tank also cited Pakistan's development of short-range tactical nuclear weapons—which in theory could be used to stop any conventional Indian armoured advance into Pakistani territory as a particular cause of concern.[94] "The continuing expansion of Pakistan and India nuclear capabilities created ever greater concern about an intensifying nuclear arms race in South Asia,"[95] the IISS warned in its annual strategic survey".[96] Mr. Alex P. Schmid and Ms. Charlotte Spencer-Smith (2012) shared the same concern about the security of nuclear weapons in South Asia:

> On March 26 2012, leaders of 53 countries met in Seoul, Korea, in the framework of the American initiative to reduce and secure scattered nuclear materials which could offer terrorists an opportunity to acquire uranium or plutonium for exploding a

nuclear weapon. It takes less than 25 kilograms of highly enriched uranium (HEU) and less than eight kilograms of plutonium for constructing a viable atomic bomb. There are still between 1.300 and nearly 1.600 tons of highly enriched uranium and nearly 500 tons of plutonium stored in Russia and the United States and, to a lesser extent, in some 30 more countries. While the more than 100 military storage sites which contain some 19,000 assembled nuclear weapons (all but about 1.000 in the USA and Russia) are generally well-protected, some of the ca. 500 civilian nuclear power stations and some of the ca. 120 academic HEU-powered research reactors are in a number of cases much less well protected. Some of the latter are badly in need of better security than a chain-lock at the gates and a single night watchman on duty. There have been some twenty known cases of theft of plutonium and highly enriched uranium since 1990 and many more of other radioactive materials.[97]

On April 2014, Bloomberg TV reported former Pennsylvania resident and two Pakistani nationals were indicted by a federal grand jury for smuggling technology to Pakistan, highlighting the U.S. Justice Department's focus on illegal exports that might be used for weapons of mass destruction.[98] The men, the report stated, used two corporations, Optima plus International, and Afro Asian International to export "dual-use" items, with both commercial and military or nuclear applications, for resale to the Pakistan Atomic Energy Commission, an arm of the Pakistani army, prosecutors said.[99] Those indicted were Pakistanis; Shafqat Rana, formerly of Lancaster, Pennsylvania, and Abdul Qadeer Rana and Shahzad Rana, both belonged to Lahore, Pakistan.[100]

On 22 June 2014, Daily the Frontiers Post reported the Modi government's announcement about the ratification of International Atomic Energy Agency (IAEA) Additional Protocol.[101] According to the newspaper report, India had signed the IAEA Additional Protocol on 15 March, 2009, which was ratified after more than four years.[102] The security of Pakistan's nuclear program has always received attention from international media due to domestic political instability and growing internal militant threats. In contrast, the security of the Bhabha Atomic Research Centre has been breached many times but there is little public discussion about threats to the security of India's huge civilian and military nuclear infrastructure. Instead, an overriding assumption exists that relevant agencies in India provide enough security to nuclear infrastructure.[103]

The issue of making nuclear devices by terrorist organizations has become very complicated. Terrorists have the skills to prepare Improvised Nuclear Device. In their comprehensive report (Future World of Illicit Nuclear Trade) for the Institute of Science and International Security (2013), David Albright, Andrea Stricker and Houston Wood warned that the theft of nuclear materials and, cyber-theft and espionage pose new threats of leakage of sensitive information important to the development of nuclear weapons and the means to make them:

> In the future, there could be a greater availability of classified, proprietary, and other sensitive information about the technologies used to make HEU and plutonium and build nuclear weapons. For almost all proliferating states during the last several decades, their progress benefited from access to another country's classified information about nuclear weapons or the means to make HEU and plutonium. More recently, cyber-theft and espionage pose new threats of leakage of sensitive information important to the development of nuclear weapons and the means to make them. In addition, there are many dual-use technologies used in modern industries that are sensitive or proprietary and sought by other states. Some of these are critical to the development of a capability to make nuclear weapons, plutonium, or HEU. Preventing the unauthorized spread of classified, proprietary or other sensitive information will remain a difficult challenge. States and terrorists will likely continue to try to gain access to such information in their quest for nuclear capabilities.[104]

Five Eyes Intelligence Alliances continues to focus on Pakistan as a potential source of nuclear bomb material. Yet unsecured highly enriched uranium elsewhere has been a worry for many years.[105] Of particular concern have been the vast amounts of weapons-grade uranium that were left relatively unguarded in Russia, Ukraine, Belarus and Kazakhstan after the break-up of the Soviet Union.[106] There are speculations that after the 9/11, the United States ordered General Musharraf to hand over all nuclear weapon to the US Special Forces as the threat of nuclear terrorism intensified. Some experts believe that the US safely controlled Pakistan nuclear weapons. In his research paper, published in World Affairs Journal (2011), Neil Padukone argued that Lashkar Toiba's violent threat to peace and stability in South Asia:

> Global scrutiny after the 11/26 Mumbai attacks pressured the ISI to make Lashkar put its violent activities on temporary hold. But JuD (which after 2009 went by the name Tehreek-e-Tahaffuz Qibla Awal) has used the intervening time to build up a vast social services infrastructure that has solidified a broader Islamist movement throughout much of Pakistan. This movement recruits not only impoverished youth but highly skilled professionals. According to the Strategic Foresight Group, as early as 2005 LeT's assets included a 190- acre campus in Muridke, outside of Lahore, complete with 500 offices, 2200 training camps, 150 schools, 2 science colleges, 3 hospitals, 34 dispensaries, 11 ambulance services, a publishing empire, garment factory, iron foundry, and woodworks factories. It had more than 300,000 cadres at its disposal and paid salaries to their top bracket functionaries that were 12-15 times greater than similar jobs in the civilian sector.[107]

Terrorist groups, such as Islamic State (IS), Taliban and Mujahedeen Hind are seeking to acquire the ability to build "improvised nuclear explosive devices," or crude atomic bombs. Research scholar, Samuel Kane suggested that Pakistani extremist groups have the capabilities to attack the country's nuclear installations. He also warned that several factors are involved in extremist's attacks on Pakistan nuclear installations:

> In Pakistan, the threat of nuclear materials falling into terrorist hands is a multi-faceted danger, composed of several different scenarios; such as (1) insiders within the Pakistani nuclear program proliferating nuclear assets and knowledge to terrorist groups; (2) a terrorist group stealing nuclear materials from a Pakistani facility; and (3) a radical Islamist group seizing control of the Pakistani government and nuclear arsenal, through a coup or democratic elections.[108]

International media continues to highlight the threat of nuclear terrorism emanating from the consecutively expanding network of Pakistan's nuclear weapons. Pakistani journalists and writers are not in position to criticize the network of Pakistan's nuclear weapons smuggling due to the fear of their country's action against their families.

Moreover, the biggest threat to Pakistan's nuclear weapons emanates from jihadists organization in and outside Pakistan, and in South and Central Asia. Federation of American Scientists published numerous articles and research papers on the prospect of nuclear terrorism in South Asia, in which experts raised important questions about the safety and security of Pakistan's nuclear weapons.

Charles P. Blair noted the looming threat of the country's nuclear jihad and its fatalities in his paper. The Chatham House writers also raised the same questions in their research paper (Too Close for Comfort Cases of near Nuclear Use and Options for Policy, April 2014). The authors highlighted Pakistan's nuclear command and its gradual development:

> Pakistan's nuclear command-and-control structure is officially divided between three authorities. The first is the National Command Authority, which is chaired by the prime minister. The second is the Strategic Plans Division (SPD), a body comprising government and military representatives set up as the result of command-and- control reforms between 1999 and 2001. The third is Strategic Forces Command, comprised of the military. The storage status of Pakistan's nuclear weapons during peacetime has not been explicitly clarified, but it is widely believed that the SPD exercises heightened vigilance against the possibility that they could go missing. Reports indicate that Pakistan does separate its warheads from its delivery systems, and that the warheads themselves are separated by 'isolating the fissile "core" or trigger from the weapon and storing it elsewhere.' While Pakistan's nuclear weapons are therefore not susceptible to being used while on a hair-trigger alert, the warhead's components are nevertheless stored at military bases and can be put together at short notice.[109]

In 1999, during the Kargil war, and in 2008, after the Mumbai attacks, Pakistan and India were on the verge of a military confrontation. Pakistan refused to restrain Lashkar-e-Toiba, and those involved in the Mumbai attacks, while India was adamant not to extend the hand of cooperation to Pakistan unless the Mumbay attackers are bring to justice. In his research paper on Pakistan's nuclear Blackmailing, Dr. Rajesh Kumar Mishra (2002) argued that the threat of Jihadist groups to Pakistan's nuclear installations is intensifying:

Jihadist zealots inside Pakistan as the epicenter of global terrorist network defy any international suggestion for peaceful resolution of disputes. They wield double-edged sword of terror—jihadist terrorist strikes and nuclear attacks, not only for India but also for the whole world. While speculations are still rife of possible use of nuclear weapons by Pakistan, the international apprehension of terrorists developing or using "dirty" bombs has also to do a lot with the so-called Jihadist sympathizers in Pakistan. Indo-Pak nuclear war remains only one aspect of nuclear terror. The potential nuclear terror if unleashed by Jihadist elements in Pakistan would be equally devastating for both India and the world community. Domestic and international illegal connection that prompts Pakistan to perpetuate nuclear terror may hardly ensure long lasting security and, so, requires timely international attention".[110]

Sometimes, Pakistani columnists dare to criticize their country's rogue army, and intelligence agencies for their atrocities against innocent civilians. Former member of the Pakistan Foreign Service, Asif Ezdi's article in the News International narrated an interesting story of India's agreement with International Atomic Energy Agency that gives nuclear weapons inspectors the right of access to its civil nuclear sites. This is an important development, and is an ordeal for Pakistan:

> The agreement, called the Additional Protocol in IAEA terminology, was concluded as part of the India–US nuclear deal of 2008 under which India received a waiver from the Nuclear Suppliers Group's restrictions on the export of nuclear material and technology to countries that do not accept full-scope safeguards on their nuclear program. Far from being aimed at providing transparency of India's nuclear program, the main purpose of the additional protocol was to provide the US with another excuse, however threadbare, for its claim that exempting India from the NSG's restrictions on nuclear trade would "bring the country into the international non-proliferation mainstream.[111]

Chapter 10

General Raheel Sharif, War Crimes in Waziristan, FATA, and Forced Disappearances in Baluchistan, Sindh and Khyber Pakhtunkhwa

In a restaurant owned by Tufail Dawar of North Waziristan, 20 truck drivers were lined up and then shot in their heads by Pakistan army.
– Wall Street Journal, 19 December 2013

On 27 November 2013, Prime Minister Nawaz Sharif appointed General Raheel Sharif as a Chief of Pakistan Army, who later on resisted his government pressure to introduce security and intelligence sector reforms.[1] This change of face didn't make effective war against Taliban.[2] General Raheel's mission of killing innocent Pashtuns in Waziristan failed with the sacrifices of thousands soldiers and officers. Moreover, a large number of his army officers and soldiers refused to fight against civilian population.[3] Mr. Sharif refused to negotiate with tribal leaders, and refused to respect parliament and democratic norms. He himself designed the policy of kill and shot for Waziristan; killed women and children with impunity, and kidnapped tribal elders.[4] His appointment as an Army Chief further complicated the prospect of cold war within the military headquarters-General Haroon Aslam resigned in protest, when he was superseded by his two juniors.[5]

General Aslam also skipped the farewell dinner of General Ishfaq Kayani, arranged by Prime Minister. Some of his colleagues inveighed against the decision of the Prime Minister.[6] In army headquarters, the pace of ethnic antagonism adversely affected civil military relations. Pashtun officers showed reservation on the killing of innocent civilians by General Raheel Sharif while military experts did not expect any radical shift under is command. He needed to adapt a new military strategy as defined in the Green Book, but his ethnic role raised some important questions.[7]

Raheel Sharif was adamant to complete the transfer of purchased nuclear weapons plus ballistic missiles to Saudi Arabia, under the Defense pact between the two states signed in 2004, but it became impossible when Prime Minister Nawaz Sharif resisted and decided to bring the army and spy agencies under democratic control.[8] General Sharif's secret plan of overthrowing the Nawaz government was brought to light by Intelligence Bureau (IB). The agency retrieved audio of the ISI chief instruction invisible forces. The army later on decided to remove Muhammad Nawaz Sharif from his office through Supreme Court of Pakistan.[9]

On 28 July 2017, Supreme Court of Pakistan disqualified Prime Minister Nawaz Sharif from holding public office in a landmark decision on the Panama Papers case.[10] Justice Ejaz Afzal Khan, who headed the apex court's implementation bench following its April 20 order on the Panama Papers case, announced that the larger bench had unanimously deemed PM Sharif unfit for holding office and would also order an accountability court to open references against him and his family, and other respondents.[11] In Pakistan's 70 years of existence, no single Prime Minister served a full five-year term. They were fired by governor-generals and army chiefs and judges. So it was always fruitless. The Supreme Court didn't find Sharif guilty of corruption per se, but instead declared that he had violated Articles 62 and 63 of Pakistan's Constitution, which demand that members of parliament be "Sadiq" and "Ameen"-"truthful" and "righteous."[12] These were made into requirements by one of Pakistan's many past military dictators, presumably as a way of controlling legislators.[13] The conditions were usually used as a way to humiliate and harass candidates; this is the first time they have been used to disqualify a member of parliament retrospectively. It doesn't take a genius to see Sharif is being singled out using a particularly dangerous and illiberal constitutional clause.[14]

However, General Raheel ordered armed forces into North Waziristan, and shifted Afghan Taliban commanders to safe houses. The challenge to Pakistan's sovereignty in Swat and Buner was addressed with brute force only after the Taliban appeared to be on a triumphant march to Islamabad.[15] The insurgency in South Waziristan was tackled on a war footing after years of procrastination, but the writ of the Tehrik-e-Taliban Pakistan still runs in North Waziristan. The issue of ethnic representation within the armed forces also raised serious concerns. Some experts say this is not a national army and view it as the club of Punjabi generals.

The army failed to develop a true ethnic representation process or motivate Baloch and Sindhis to join the ranks of armed forces, but gained a good experience in killing of innocent civilians. In Baluchistan, thousands Balochs men and women disappeared in a so called military operations during the last 15 years, while bodies of thousands of missing persons began turning up on roadsides. Since the killing of Akbar Bugti in 2006, more than 25,000 Balochs men were kidnapped or forcefully disappeared by Pakistani intelligence agencies and the police, in which of them 1500 were students and teachers. On 29 November 2013, nineteen personnel of Paramilitary force, who had allegedly taken away 35 detainees, were directed by the Supreme Court to appear before the CID office in Quetta.[16]

There are numerous stories of Pakistan army war crimes in North Waziristan and Baluchistan province circulating in print and electronic media showcase the real hidden agenda of Miltablishment. In Baluchistan, thousands innocent Balochs were killed, kidnapped, and their houses were destroyed. Pakistani intelligence agencies and the police created bigger problems of ethnicity and sectarianism by kidnapping, torturing and forcefully disappearing Baloch and Pashtun leaders in Khyber Pakhtunkhwa and Baluchistan provinces. On 25 September 2017, Dawn reported the Senate Functional Committee on Human Rights Chairperson, Nasreen Jalil, accusations against law enforcement agencies of abducting people and "asked" them to investigate the missing person's case.[17] "They [disappeared individuals] are not even presented in court and [only] their tortured corpses are found later," she alleged.[18] The PPP leader, Senator Mr. Farhatullah Babar also warned that parliament, Supreme Court and other institutions have failed to resolve the issue. "The people involved in abductions are not punished despite the evidence against them," he said.[19] In his article, prominent Pakistani analyst I.A Rehman spotlighted some weaknesses of the government and law enforcement agencies in resolving the issue of missing persons:

> The horrible phenomenon of enforced disappearances in Pakistan has been in public debate for more than 25 years and there is hardly any aspect of the matter that has not been discussed threadbare and from different points of view. If the demand for an end to enforced disappearances, criminalization of the practice punishment of the perpetrators and payment of compensation to victim families has been made from various national and international forums, there have also been suggestions, though from a tiny minority, for giving the security forces powers to detain indefinitely dangerous criminals who in many cases are victims of enforced disappearance (ED).[20]

Court proceedings after 9/11, and the information provided by different authorities confirm that ISI and the army had adopted the policy of enforced disappearances as a long term measure for 'national security'/counter-terrorism strategy.[21] Enforced disappearances have been adopted as a strategic tool as opposed to a mere short term tactic.[22] This is supported by the fact that in several legislative measures introduced at the behest of the national security institutions, the focus has been to provide 'legal' cover rather than prohibit and criminalize the practice as required under the constitutional framework and international law.[23] In his recent article in the News International, Mr. Sher Ali Khalti noted important facts of missing persons in Baluchistan and Khyber Pakhtunkhawa provinces:

> According to data available with TNS, the Commission received 4113 cases of missing persons up till June 30, 2017. About 2857 out of 4113 cases were disposed of till July 30, 2017. Around 377 hearings were held in the country and despite that 1256 persons are still missing in the country. In Khyber Pakhtunkhawa, 1582 cases of missing persons were received. Around 666 missing persons were traced and 831 cases were disposed of till July 30,

2017 yet 751 missing persons are to be produced. In Punjab, 862 cases of missing persons were received, 450 missing persons traced and 617 missing persons' cases were dispose of while 245 persons are still missing. Sindh Province ranks second on the list of missing persons. 1055 cases of missing persons were received, 766 traced and 1005 cases of missing persons were disposed of and 50 persons are still missing. In Baluchistan 291 cases of missing persons were received, 108 missing persons traced and 193 cases of missing persons were disposed of and 98 persons are still missing. 45 people in Islamabad, 48 in Fata, 5 in Gilgit Baltistan and 14 persons in Azad Jammu Kashmir are still missing.[24]

Pakistan is notorious for widespread enforced disappearances, with state agents finding it an easy way to keep persons in their custody indefinitely, torture and kill them without any evidence. Since 2001, the higher courts failed to recover missing persons; the military and other institutions, accused of enforcing disappearances, have arrogantly refused to obey court orders.[25] The case of Zeenat Shahzadi, who was pursuing Ansari's case, is no less serious than Qandeel Baloch's, the model who was killed because she wanted to live by her own lights.[26] On 07 January 2017, social activist Samar Abbas reportedly went missing. He was one of the founders of the Civil Progressive Alliance, a campaign created to counter the dominant public narrative after the Peshawar Army Public School attack in 2014, when six gunmen affiliated with the Tehrik-i-Taliban killed 141 people, including 132 schoolchildren.[27] On 30 August 2017, World Sindh Congress and Asian Human Rights Commission (AHRC), Voice of Baloch Missing Persons (VBMP) and Right snow in their joint statement on the International Day of the Victims of Enforced Disappearances reported thousands cases of forced disappearance in Pakistan:

From 31st December 2010 to 31st March 2017, the highest number of enforced disappearance cases was reported from Khyber Pakhtunkhwa province (1486 cases), followed by Sindh (1031), Punjab (819), Baluchistan (282), Islamabad Capital Territory (138), Federally Administered Tribal Areas (113), Azad Jammu & Kashmir (40) and Gilgit-Baltistan. The Edhi Foundation has reportedly buried a total of 58,261 unidentified and unclaimed bodies between 2005 and 2012 in the country, including 12,561 bodies in 2005, 4,819 bodies in 2006, 6,611 in 2007, 6,692 in 2008,

6,491 in 2009, 6,493 in 2010, 7,854 in 2011 and 6,738 in 2012. The Edhi Foundation claimed that they used to bury more than 100 unclaimed bodies a month in Karachi during this period.[28]

On 30 July 2017, MQM held a large demonstration in front of White House against paramilitary operation to suppress Mohajirs, enforced disappearances and extra judicial killings of MQM workers in Karachi.[29] The demonstration was attended by MQM Convener Nadeem Nusrat, members of Coordination Committee; office bearers along with large numbers of workers, supporters and members of Pakistani Diaspora from all walks of life, including ladies, elders and youth.[30] The demonstrators demanded that Pakistani establishment should stop these cruel tactics of "unlawful kidnapping" of Mr. Hussain's relatives in order to cause him to bow his head down, a wish of their which will never fulfill. They held banners and placards demanding US government to take notice of worst form of human rights violations, enforced disappearances, extra judicial killings, inhumane torture, ban on political and social activities of MQM, Media blackout of MQM's founder and leader Altaf Hussain.[31] MQM's founder Altaf Hussain joined the participants via tele-conferencing and addressed the participants in a brief speech. In this address, he went on to condemn the role of Pakistan Army and ISI in Karachi, particularly against the Muhajir community.[32]

A fact-finding mission of the Human Rights Commission of Pakistan to Swat documented accounts of extrajudicial killings by the rogue Pakistani army in 2009. However, discovery of mass graves in Swat points to the unabated suffering of the civilian population. The report of the three-day mission documented a number of Swat residents evidences of having seen mass graves in the area, including at least one at Kookarai village in Babozai tehsil and another in an area between Dewlai and Shah Dheri in Kabal tehsil. The witnesses to mass burials said at least in some cases the bodies appeared to be those of Taliban militants.[33] The mission expressed grave concern over the "worrying development and also over credible reports of numerous extrajudicial killings and reprisals carried out by the security forces. Bodies were dumped throughout the valley – bloated corpses were found floating down the rivers while others dangle from electricity poles with notes warning of dire consequences for the Taliban and its supporters. Some villagers claimed that state security forces even warned them against giving a Muslim burial to fallen Taliban fighters – in Islam the dead must be buried immediately".[34]

Since the discovery of the mass graves, government remained unhelpful in getting to the truth behind the mass graves. The government sometimes deviated from the actual issue by disputing the actual number of the bodies found in the mass graves while, on other occasion, it blamed India for being involved in this gruesome episode.[35] A mass grave was discovered in Tootak, Khuzdar by a shepherd after which the locals converged there to recover bodies.[36] The number of the bodies found, which the middle class government representatives are at pains to limit to 13, while reports filtering out put the number at around 150 and more. The Baloch are systematically being marginalized to make their suppression easier and the illegal exploitation of their resources justifiable.[37]

The killing of thousands of tribal leaders in FATA destroyed leadership among the ethnic Pashtuns. For more than a decade, Pakistan army in Federally Administered Tribal Areas (FATA) relied on the targeted assassination of powerful tribal chiefs as a cornerstone of its strategy to establish control and protect the sanctuaries of terrorists.[38] On 15 November 2017, Dawn reported fifteen bullet-riddled bodies were discovered by the Levies force in Baluchistan's Kech district. A senior administration officer who spoke to Dawn News on condition of anonymity said that the Levies found the bodies in the Gorak area of tehsil Buleda. "All the victims received multiple bullets from a close range," he said.[39]

On 11 February 2015, after learning that 4,557 bodies were found in the country over the past four years, the Supreme Court asked the federal government to effectively address in a coordinated manner the handling of unclaimed bodies as well as the issue of missing persons.[40] A bench comprised of two-judges of Supreme Court, headed by Justice Jawad S. Khawaja, took up an application of Nasrullah Baloch, chairman of the Voice for Baloch Missing Persons, who invited attention of the court towards lack of a proper system for handling of mutilated or unclaimed bodies found at different places in Baluchistan.[41]

The detainee men, women and young children were abused, raped, humiliated and then killed in secret prisons established by Pakistani intelligence agencies and the army in Waziristan, FATA, and Baluchistan. Soldiers and officers of Pakistan army kidnapped girls and women from Swat, Momand and FATA as well. Minor children were killed in front of their parents. The FATA Senator Maulana Gul Naseeb accused rogue army of kidnapping girls and women from Swat and Momad agencies. Moreover, Supreme Court of Pakistan ordered law enforcement agencies to arrest those criminal army officers responsible for the enforced disappearance, but they didn't arrest them because of their affiliation with ISI and military intelligence.[42] The army has been facing many difficulties in conducting effective counter-insurgency operations, even though, it has deployed more than 150,000 soldiers in the Khyber-Pakhtunkhwa and FATA, and has suffered over 15,700 casualties, including over 5,000 dead since 2008. Total casualties including civilians numbered 80,000 since 2001.[43]

This brutal and aimless war against their own people caused officers and soldiers of the army deep frustration and mental-illness. Their desertion greatly disturbed military leadership. There were reports that more than 3000 soldiers joined Taliban while a good number of soldiers and officers deployed in Waziristan, FATA, Mohmand, Dir, and Swat refused to fight against their own people. In South Waziristan agency, journalist Amir Mir reported, more than 400 Pakistani soldiers joined Taliban in 2007. Many of the army officers do not want to fight against the Taliban. Army Chief, warlord Raheel Sharif never been succeeded to address this issue immediately due to his resentment towards Pashtuns.

After the killings of 2,500 innocent Pashtun children by General Musharraf in Red Mosque in Islamabad, majority of militant groups pulled out of peace treaties. Military spokesman Maj. Gen. Waheed Arshad once confirmed the desertions in the army in large number. The number of army soldiers killed at the hands of Taliban and sectarian groups in FATA, Waziristan, and Swat crossed the number of those killed in the wars (1965 and 1971) against India. An intelligence report presented to top military brass in Islamabad confirmed the desertion of 900 soldiers who join the Taliban network. There were reports that Pashtun and Punjabi officers refused to see each other, while the reports of infighting are more heartbreaking. Moreover, cases of soldiers killing their own colleagues in FATA, Kurram and Waziristan agencies were on the rise.[44]

Chapter 11

Involvement of Pakistani Intelligence Agencies and the Army Generals in Extrajudicial Killings, Forced Disappearances and Terrorist Attacks in India and Afghanistan

After the 16 December 2014 terrorist attack in Peshawar school, the army started the ball rolling to legalize enforced disappearances and kidnapping by exerting pressure on Prime Minister Nawaz Sharif to announce National Action Plan (NAP), the license of kill and dump.[1] On 06 January 2015, Pakistan National Assembly and the Senate passed the 21st Amendment to constitution, which formally established Military Courts.[2] The NAP was established on 25 December, 2014, in reaction to 133 children being murdered by terrorists. The first point in the NAP is the controversial lifting of the moratorium on the death penalty. After the establishment of NAP, the army began punishing innocent Pashtuns in Waziristan, Baluchistan and FATA, and political activists in Sindh and Punjab.[3]

Thousand were forced to leave their houses, and thousands were killed and kidnapped in daylight-bombed their houses, and kidnapped their relatives. Torture cells were established and law enforcement agencies were empowered to kidnap citizens with impunity.[4] Pakistani

American analyst, Shuja Nawaz in his research paper raised important points about the disengagement of parliament and civil society in the war against militancy and terrorism:

> But there were few opportunities for the public to understand the details of what was being done and the relationship between the actions of the military inside FATA and the actions being taken by the civilian authorities in the rest of the country. Periodic meetings between the civil and military leaders were reported briefly, largely through the shorthand tweets from the military PR outfit. Parliament did not appear to seek, nor was it granted, regular briefings or reports on the ongoing operations. Against this backdrop, it was not surprising that the general public was not fully engaged in the effort against militancy and terrorism.[5]

In December 2017, after announcing a 23-party "grand alliance" called the Pakistan Awami Itehad (PAI), Asia Times reported former military dictator General Pervez Musharraf admitted that he had been the greatest supporter of Lashkar-e-Toiba (LeT) in the past. The rise of Hafeez Saeed's MML, and the Tehrik Labbaik Ya Rasool Allah (TLY) against PML-N can be attributed to the military establishment's bid to contain the civilian leadership.[6] Miltablishment shamelessly supported Faizabad set in and in the tail-end, gave money to every participant. Security experts view these counter-measures as flawed and brutal for the reason that this unprofessional security approach cannot restore the confidence of minorities, ethnicities and political parties. Notwithstanding the enforced disappearances of thousands innocent people in Punjab, Khyber Pakhtunkhwa, Baluchistan and Sindh provinces, lawlessness, terrorism, target killings, insurgency and alienation of citizens from the tattering state still exist in different forms, and the side-effects of their proposed panacea further aggravated and conflagrated.[7]

Writers, bloggers, commentators, and columnists who have been lambasting and disparaging the role of Pakistan army, and law enforcement agencies in enforced disappearance, torture, and extra-judicial killings in four provinces receive death threats, or kidnapped by agencies since the past two decades.[8] The exponentially growing trends of kidnapping for ransom by police and intelligence agencies is a new development in Pakistan, which further exacerbated the pain of political activists, members of human rights groups and civil society.[9] This campaign of consternation now reached at a crucial stage where political workers and parliamentarians have raised this issue on various forms, and besmirched the criminal inattention of the country's armed forces, judiciary and political parties.[10]

Pakistani intelligence agencies kidnap journalists, and political activists to establish a new concept of counter terrorism. In Baluchistan, FATA, Waziristan and Sindh, thousands missing persons never returned their home safely. In this business of killing and torture, intelligence agencies are backed by the army and paramilitary forces. On March 2017, journalist Kiran Nazish in her investigative report on forced disappearance in Pakistan astonished civil society about the male practiced of police and intelligence agencies: "On December 2, 2017, 40 years old Raza Khan, a Pakistani political activist, disappeared from his home. When Raza wouldn't answer his phone, Khan's brother went to his residence in Lahore. He found the lights on, the curtains drawn and the doors locked-but no sign of Raza. The intelligence agencies hold so much power that even the police can't touch them, an officer at Peshawar police headquarters told me the police see several abduction cases a week but can't write up official police report. "We have orders not to meddle in such cases that might be part of anti-terror campaign" he told me.[11]

The issue of secret prisons managed and established by police, army, and intelligence agencies still remains untouched, while the conscience of Pakistani politician, religious clerics, mullahs and so-called jihadists have died, and they have criminally kept close-mouthed.[12] There are numerous secret prisons managed by intelligence agencies in houses, field-intelligence-units, secret basements, military farms, forests, their offices and deserts, where men and women are tortured and sexually abused.[13] This wave of harassment and consternation has ruined the lives of millions Pakistanis, who never liked the way intelligence agencies and the armed forces maintain security and law and order management in the country. Civilian and military intelligence agencies are deeply involved in kidnapping of writers, journalists, and critics of military establishment and since the promulgation of National Action Plan (NAP).[14]

In history of law enforcement, and counterinsurgency operations across the globe, no match of Pakistani methodology, modus-operandi and flawed security approach can be found.[15] Thousands young girls, boys, students, adults, political workers are missing, while bodies of thousands innocent men and women have been found in hospitals, farms houses, roadside, deserts, forests and plains in Baluchistan and Khyber Pakhtunkhwa provinces.[16] In March 2014, after repeated court orders, Minister of Defence registered First Information Report (FIR) against the army officers allegedly responsible for the disappearances of innocent citizens.[17]

On 29 August 2013, the News International reported a gang of Pakistan's naval intelligence involvement in kidnapping for ransom in Karachi: "Some officers and an activist of the naval intelligence had formed a gang which was kidnapping traders and industrialists and receiving a huge ransom. The kidnapped persons used to be kept in the headquarters of naval intelligence, adjacent to the Chief Minister's House, the newspaper reported".[18] The News International also reported fisheries trader, Mr. Javed's kidnapping for ransom.

> His life was spared after immediate payment of Rs2 million and some negotiations in which it was also agreed that he would be freed after a payment of another Rs3 million. Subsequently, the members of Javed's family boarded a taxi and arrived at the Nehr Khayyam in Clifton in pitch darkness where they found a motorcyclist who had covered his face and who had come to receive the ransom payment. The News noted.[19]

However, on 29 August 2013, the News International reported the involvement of a gang of Pakistan naval intelligence in kidnapping for ransom:

> In the meantime, the SSP South, Nasir Aftab, who had been present in plainclothes along with the family of the kidnapped man, opened fire on the man who was going back after receiving the ransom money. A bullet hit him on his leg and he fell. Nasir Aftab and some cops, who had been hiding in a bush, then grabbed the accused. He was taken to the Clifton police station in an injured condition, and during initial investigations made a shocking disclosure that he belonged to the naval intelligence

and that two assistant directors of the naval intelligence, Ashfaq and another unknown, had been present at the venue where the accused had gone to receive ransom money, but they escaped from the venue when they heard the gunshot, the SSP and a CPLC team contacted the high officials of naval intelligence and recovered the kidnapped person from the headquarters of the naval intelligence. The SSP Nasir Aftab and CPLC chief Ahmed Chinoy confirmed the arrest of the accused and the involvement of assistant directors in the gang, but they refused to divulge more information". The Newspaper reported. After this report, leader of Awami National Party (ANP), Senator Zahid Khan called for the court martial of intelligence officials if they are found to be involved in extortion. JUI-F leader, Senator Haji Ghulam Ali questioned how intelligence agencies could stop India if they could not even stop kidnappers entering their headquarters. The Newspaper reported.[20]

However, Pakistan Air Force officers are also involved in corruption cases. On 01 April 2018, Dawn reported the mysterious death of Rezwan Attique, a Group Captain of Pakistan Air Force. His wife had submitted petition to the Islamabad High Court along with attached copy of Punjab Forensic Science Laboratory, which spotlighted injury marks on her husband body. The petition cited Secretary of Defence, Chief of Air Staff, and Deputy Chief of Air Staff, and Air Intelligence Director General as respondents. The officer wife requested Islamabad High Court to form a joint investigation team. In response to a petition filed by Attique's widow, Tanzeela Khan, PAF's director legal service Sohail Ahmed stated that the woman's husband had committed suicide as he feared the consequences of an inquiry into his alleged corruption. The PAF Director Legal stated: "During his service, the petitioner's husband became involved in embezzlement, misappropriation, malpractices and collusion with various civilian contractors against service interests. Consequently, a board of inquiry was ordered at the Air Islamabad, on July 5, 2017 to probe into his alleged illegal activities".[21]

Pakistani human rights groups have remained hushed and wordless. They were under threat and under pressure from the army and intelligence agencies-taking the issue of forced disappearance and kidnapping to the court. Similarly, courts are tight-lipped, close-mouthed, and tongue-tied to investigate cases of extra-judicial killings of innocent Pashtun and Baloch activists. They are frightened and panic-stricken to raise the issue of mass graves, torture and humiliation by police and law enforcement agencies. Prominent human right activist and senior journalist, I.A Rehman also noted the attitude of law enforcement authorities to recover missing persons:

> The lack of satisfactory progress on affording relief to the victims of enforced disappearance makes it necessary to revisit their case. The more one looks at the monthly reports on the cases pending before the Commission of Inquiry on Enforced Disappearances, the more alarmed at the unmitigated suffering of the people affected one becomes. Let us look at these reports for the last three months — December 2016, January and February 2017. The commission inherited 138 cases from the earlier body. It has received 3,718 complaints since March 01, 2011, when it started working, raising the total number of cases to 3,856.[22]

Mr. I.A Rehman also uncovered more details about forced disappearances in Khyber Pakhtunkhawa, Baluchistan and Waziristan, where rights groups and journalist were not allowed to report war crimes:

> The commission claims to have traced 1,953 people in all. Three hundred and fifty-four cases have been deleted from the list on the ground that information about the disappeared persons was incomplete and another 309 cases were dropped for other reasons. The largest group of persons traced so far belonged to Sindh (714 out of 1,025 people reported to have disappeared), followed by KP (626 out of 1,461), Punjab (398 out of 799), Baluchistan (102 out of 281), Fata (51 out of 113), Islamabad (49 out of 131), and Azad Kashmir (13 out of 40). As for Gilgit-Baltistan, none of the six disappeared have been traced.[23]

On 06 January 2017, Dawn reported 728 kidnapped Pakistanis were added to the list of missing persons in 2016--the highest in at least six years--taking the total to 1,219. In 2015, as many as 649 cases of missing persons were registered.[24] However, on 12 October 2017, Dawn reported Chief of the Commission on Enforced Disappearances Justice (Retd) Javed Iqbal repudiated the claim made by Mama Qadeer about missing of 25,000 people in Baluchistan.[25] According the Dawn report,

Justice Javed Iqbal told the Senate's Human Rights committee that the statistics of the missing persons in Baluchistan are highly exaggerated. He said those who had made such claims have not provided list of the missing persons to the Commission so far. Senator Farhatullah Babar said the status of the lists of missing persons was controversial. He said the situation would have been different had the Commission on Enforced Disappearances asked critical questions from concerned institutions instead of Mama Qadeer. He criticized the commission for not presenting its initial report despite six years of its creation which is a matter of grave concern, Dawn reported.[26]

On 30 October 2017, Outlook India reported the abduction of Dr. Allah Nazeer Baloch's wife and daughter, Fazeela and Popal, along with three other woman and children by Pakistani security agencies.[27] In a separate incident on Saturday 28 October 2017, Muhammad Nawaz Atta, information secretary for Baloch Human Rights Organization and eight other students and children were taken into custody. Since the enforced disappearances, no information on their well-being has been heard.[28] UNPO unequivocally condemned this crackdown and called for their immediate release. The organization, Voice for Baloch Missing Persons (VBMP) warned that civil society, journalists and human rights organizations were also responding improperly about human rights abuses in Baluchistan.[29] In March 2017, South Asia Terrorism Portal reported militant's attacks on Army vehicle with an Improvised Explosive Device (IED) in the Awaran District, killing one soldier.

On February 28, 2017, at least three FC personnel and one civilian were injured in an IED blast on the Sariab Road in Quetta, the provincial capital of Baluchistan. The bomb, which was planted on the roadside, targeted an FC vehicle while it was on patrol. The explosion left the vehicle partially damaged. On February 16, 2017, three Army personnel were killed when an IED, targeting an Army convoy, exploded in Awaran town. The dead were identified as Captain Taha, Sepoy Kamran Satti and Sepoy Mehtar Jan. Another two soldiers were also injured in the attack.[30]

However, head of Free Baluchistan Movement (FBM), Hyrbyair Marri in a statement warned that abduction of women and children from different areas of Baluchistan was part of Pakistan's ongoing campaign of enforced-disappearances in the restive province. Pakistani intelligence agencies are afraid of Baloch liberation struggle and now they started abducting Baloch children. They fear that these children will grow up to resist China-Pakistan brutalities in Baluchistan," he said.[31]

Targeting Pakistani intelligence agencies, Baloch leader Mr. Marri said they were violating Islamic principles for their own evil interests and for expansion of their religious extremist ideology in the world.[32] According to the International Convention for the Protection of All Persons from Enforced Disappearance (ICPPED): "enforced disappearance is an ongoing crime for as long as the victim's fate or whereabouts remains unknown, meaning that states cannot invoke the principle of non-retroactivity with regard to domestic laws that criminalize enforced disappearance". A forced disappearance generally leads to murder. The victim is abducted, illegally detained and tortured, then killed and the body is kept hidden.[33] In August 2017, International Commission of Jurists in its comprehensive report on enforced disappearances in South Asia warned that enforced disappearance and kidnapping are serious violation of human right:

> The International Convention for the Protection of All Persons from Enforced Disappearance (ICPPED) defines enforced disappearance as the "arrest, detention, abduction or any other form of deprivation of liberty by agents of the State or by persons or groups of persons acting with the authorization, support or acquiescence of the State, followed by a refusal to acknowledge the deprivation of liberty or by concealment of the fate or whereabouts of the disappeared person, which place such a person outside the protection of the law." The UN General Assembly has repeatedly described enforced disappearance as "an offence to human dignity" and a grave violation of international human rights law.[34]

In its report, International Commission of Jurists also elucidated kidnapping and abduction within the matrix of Pakistan's Panel Code:

> Pakistan's Penal Code Sections 359 to 368 relate to the crimes of "kidnapping" and "abduction". The crime of kidnapping is of two kinds: kidnapping from Pakistan and kidnapping from lawful guardianship, and is punishable with a maximum of seven years imprisonment and a fine. The crime of "abduction" is regulated

by section 362 of the Penal Code and is defined as "whoever by force compels, or by any deceitful means induces, any person to go from any place." Section 364 prescribes a punishment of ten years imprisonment for the crime of "kidnapping or abducting in order to murder". Section 365 relates to kidnapping or abducting "any person with intent to cause that person to be secretly and wrongfully confined" and prescribes a punishment of a maximum of seven years imprisonment.[35]

However, Amnesty International in its report warned that enforced disappearances caused serious violation of human right, and called on Pakistani authorities to immediately carry out independent and effective investigations with a view to determining the fate and whereabouts of all missing people.[36] Moreover, on 07 December 2017, Dawn reported Amnesty International demanded recovery of missing social activist Mr. Raza Khan. Amnesty in its statement demanded Pakistani government to immediately ensure the recovery of missing Lahore-based activist Raza Khan.

The Pakistani authorities must take all measures as may be necessary to investigate Raza Khan's fate immediately", Amnesty's Deputy South Asia Director Dinushika Dissanayake said.[37] Many cases of disappeared social activists come to light recently, and many of them appeared on social media. In 2017, the news of five activists going missing had evolved a strong response from activists in Pakistan and abroad. While four of them were later returned, Syed Samar Abbas, President of the Civil Progressive Alliance Pakistan, remains missing.[38]

On 07 December 2017, Dawn reported the Senate Standing Committee on Human Rights decision to summon recovered missing persons for an in-camera session to ask them directly who they had been picked up by. The committee also decided that once the victims have recorded their statements, representatives of the apex Intelligence Agencies; Inter-Services Intelligence, Military Intelligence and the Intelligence Bureau must be summoned before the committee and asked to explain their actions.[39] Having briefed the committee, Dawn reported Additional Interior Secretary of Baluchistan admitted that 136 more people were missing in the province. "He added that bodies of 27 people were found, while 104 people were recovered alive. He added that attempts were being made to gather information on those who had returned home but had not been willing to record statements on the matter".[40] In January 2015, Pakistan empowered military courts to try civilians for terrorism-related offences. These courts have since sentenced and hanged hundreds of citizens. After grossly unfair trials without possibility of appeal to any civilian courts, including the Supreme Court, relatives of these people alleged that some of those tried had been subjected to enforced disappearance by military authorities, and military control over the proceedings leaves the family and victim without effective remedy.[41]

Asian Human Rights Commission that celebrated the International Day of Victims of Enforced Disappearance on 30 August 2016 spotlighted Pakistan as a notorious country for enforced disappearances of individuals: We have also found the mass grave of disappeared persons particularly from Baluchistan. We found grave of over 100 persons that were recorded, there was an inquiry ordered but the report has not been made public. Interior Minister of Pakistan said that there are around 1,000 bodies that have been found in a mass grave", senior researcher at Asia Human Rights Naved said.[42]

On 20 September 2017, Outlook India reported World Sindhi Congress (WSC) protest at Broken Chair in front of United Nations in Geneva highlighting the issue of enforced disappearances, extrajudicial killings and targeted killings of political activists in Pakistan's Sindh province.[43] Protesters called Pakistan a 'terror state'. "We are protesting here as there is huge surge of disappearances in Sindh. Any activist who raises their voice for protection of Sindhi rights has been disappeared," Dr. Hidayat Bhutto said. He accused Pakistani authorities of forcefully abducting activists in the region.[44] "We are peaceful and non violent people, raising our demands to release political activists in front of UN," Dr. Bhutto said, adding that: "Our protest is focused on enforced disappearance of Sindhi people.[45] In Pakistan, most serious human rights problems are extrajudicial killing, disappearances; lack of rule of law, and gender inequality. Other human rights issues involved poor prison conditions, arbitrary detention, a weak criminal justice system, and lack of judicial independence.[46]

On 09 February 2018, Dawn reported attention of US Congress to the forced disappearances of political activists in Pakistan.[47] That special hearing of the House Subcommittee on Asia and the Pacific, lawmakers also accused Pakistan of continuing to allow Afghan extremists to destabilize the government in Kabul, a charge raised at a Senate hearing as well.[48] Dawn noted lawmakers also backed President Donald Trump's 04 Jan 2018 decision to suspend security assistance to Pakistan.[49] In recent years, the newspaper reported intelligence agencies responsible for these disappearances broadened their crackdown to include social media and other political activists, rights defenders, and reporters.[50] On 19 February 2018, Daily Times reported the illegal detention and forced disappearance of several political activists by intelligence agencies in Gilgit Baltistan.

> Several political activists, led by the iconic Baba Jan, who had raised voice for those displaced in the Atta bad lake fiasco, remain incarcerated on charges of terrorism. That our law enforcement apparatus can charge GB residents with terrorism for exercising civil liberties that the rest of us, in mainland Pakistan, take for granted should be a moment of shame for those representing the Pakistani public in Islamabad. Incidentally, Pakistan's greatest champion for human rights who left us last week, Asma Jahangir, had condemned the authorities for Baba Jan's incarceration and sought a fair and speedy trial for GB's political prisoners", the newspaper reported.[51]

Daily Times also reported the arrest President of Gilgit Baltistan Supreme Appellate Court Advocate Ehsan Ali. He was held for re-sharing a photo from recent Iranian protests on social media.[52] Ring of fear and consternation continues to resonate in the ears of every educated political activists, bloggers, writers, columnists, and separatists as Pakistan intelligence agencies and law enforcement agencies intensified campaign of enforced disappearance across the country.[53] Pakistani intelligence agencies have long been accused of using "enforced disappearances" as a tool for warning or punishing critics of their unethical behaviour, villainy, misbehavior, and mischief.[54] Just since 2011, Human Rights Commission of Pakistan reported more than 3,500 cases of enforced disappearances. Dr. Pervez Hoodbhoy, an outspoken Pakistani physicist warned in his critical comment: "The kidnappings were designed to eliminate the tiny sliver of cyberspace that activists currently have."[55]

Analyst Mr. Najam Sethi was also under intense pressure while charges of blasphemy and sedition were filed against him. He registered complaints with Pakistani rights groups and the international Committee to Protect Journalists, alleging that he was being denigrated in a life-threatening campaign. Mr. Najam Sethi said the condemnation and denunciation focused on his critical comments of the military establishment, and the blogger case. In September 2017, activists of UK-based Baloch and Sindhi groups staged a demonstration in front of 10 Downing Street, over the extrajudicial killings and enforced disappearances being carried out in Pakistan.[56]

In January 2018, law enforcement authorities killed Prof Dr Hasan Zafar Arif and Mr. Naqeebullah, a young man from Waziristan in a fake encounter in Karachi. Sindh Home Minister Sohail Anwar Siyal took notice of the death of Mr. Naqeebullah, and ordered Deputy Inspector General South to personally conduct a "clear and unbiased" inquiry into the matter and submit a detailed report to the Ministry. Mr. Naqeebullah was killed by SSP Rao Anwar, in a fate encounter. The police claim that the deceased was a militant affiliated with the banned Tehreek-i-Taliban Pakistan (TTP) but it is totally baseless, while relative of Mr. Naqeebullah disputed SSP Anwar's claim.[57]

After his extrajudicial killing, youth from Waziristan started a long march from D.I. Khan—Southern Districts of Khyber Pakhtunkhwa on 26 January 2018 against the ongoing slow motion Pashtun genocide in Pakistan, human rights violations in FATA and State imposed terrorism and militarism.[58] Protesters claimed and loudly chanting slogans that Pakistan's security agencies have been harboring, sheltering and conducting terrorism in FATA and Afghanistan, aimed at de-Pashtunization and undermining US led war on terror.[59] The long march by the youth of Waziristan was warmly welcomed in Lakki Marwat, Bannu, Kohat, Peshawar, Charsadda, Mardan and Sawabi districts of Khyber Pakhtunkhwa where a large number of Pashtuns joined the protest and entered Islamabad on Thursday where sit-in continues.[60] Moreover, the head of Pakhtunkhwa Wolesi Tahreek Dr. Said Alam Mahsood in his address to the historic Pashtun procession in Islamabad said, "Our sit-in will continue until we find justice for Naqeeb and favorable solutions to other problems of Pashtuns, posed by the State of Pakistan."[61]

DG ISPR and ISI admitted to the atrocities committed against the Pashtuns, but requested him not to insisted on putting to writing those admissions in the interests of "Mulk Ki Slamati and Fooj ki Badnami.[62] On 18 February 2018, Dawn Newspaper published a detailed Investigation report about Mr. Rao Anwar and the killing fields of Karachi, which painted different story of Mr. Naqeebullah Mehsud extrajudicial murder:

> Until Naqeebullah's murder, Sindh's so-called encounter specialist had not faced any inquiry over the number of encounter killings to his 'credit'. Not a single inquiry — despite having slain at least 444 people between 2011 and 2018, according to the police's own records. Not a single policeman was even injured, let alone killed, during the 745 encounters. The Rangers-led operation in Karachi, which began in late 2013, gave fresh impetus to police encounters in district Malir during Rao's tenure. The current law enforcement system is simply not capable of telling us as to how many innocents like Naqeebullah were among those mowed down. "He led a team of killing machines. There was no one to stop him," says a senior police official. "Why was no notice taken of his actions earlier? The truth is, everyone knows everything, but even the police command is afraid of him because of his close connections with criminal political bosses and within the security establishment.[63]

Meltablishment in Pakistan treats Gilgit-Baltistan vexatious and harrowingly. The army has established secret prisons in the region where political prisoners, writers and journalists are being tortured. On 19 February 2018, Daily Times editorial uncovered some details of state attitude towards the region:

> Instead of trying to address the grievances of the region, the authorities continue with their undemocratic practices in the region. The latest example is the arrest of the president of Gilgit Baltistan Supreme Appellate Court Advocate Ehsan Ali. He was held for re-sharing a photo from recent Iranian protests on social media. The photo showing a woman protester sitting on the platform meant for prayer leaders in a mosque had become a symbol of defiance of ordinary Iranians against the clerical regime.

There was hardly anything derogatory about the photo but Ali reportedly still took it off from his social media profile and also apologized for re-sharing it. He was still arrested and remains behind bars. Meanwhile, protests have been held against his arrest in GB as well as in major cities across the country. The protesters, including a large body of students from GB, have sought an end to our double standards vis-a-vis the region. The authorities in Islamabad will do well to listen to these youngsters of GB for this lopsided relationship of Islamabad with the region and its people needs to end.[64]

Chapter 12

The Inter Services Intelligence (ISI) and Intelligence Bureau (IB) Support to Terrorist Organizations in India, Afghanistan and Central Asia

Pakistani intelligence agencies have lost the confidence of civil society, parliament and judiciary by reason of their atrocities and against civilian. Internal fight and their support to terrorist organization in Afghanistan and India deeply weaken their operational capabilities. The ISI and the IB established secret prisons, tortured and killed writer, bloggers, journalists and tribal leaders across the country. They never allowed democratic governments to complete their terms, and never allowed legislatures to introduce intelligence reforms, or bring agencies under democratic control. On 14 August, 2015, Federal Minister of Climate Change Mushahidullah Khan told news channels that former Director General of Inter-Services Intelligence (ISI), Lt. General Zaheerul Islam had planned to overthrow democratic government and take over the country.[1]

He categorically indicated that Prime Minister Nawaz Sharif had played the audio tapes of former DG ISI to former Army Chief General Raheel Sharif. General Raheel didn't spurn disdainfully because he wanted to derail democracy and disrupt whatever achieved by the government.[2] In an interview to British Broadcasting Corporation

(BBC), the PML-N Senator said that former chief of ISI had hatched a conspiracy against the government during the sit-ins of Pakistan Tehreek-i-Insaf (PTI) and Pakistan Awami Tehreek (PAT) through which he wanted to take over power.[3] He told that this conspiracy was exposed by Intelligence Bureau's (IB) recording. The senator said that these tapes and other information that the government was receiving through some other sources were extremely horrible and the conspiracy prepared at that time would have brought devastation.[4]

Mr. Mushahidullah Khan said; "The PTV building had already been occupied by then and the people were moving towards the PM House. The government had no other option at that time but to shift the PM to some other place. Mr. Mushahidullah Khan said that PML-N knew some ISI officers were present in the meeting between PTI and PAT chiefs, Imran Khan and Dr. Tahirul Qadri. "We also knew what was decided upon in this meeting. Who would leave Lahore at what time and where they would reach and what they will do", he said.[5]

In this chapter, I want to highlight some aspects of the ISI and IB and MI war and their support to worldwide terror organizations. Some recent developments and reports of the involvement of 37 Pakistani parliamentarians in supporting, financing and facilitating terrorist organizations, and the involvement of Intelligence Bureau and ISI officials in terror-related incidents, generated countrywide debate about the competency, professionalization and politicization of intelligence agencies. On 26 September 2017, Dawn reported a serving Assistant Sub-Inspector of Intelligence Bureau (IB), Mr. Malik Mukhtar Ahmed Shahzad, incriminated senior officers of Intelligence Bureau of not taking action against terrorism suspects and filed a petition before the Islamabad High Court (IHC) requesting the matter to be referred to Inter Services Intelligence (ISI) for a thorough investigation.[6] The Assistant Sub-Inspector (ASI) told the court that he had often reported the link of IB officers and terrorist groups from various countries but no action was taken. "However, to the petitioner's utter dismay, no action was ever been taken by IB in this respect despite concrete evidence provided to it in the form of the intelligence reports", the petition said.

Upon thorough intelligence gathering process, it transpired that certain high officials of the IB themselves are directly involved with the terrorist organizations having linkages with hostile enemy intelligence agencies" the petition warned. He said that the matter was even reported to the IB director general, who also did not take any steps.[7] It the petition, he warned that some IB officials travelled to Israel and had direct links with Afghan intelligence which, it was found later, had links with another terrorist group from Kazakhstan. "These terrorists used to disguise themselves as citrus dealers in Kot-Momin and Bhalwal, Sargodha. The business was a mere camouflage," the petition warned.[8] According to his petition, the son of Joint Director Intelligence Bureau (Punjab) was dealing with the said terrorist groups.[9] The petition claimed that some officials of Afghan and Iranian intelligence used to take refuge in the places of the citrus dealers. The petition names certain IB's officials who were on the payroll of foreign intelligence agencies which included a Joint Director General, Directors and Deputy Directors. The petitioner said that senior IB officials also facilitated Afghan nationals in getting Pakistani nationality.[10]

On October 01 2017, Intelligence Bureau (IB) told Islamabad High Court (IHC) that this argument or answering the queries posed by one of its officials would affect Pakistan's relations with several countries and compromise the secrecy of the agency's internal structures.[11] The bureau submitted its reply in response to the petition of Malik Mukhtar Ahmed Shahzad that accusing senior IB officials of having links with different terrorist organizations from neighbouring and Central Asian countries, as well as protecting terrorists. In its reply, IB claimed that the official seeking an Inter-Services Intelligence (ISI) probe against senior bureau officials was a habitual litigant and had tried to tarnish the repute of the intelligence agency in the past as well.[12] The issue was also highlighted by some parliamentarians like Senator Farahatullah Babar who moved a calling attention notice urging the Interior Minister to take notice of the IB official's allegations. The calling attention notice pointed out that the head of the banned Jaish-i-Muhammad Maulana Masood Azhar and Afghan Taliban chief Mullah Mansour Akhtar were facilitated by certain quarters. Mr. Babar also claimed that during NA-120 by-election in Lahore, a candidate backed by banned militant outfits was allowed to contest, in violation of the law.[13]

"The petition should be dismissed on the grounds of being frivolous, as it demands the disclosure of details pertaining to secret operations and task objectives,"[14] The News quoted the IB as stating in its reply. "If disclosed, these details will compromise national security as they will expose the administrative units of the department," the reply further said.[15] The News International also mentioned that IB's response claims that the employee in question has "frequently caused trouble" for the department, having submitted 14 petitions against the agency in the past.[16] On 28 September 2017, Dawn reported Islamabad High Court warning about the intelligence war in the country. Mr. Justice Shaukat Aziz Siddiqui sought a reply from the Interior Secretary to the petition filed by an IB assistant sub-inspector.[17]

The agency, Dawn noted came under fire from Pakistan Tehreek-i-Insaf (PTI) leader Imran Khan after its head allegedly met ousted Prime Minister Nawaz Sharif in London. A list of politicians allegedly having links with terrorists was also attributed to the IB.[18] The Nation reported petitioner's allegations that he received threatening calls after having filed the petition and requested the court to provide him and his family members with security. Justice Siddiqui then ordered police to deploy reasonable security for the protection of the petitioner and his family.[19]

On 27 September 2017, a news item in Dawn further conflagrated war between military and civilian intelligence agencies. Members of the Federal Cabinet took serious notice of the airing of a "false report" on a private television channel claiming that former Prime Minister Nawaz Sharif had directed the Intelligence Bureau (IB) to keep vigilance over some 37 legislators, mostly belonging to the ruling PML-N, allegedly for having links with banned terrorist and sectarian outfits, Dawn reported.[20]

The Prime Minister later directed Law Minister Hamid to probe the issue and ensure action against the channel through the Pakistan Electronic Media Regulatory Authority (Pemra) for the "malafide reporting". Dawn reported.[21] On 06 October 2017, Prime Minister Shahid Khaqan Abbasi met the Director General of the Intelligence Bureau (IB), the law Minister along with several members of parliament allegedly investigated by the Intelligence Bureau (IB) for links to terror outfits.[22] DG IB Aftab Sultan briefed members of parliament on the issue, clarifying once again that the bureau is not responsible for the list, which purportedly names lawmakers with links to terrorists and was alleged to have been sent to IB by Prime Minister House when Nawaz

Sharif was in office.[23] The civilian-military distrust can also be seen in Dawn's report as the IB often accuses ISI of interfering in its affairs. A former top intelligence chief told TFT that according to the Telegraph Law, "only Intelligence Bureau (IB) is allowed to tap someone's phone, and that too, only based on real fears, only after the prime minister's permission."[24]

Experts view these developments in Pakistan's intelligence infrastructure as a bigger bang that shocked the whole region. These developments gave India more courage to tell international community that Pakistan had been the exporter of terrorism since 1980s. However, on 23 September 2017, Indian Minister of External Affairs Sushma Swaraj in her address to the 72nd Session of the United Nations General assembly warned that Islamabad had given the world "terrorists" while India was producing top-notch doctors and engineers.[25] "Why is it today India is a recognized IT superpower in the world, and Pakistan is recognized only as the pre-eminent export factory for terror?" Sushma Swaraj told the General Assembly. "We produced scholars, doctors, engineers. What have you produced? You have produced terrorists," she said. Indian Prime Minister Narendra Modi stepped up a drive to isolate Pakistan diplomatically after the Uri army base attack in Sept 2016 in which 19 Indian soldiers were killed.[26]

On 06 October 2017, Pakistan army admitted the association of Inter-Services Intelligence (ISI) with terrorist organizations.[27] However, it added that the "links" did not necessarily mean "support" of the terror organizations. Pakistan Army spokesperson Major General Asif Ghafoor, while addressing a press conference said, "There's a difference between support and having links. Name any intelligence agency which does not have links. Links can be positive."[28] Recent incidents involving young extremists, and the advent of Ansar-ul-Sharia (ASP), point unequivocally to the transformation of educational institutions into terror-producing factories. On 07 September 2017, two ASP operatives, from the Quetta and Pishin districts of Baluchistan, were arrested. They were identified as Professor Mushtaq, a teacher at the department of Information Technology, Engineering and Management Sciences (BUITEMS) Baluchistan University, and Mufti Habibullah, who was running seminaries in Karachi and Hyderabad. Both were accused of hatemongering and spreading militant ideas among students.[29]

Involvement of former ISI chief Lt Gen Rizwan Akhtar in corruption cases was also reported by Pakistani and international media. He was later on, forced to take early retirement due to his brother's involvement in huge corruption cases. Former Inter-Services Intelligence (ISI) Chief Lt Gen Rizwan Akhtar requested early retirement from the Pakistan Army citing "pressing personal commitments". Gen Akhtar, in a letter, asked for "premature release" starting Oct 9, 2017, after nearly 35 years of active commissioned service in the armed forces. "I want everyone [...] to respect my decision and not succumb or resort to speculation in any domain.[30] However, On 10 October 2017, NAB and FIA directed to probe PIA plane's 'mysterious' sale to Germany by General Rizwan's brother. Two separate inquiries were ordered into the 'mysterious' sale of a Pakistan International Airline (PIA) plane to a museum in Germany.[31]

Postscript

The boiling and fiercely churning pot of transmogrified jihadist ideology of Pakistan is now out of control as the army refused to relinquish sleepwalking to hell. Every month, the corps commander conference ends with castigation, slander and scornfulness. Patience and tolerance of Pashtun generals has now dematerialized and vanished. The killing and abduction of Pashtun men and women by intelligence and law enforcement agencies, sexual abuse of young girls and women by army officers in secret prisons have further exacerbated their pain.[1] Pakistani intelligence agencies and their controversial analysis of terrorism and jihadism are no more valid in international community. Intelligence of the country has grown into a militarized and politicized form, that views neighbouring states as enemies through military glasses, and misguiding their military, parliament and policy makers. Their affiliation with the country's political and religious leadership is making thing worse. The ISI never allowed civilian governments to adopt a positive approach towards neighbours, while every year, the agency paints a new ugly picture of India and Afghanistan.[2]

During the Zia military regime, radicalization-virus spread within intelligence infrastructure and military ranks, while a major change occurred when General Zia-ul-Haq instructed military and intelligence units to take on combatant mullahs with them to the frontline. Soldiers and officers were also required to attend classes of Tablighi Jamaat and other religious ceremonies.[3]

The purpose of this process was to indoctrinate young officers of armed forces and military intelligence agencies. Many of these young officers later on took control of higher sensitive positions and introduced sectarian Islam into their ranks. Sunni, Shia and Salafi brigades were established and their transmogrified version of religious ideology was promoted.[4] Within the army and intelligence quarters, different religious mosques were established. In 1992, after the fall of Dr. Najibullah government in Afghanistan, the decline of Pakistani intelligence agencies began when military establishment decided to directly intervene in the Afghan civil war by providing military and financial support to specific religious groups.[5]

The establishment of Shia and Salafi and Tablighi brigades in the army caused deep loathing of Pakistan among Afghans. General Javed Nasir of Tablighi Jamaat became the ISI's chief. He adopted an anti-Wahabi and anti-Deobandi policy in Afghanistan. He nominated Sabghatullah Mujaddidi—a Barelvi Pir—as President of Afghanistan for two months.[6] In 1994, Taliban emerged with their transmogrified version of religion, and later on defeated the Barelvis in the Southern and Eastern provinces of Afghanistan. In 1996, Taliban entered Kabul and established an Emirat-e-Islami government (Deobandi) in Afghanistan while Pakistan's intelligence infrastructure also became radicalized, ethnicised and sectarianised.[7]

In another u-turn, in 2001, the army and intelligence agencies supported the CIA and Pentagon, and declared war against their Deobandi colleagues. In their third u-turn, from 2001 to 2014, the army and ISI again started supporting Barelvi groups to de-radicalize the intelligence and military command of the country. Salafis and Deobandis were arrested one-by-one and handed to CIA and Pentagon in Afghanistan. This resulted in sectarian war in Pakistan. Baluchistan and Karachi have been the two most active zones of violence with roughly equal numbers of fatalities as a result of confirmed and suspected sectarian attacks in 2013 and 2014.[8] Journalist James M. Dorsey in his article spotlighted General Bajwa's anxiety about the exponentially growing sectarianism and jihadism in Pakistan: "Pakistan's Army Chief Gen Qamar Javed Bajwa recently expressed support for religious seminaries or madrassas, many of which are run by militants, but insisted that they expand their curriculum to ensure that graduates become more productive. With millions attending seminaries General Bajwa asked: "So what will they become: will they become Maulvis (clerics) or they will become terrorists?" He noted that Pakistan could not build enough mosques to employ the huge number of madrassas students. General Bajwa went on to say that more religious seminaries than mainstream schools had been established in Baluchistan in the past four decades. "Only religious education is being imparted to the students at all these seminaries and thus the students are left behind in the race for development," the general cautioned. Saudi-funded ultra-conservative Sunni Muslim madrassas operated by anti-Shiite militants dominate Baluchistan's educational landscape, according to Pakistani militants. "A majority of Baloch schoolchildren go to madrassas. They are in better condition than other schools in Baluchistan. Most madrassas are operated by Deobandis and Ahl-i-Hadith," said the co-founder of a virulently anti-Shiite group that is believed to enjoy Saudi and Pakistani support.[9]

However, Canadian Security Intelligence Service in its report "Pakistan's Security-Today and tomorrow" spotlights several complex challenges of Pakistan's national security: "Pakistan faces several complex and interdependent challenges; the country's history has been marked by political instability, sectarian and tribal violence, as well as regional conflicts with lasting negative effect. Today, economic difficulties and, again, political instability present problems; Pakistanis do not appear united in tackling these issues, with sub-nationalism and ethno-linguistic regionalism dominating everyday life. These problems are exacerbated as the rule of law and democratic civilian institutions remain underdeveloped, while the central government's weakness in comparison to the military results in the latter dominating politics generally. Currently, large areas of the country are beyond the control of government, with different groups having taken advantage of a porous border with Afghanistan. Pakistan's frontier and tribal areas have been used by insurgent movements, including the Taliban and Lashkar-e-Taiba (LeT), to support their terrorist activity in both Pakistan and Afghanistan. Despite its wide-ranging powers, the military has been unable to counter rising insurgency and cross-border terrorism into Afghanistan and India. A wide variety of regional issues further complicate the situation. Chief amongst these is Pakistan's complex and mostly antagonistic relationship with India. In the latest episode of this relationship, India alleged Pakistani involvement in a series of terrorist attacks on Indian targets, including the attacks in Mumbai in November 2008. Given the history of conflict as well as the nuclear capabilities of both South Asian states, rising tensions between the two are of serious concern".[10]

Pakistani scholar and professor Pervez Hoodbhoy in his research report uncovered the clandestine support of armed forces to sectarian religious groups against the democratic governments: "For three decades Pakistan's military establishment has stoutly denied supporting violent religious groups irrespective of whether a group's target lay across national borders or, instead, its goal was to achieve specific political objectives within Pakistan. But today the military's attitude is more ambivalent. Both serving and retired senior army officers are now openly expressing support for some groups. These include the newly emerged religious parties opposed to the PML-N government, notably Hafiz Saeed's Milli Muslim League (MML) and Khadim Hussain Rizvi's Tehreek Labbaik Ya Rasool Allah (TLYRA). Religious groups have already made their debut on the national scene and their initial successes — as in the NA-120 by-elections — are considerable. In a video that went viral, the serving DG of the Punjab Rangers, Maj-Gen Azhar Naveed, can be seen handing out coupons of Rs1000 to TLYRA demonstrators while assuring them support—"kya hum bhi aap kay saath nahin hain?" The demonstrators had tortured policemen while protesting a religious issue subsequently corrected by the government. Their dharna had been declared illegal by the Islamabad High Court which had specifically criticized COAS Gen Qamar Jawed Bajwa for opting to act as a mediator rather than follow the government's orders. Mainstreaming jihad: why now?[11]

On 14 December 2017, the Muttahida Majlis-i-Amal (MMA), an alliance of extremist parties emerged on the country's political horizon by contesting the 2002 general elections was revived. The decision to revive the alliance was announced by Jamiat Ulema-i-Pakistan (JUP) chief Shah Ovais Noorani in Karachi. Extremist parties They include Maulana Fazlur Rehman of the Jamiat Ulema-i-Islam-Fazl, Sirajul Haq of the Jamaat-i- Islami (JI), Allama Sajid Mir of Jamiat Ahle Hadith (JAH) and Allama Sajid Naqvi of Tehreek-i-Islami (TI).[12]

On 25 December 2017, Afghan Minister of Interior, Wais Ahmad Barmak warned that Daesh in Afghanistan receive support from Pakistan and the majority of the fighters belong to Afridi and Orakzai tribes based in Pakistan.[13] Mr. Zamir Kabulov, Russia's special presidential envoy for Afghanistan said that Moscow was worried about an increasing foothold of Daesh militants in northern Afghan provinces bordering

Baluchistan. However Pakistan Security Report for 2017 revealed: "The IS has claimed responsibility for just six terrorist attacks in the country, but they were the most deadliest ones, such as attacks on the convoy of Senate Deputy Chairman Abdul Ghafoor Haideri, Sehwan shrine, Shah Noorani shrine in Lasbela, Bethel Memorial Methodist Church in Quetta and Dargah Pir Rakhyal Shah in Fatehpur area of Jhal Magsi district and the abduction and killing of two Chinese nationals." The report claimed that despite a 16 per cent decline in terrorist attacks in 2017, Tehreek-e-Taliban Pakistan (TTP) and its associated groups remained the most potent threat. They were followed by nationalist-insurgent groups, especially Baluchistan Liberation Army and Baluchistan Liberation Front."[19]

On 28 January 2018, in his Dawn article, Amir Rana uncovered the hidden agenda of Pakistani sectarian groups: "Most importantly, these groups are a major source of confusion at multiple levels. When they take refuge under the cover of nationalist agendas, ambiguities are created in the public perception. On the social media, members of banned groups portray themselves as the 'ultra-patriotic' custodians of the ideology of Pakistan and defenders of the country's borders. The silence of state institutions regarding their activities in cyberspace creates fear amongst ordinary citizens".[20]

On 30 January 2018, Afghanistan's Permanent Representative to the United Nations Mahmoud Saikal accused Pakistan's premier intelligence network of training one of the Kabul attackers. "Abdul Qahar, father of one of the terrorists involved in last week's attack on Kabul Intercontinental Hotel, concedes his son was trained in Baluchistan province by the ISI," Saikal tweeted.[21] A mid-level diplomat at the Afghan embassy in the US alleged the attack was planned by Pakistan. "A clear proof that the attack on the hotel was planned in a madrasa on Pakistan's soil: Abdul Qahar, father of one of the suicide attackers, is an eyewitness of the story," said Majeed Qarar, cultural attaché at the embassy of Afghanistan. "The night vision goggles found with Taliban attackers in maiwand's ANA base were military grade goggles (Not sold to public) procured by Pak army from a British company & supplied to Lashkar-e-Taiba in Kashmir & Taliban in Afghanistan," he said.[22]

In reaction to the deadly wave of terrorist attacks across the country, especially in capital, Kabul, Afghanistan Times reported

President Ashraf Ghani urging the political elite in the country to rise above petty politics and unite to defend the Afghan nation and country against state-sponsored terrorism. "Those who consider themselves Muslims and Afghans must now separate themselves, in words and actions, from those barbaric puppets of religious manipulators and intelligence agencies," President Ghani warned. President Ghani's call for unity was just a call, practically; he did not approach political leadership of the country. "We all know that unity gives us courage, power and strength. Even in local trains people create groups so that they can help each other". Ghani said.[23]

However, Donald Trump accused Pakistan of "lies and deceit", saying America was foolish to have given Islamabad more than $33bn in aid. Trump began the New Year (2018) by launching an attack on Islamabad in his first tweet, saying Pakistan was providing "safe haven to the terrorists we hunt". "The United States has foolishly given Pakistan more than 33 billion dollars in aid over the last 15 years, and they have given us nothing but lies & deceit, thinking of our leaders as fools," he wrote. "They give safe haven to the terrorists we hunt in Afghanistan, with little help. No more."[24]

The New York Times reported that the Trump administration was considering withholding $255m in aid to Pakistan over Islamabad's failure to confront terrorism in the country. Pakistan had refused to allow the US access to a captured militant from the Taliban-linked Haqqani network. The militant was arrested in October 2017 by Pakistani troops as they rescued a Canadian-American couple who had been held captive for five years.[25]

Moreover, on 04 January 2018, Express Tribune reported Pakistan's brave Foreign Minister Khwaja Muhammad Asif warned the US; "You have asked what we did? A dictator surrendered on a single phone call, our country witnessed the worse bloodbath, you carried out 57,800 attacks on Afghanistan from our bases, your forces were supplied arms and explosives through our soil, thousands of our civilians and soldiers became victims of the war initiated by you." Asif said.[26] Former President Pervez Musharraf categorically admitted Pakistan's support to terrorist groups like Lashkar-e-Taiba (LeT) in 1990s to carry out attacks in Kashmir. From 1979, Pakistan was in favour of religious militancy."The Kashmiri freedom fighters including Hafiz Saeed and Lakhvi were our heroes at that time. We trained Taliban and sent them to fight against Russia. Taliban, Haqqani, Osama Bin Laden and Zawahiri were our heroes then. Later they became villains". Pervez Musharraf said.[27]

On 17 January 2018, Pakistani newspapers reported President Mamnoon Hussain called the unanimous Fatwa issued by Pakistani ulema as representation of different schools of thought. He was speaking at the launching ceremony of the Fatwa, called Paigham-e-Pakistan at a ceremony in Islamabad. He said issuance of the unanimous Fatwa through consultations is a step in the right direction and it would go a long way in projecting soft and positive image of Pakistan in the comity of nations. He said this would also highlight the fact that Islam is a religion of peace, brotherhood, tolerance and accommodation. He said the Fatwa represent true teachings of Islam.[28]

The "Fatwa" (decree) signed by eminent religious scholars and heads of major religious schools across Pakistan, was issued at a gathering at the President House in Islamabad in the presence of President Mamnoon Hussain, religious scholars, diplomats, teachers, ministers and lawmakers. The 9-point decree "declared that suicide attacks are forbidden in the light of the Holy Quran and the Sunnah ," which are "already adversely affecting the country and its society by causing disorder and mayhem in Pakistan; advantages of which is being taken by the enemies of Islam." "We unanimously reject extremist ideology and extremism in all its form a manifestations. Wherever exists, this is an evil ideology, therefore, shall be dealt with as a religious obligation through all means available i.e. ideological, kinetic and non-kinetic," the decree said.[29]

On 02 February 2018, Afghan President Ashraf Ghani said eleven suspects had been arrested in connection with the recent spate of deadly attacks and vowed the Afghans would take revenge event if it takes a hundred years. In a televised address to the nation President Ghani said a new security plan for Kabul was a must. The President said Pakistan was 'the centre of Taliban' who was responsible for the recent deadly attacks that killed and wounded nearly 500 people. "Now the decision rests with Pakistan, whatever it (Pakistan) likes for itself, it should like the same for others," Ghani said. "No one can defeat us, we are unconquerable. Today is the time to change our grief into determination." "Islam does not differentiate between black and white, it is a universal religion and the Taliban who claimed the latest attacks do not believe in Allah and His Prophet", Ghani remarked, declaring the Afghans were not only winning the war but also on the reconciliation front.[30]

On 31 January 2018, Dawn reported the arrival of Afghan Spy Chief Visit to Pakistan. The visit came amid anger in Afghanistan over an attack on a luxury hotel and a car bomb in the capital, Kabul, which killed more than 120 people, which the government blamed on Haqqani network militants believed to operate out of Pakistan. The Afghan team presented documentary evidence and phone tap information linking individuals and groups based in Pakistan with the Kabul attacks. The delegation included Mr. Masoom Stanekzai, head of the National Directorate for Security intelligence agency, and Afghan Interior Minister Wais Barmak. "The Afghan government had requested that a high-level delegation would visit Pakistan with a message from the Afghan president.[31]

On 01 February 2018, Dawn reported the Trump administration's South Asia strategy authorized US commanders in the region that they need to deal with "terrorist safe havens in both Afghanistan and Pakistan. The strategy that President Donald Trump announced in August last year underlined the US determination to defeat the Taliban in the battlefield in order to force them to accept the current administrative set-up in Kabul.[32] On 10 February 2018, Hizbul Mujahedeen Commander wowed that his organization trained terrorists for jihad in Kashmir. "Pakistan has just ignored the Trump administration's wrong-headed decision of terming a 'freedom fighter' a 'terrorist,'" which violates United Nations resolutions and the US Constitution," he told Asia Times in an exclusive interview. "Pakistan knows very well that a 'mujahid' cannot be a 'terrorist,' [and therefore] continues to provide 'moral' and 'diplomatic' support to the forces fighting for the right of self-determination in Kashmir." His assertion reinforced India's claims that Pakistani authorities have been lending support to militant outfits in the region. 'We're still training Kashmiris for jihad: Hizbul Mujahedeen Commander laughs off his designation as a global terrorist in an exclusive interview with Asia Times.[33]

Notes to Chapters

Notes to Introduction

1   *Daily Times*, 15 July 2013

2   Ibid

3   *The Herald Magazine*, 14 September 2017

4   Iid

5   *New Delhi Times*, 23 September 2017

6   *The Nation*, 01 May 2017

7   Pakistan Troubled State, *Gallup news*, 08 March 2018

8   *Dawn Leaks*: A tweet that underscored the state within a state: No institution should have hegemony over "national interest" and "patriotism", Imad Zafar, *The Nation*, 01 May 2017, https://nation.com.pk/01-May-2017/dawn-leaks-a-tweet-that-underscored-the-state-within-a-state.

9   The Garrison State, Ishtiaq Ahmad, Oxford University Press, 2013

10 *The Nation*, 05 December 2015

11 The Afghan Intel crisis, Musa Khan Jalalzai, New York, 2017

12 The Corrosive influence of Pakistan's deep state, Imad Zafar *Asia Times*, 28 March 2018

13 A Soft Coup in Pakistan: Army Consolidate Power, Gurmeet Kanwal, 29 July 2017, https://www.thequint.com/voices/opinion/a-soft-coup-in-pakistan-army-consolidates-power

14 Ibid

15 Pakistan's Future Wars: Tackling Terrorism Within. Dhruv C Katoch, Scholar Warrior, Spring, 2016

16 Ibid

17 The Afghan Intel crisis, PP: 133

18 Ibid

19 Whose Army, Musa Khan Jalalzai 2014, New York

20 Marketing terrorism and Fear, *Daily Times*, 24 April 2016, in my fact based analysis; I spotlighted some facts about the way Afghan Taliban training and brainwashing of suicide bombers, and warned that it was not different from the suicide techniques of the Pakistani Taliban in FATA.

21 *Dawn*, 28 February 2018

22 Nuclear arms race in South Asia, in my research article of *Daily Times*, I argued that the issue of nuclear, chemical and biological terrorism in South Asia has been the centre of debate in the international press since the establishment of Islamic State (IS) in Iraq and Syria. The acquisition of chemical and biological weapons by ISIS has exacerbated the frustration of the international community that these weapons have fallen into the wrong hands, *Daily Times*, 06 July 2015

23 In my previous analysis in 2013, I warned that availability of biological and nuclear explosives in South Asian markets, the nuclear arms race between India and Pakistan and their changing relations with China, the US and Russia have raised serious questions about the jihadists' intentions of retrieving modern nuclear missile technologies. Pakistan and India have been updating their nuclear arsenal for a decade. *Daily Times*, 06 July 2015

24 Ibid

25 Father of Pakistani Bomb Sold Nuclear Secrets, Karen Yourish and Delano D Souza. Arm Control Today, Arms Control Association. 01 March 2004, https://www.armscontrol.org/act/2004_03/Pakistan

26 Ibid

27 *The New Yorker*, March 08, 2004, The Deal: Why is Washington going easy on Pakistan's nuclear black marketers? Seymour M. Hersh, this story uncovered Pakistan's illegal nuclear black marketing across Asia.

28 Bush handed blueprint to seize Pakistan's nuclear arsenal: Architect of Iraq surge draws up takeover options. US fears army's Islamists might grab weapons, Adrian Levy and Cathy Scott-Clark, *The Guardian*, 01 Dec 2007, https://www.theguardian.com/world/2007/dec/01/pakistan.iraq

29 Keeping Pakistan nuclear weapons out of the hands of terrorists, The Heritage Foundation September 18, 2007 Lisa Curtis and Delivered June 27, 2007. https://www.heritage.org/about-heritage/mission

30 *The Nation*, 31 August 2017

31 Dr AQ Khan provided centrifuges to N. Korea, *Dawn*, August 25, 2005

32 *New York Times*, February 2004

33 01 September 2017, *Dawn* reported Veteran politician Javed Hashmi meeting with Dr Abdul Qadeer Khan who told him that a group in the army was not in favor of Pakistan's nuclear tests.

34 On 30 August 2017, *Dawn* reported the PPP Senator Farhatullah Babar call for an investigation into nuclear proliferation by Pakistan under the rule of former president Pervez Musharraf.

35 *The News*, 21 May 2009

36 *Times of India*, 11 August 2009

37 BBC, 21 August 2008

38 Thinking about Pakistan's Nuclear Security in Peacetime, Crisis and War, Christopher Clary, Institute for Defense Studies and Analysis, 17 July, 2009

39 Daily Times 21 July 2014

40 Ibid

41 Ibid

42 India's experience with the limited conflict in Kargil suggests to Indian strategic elites that "limited war" is indeed possible. C. Christine Fair, Keith Crane, Christopher S. Chivvis, Samir Puri, Michael Spirtas. The RAND Corporation-2010, Pakistan was defeated by Indian army in Kargil conflict in 1999.

43 Sajid Farid Shapoo, *The Diplomat*, 01 February 2017

44 *Hindustan Times*, 13 October 2016, Mr. Shivshankar Memon warned that the real threat to Pakistan nuclear weapons is from rogue elements inside its military rather than from the terrorist outfits.

45 The October 2006 and May 2009 North Korean tests took place with regular participation of scientists from a secret nuclear weapons development facility near Hyderabad, Sindh in Pakistan, Madhav Nalapat, 25 September 2016

46 The Prospect of Nuclear Jihad in Pakistan, Musa Khan Jalalzai, New York, 2015

47 Vinayak Bhat, 19 May 2017

48 On 03 March 2017, Journalist and expert, Mathew Aid in his analysis

highlighted Pakistan's support to Taliban. https://www.strategypage.com/qnd/afghan/articles/20170303.aspx

49 US Cannot Tolerate Pakistan's Support To Terrorists: Official, *ToloNews*, 17 November 2017

50 In President Karzai's times, yes, indeed, he was damaging Pakistan and therefore we were working against his interest. *Guardian* 2015

51 General Pervez Musharraf said terrorists like Osama bin Laden and the Taliban were heroes for Pakistan, *Economic Times*, India, 28 October 2015

52 Ibid

53 Musa Khan Jalalzai, the Prospect of Nuclear Jihad in Pakistan, 2015

54 On 23 June, 2011, *BBC* reported Brigadier Ali Khan's incarceration

55 The prospect of nuclear jihad in South Asia: During the Taliban regime in Afghanistan, the al Qaeda sought nuclear weapons assistance from Pakistan, Musa Khan Jalalzai, 02 October 2013

56 *PTI news*, 21 January 2014

57 Pakistan Tests Its Nasr Short-Range Ballistic Missile System, Improving Range: Pakistan extends the Nasr's range by 10 kilometers. Is that meaningful?, Ankit Panda, *Diplomat*, 10 July, 2017

58 *The Diplomat*, 10 July 2017, analyst Ankit Panda, http://thediplomat.com/2017/07/pakistan-tests-its-nasr-short-range-ballistic-missile-system-improving-range/

59 Pakistan Tests Its Nasr Short-Range Ballistic Missile System, Improving Range: Pakistan extends the Nasr's range by 10 kilometers. Is that meaningful? By Ankit Panda, *The Diplomat*, 10 July 2017, https://thediplomat.com/2017/07/pakistan-tests-its-nasr-short-range-ballistic-missile-system-improving-range/

60 *The ICG Report*, July 2016

61 On 21 June 2014, *Dawn* reported more than 600,000 people fled Waziristan. They faced grave difficulties because of transport shortages and over pricing.

62 *Daily Times* and *Pak Tribune*, 30 June 2014

63 09 February 2014, *Dawn*

64 On 22 February 2017, *Dawn* reported Punjab police started a surveillance of people belonging to the Federally Administered Tribal Areas (FATA) and decided to issue them chip-based national identity cards equipped with security features. A senior police official told *Dawn* that more than 5,400

Pashtuns living in Rawalpindi were put under strict surveillance.

65 *Dawn* 01 March 2017, Rawalpindi police began conducting surveillance of people from the tribal areas living within the Pindi-division.

66 *The Friday Times*, 03 March 2017, Fawad Ali Shah reported the humiliation of a Pashtun young man by local police

67 On 21 February 2017, *Pakistan Today* reported citizens were asked to report any persons of Pashtun descent to the Punjab police.

68 *Express Tribune*, 28 February 2017

Notes to Summary

1 Nuclear deterrence has brought stability, Asma Khalid, *Daily Times*, 28 May, 2017, https://dailytimes.com.pk/9323/nuclear-deterrence-has-brought-stability/

2 The Deal: Why is Washington going easy on Pakistan's nuclear black marketers? By Seymour M. Hersh, *New York Times*, March 8, 2004, https://www.newyorker.com/magazine/2004/03/08/the-deal-3

3 U.S. Secretly Aids Pakistan in Guarding Nuclear Arms, David E. Sanger and William J. Broad, *New York Times*, 18 November 2007, http://www.nytimes.com/2007/11/18/washington/18nuke.html. The Guardian reported that Pakistani generals 'helped sell nuclear secrets. North Korea paid senior figures $3.5m. Letter claimed, AQ Khan 'wanted to set the historical record straight. Generals denied the allegations. Julian Borger, diplomatic editor, *The Guardian*, 07 July 2011.

4 Pakistan admitted nuclear expert traded with Iran, the Guardian reported on 10 March 2005. The newspaper, reported Pakistani authorities admitting the sale of nuclear secrets by Dr. Abdul Qadeer Khan, the father of Pakistan's nuclear programme.

5 Pakistan boasted of nuclear strike on India within eight seconds: Alastair Campbell's diaries recount warning by army general at height of military standoff between India and Pakistan, Nicholas Watt, *The Guardian*, 15 Jun 2012.

6 Forget North Korea: A Nuclear War Between India and Pakistan Should Terrify You. 27 March 2017, *Defence News*, www.*DefenceNews*,in is a dedicated online Indian Defence News portal. http://defencenews.in/article/Forget-North-Korea-A-Nuclear-War-Betweeen-India-and-Pakistan-Should-Terrify-You-251206

7 Musa Khan Jalalzai, the Prospect of Nuclear Jihad in Pakistan, PP;60

8 Ibid

9 *Hindustan Times*, 12 January 2018

10 *The News International*, 12 January 2018

11 Rule by the Generals: The Influence of Military Regimes on Pakistan's Internal Security, Farooq Sadaf, University of Reading, 2011

12 Proliferation of Weapons of Mass Destruction: Risk for Companies and Scientific Institutions, General Intelligence and Security Services (AIVD) Netherlands. July 2003 https://fas.org/irp/world/netherlands/wmdrisks.pdf

13 Countering Proliferation Finance: An Introduction Guide for Financial Institutions, Emil Dall, Tom Keating and Andrea Berger, RUSI Guidance Paper, April 2017

14 Ibid

15 Ibid, https://rusi.org/sites/default/files/201704_rusi_cpf_guidance_paper.1_0.pdf

16 What Donald Trump can Really do to rein in Pakistan, Deutsche Welle, 02, 01 2018, http://www.dw.com/en/what-donald-trump-can-really-do-to-rein-in-pakistan/a-42000916

17 Country Reports on Terrorism 2016. United States Department of State Publication Bureau of Counterterrorism, released on July 2017, Country Reports on Terrorism 2016 is submitted in compliance with Title 22 of the United Stateswhich requires the Department of State to provide to Congress a full and complete annual report on terrorism for those countries and groups meeting the criteria of the Act. ". South Asian Geopolitics Has Pakistan Lost its Plot? Abhay K. Singh.

18 *Diplomat*, 11 January 2018

19 The Only Enemy Pakistan's Army Can Beat Is Its Own Democracy: The country's prime ministers have always come and gone at the behest of the generals who really run the country. C. Christine Fair, *Foreign Policy*, 09 August 9, 2017

20 Radicalisation of the Pakistan Army Journal of Defence Studies, Vol. 5 No. 4 October 2011, Institute for Defence Studies and Analyses (IDSA).

21 Militant Groups in South Asia, Part-C Pakistan, (Jamaat-ud-Dawa or JuD—the new name of the outlawed LeT in Pakistan—has been derived from Markaz-e-Dawa-wal-Irshad (MDI), an organisation which Hafiz Mohammad Saeed and his associates established in 1986), Surinder Kumar Sharma, Anshuman Behera, Institute for Defence Studies and Analyses, New Delhi, 2014.

22 *The News International*, 05 December 2017

23 Ibid

24 Ibid

25 Ibid

26 *The Reuters*, 15 September 2017

27 Namrata Tripathi. *International Business Times*, October 6, 2017. http://www.
ibtimes.co.in/pakistan-army-admits-links-between-intelligence-agency-isi-
terrorist-groups-744558. Pakistan army pushed political role for militant-
linked groups, Asif Shahzad, Reuter, 21 September 2017,https://uk.reuters.
com/article/uk-pakistan-politics-militants/pakistan-army-pushed-
political-role-for-militant-linked-groups-idUKKCN1BW2JN

28 Ibid, 05 October 2017

29 Ibid

30 On 06 October 2017, *The News International* reported Pakistan army admitted
to associations between terrorist groups and its top intelligence agency.

31 Ibid

32 Ibid

33 Ibid

34 *Journal of Defence Studies*, Vol. 5 No. 04 October 2011

35 Pakistan Army Pushed Political Role for Militant-Linked Groups: Pakistan
Army Pushed Political Role for Militant-Linked Groups. New Age Islam,
http://www.newageislam.com/islamic-world-news/pakistan-army-
pushed-political-role-for-militant-linked-groups/d/112624

36 Inside Al-Qaeda and the Taliban: Beyond Bin Laden and 9/11, 23 May 2011,
Saleem Shehzad, Pluto Press, London

37 Ibid

38 Ibid

39 Musa Khan Jalalzai, The Prospect of Nuclear jihad

40 Musa Khan Jalalzai, The Prospect of Nuclear Jihad in Pakistan, Introduction
pages

41 Ibid

42 *The Telegraph*, UK, 01 September 2014

43 *BBC*, 23 November 2016

44 Why was Pakistan general giving money to protesters? M Ilyas Khan, *BBC
News*, Islamabad, 29 November 2017

45 Ibid

46 Ibid

47 The Only Enemy Pakistan's Army Can Beat Is Its Own Democracy: The country's prime ministers have always come and gone at the behest of the generals who really run the country. BY C. Christine Fair Foreign Policy, 09 August, 2017. http://foreignpolicy.com/2017/08/09/the-only-enemy-pakistans-army-can-beat-is-its-own-democracy/

48 Pakistani Army Delusion and Self-Destruction, Shekhar Gupta, September 24, 2016

49 A Pakistani's perspective: Why Bangladesh is doing better than Pakistan, Saquib Saeed, *Express Tribune*, 02 June 2014

50 Musa Khan Jalalzai, The Prospect of Nuclear jihad, PP: 56

51 Ibid

52 Unpacking the Pakistan Army's Twitter War With Nawaz Sharif: The Pakistan army's public rejection of Nawaz Sharif's decision to sack top aide Tariq Fatemi reveals the extent it goes to protect its control over the country's national security and foreign policies. Mohammad Taqi, *the Wire*, 02 May 2017. https://thewire.in/131004/unpacking-pakistan-armys-twitter-war-pm-nawaz-sharif/

53 Ibid

54 Pakistan Waging Dirty War on its Balochs: While Baloch people want azadi from atrocities committed by Pakistani authorities; the federal Government has unleashed State and non-State forces against them, Makhan Saikia, *The Pioneer*. 27 August 2016.

55 Mainstreaming militancy not surprising at all (The open involvement of radical, militant organisations – both religious and non-religious– in the political scene of Pakistan is a very natural outcome of what the establishment of the country has made it and its citizens go through for the past two decades and beyond). Khursheed Sardar, *Pakistan Today*, 11 October, 2017.   https://www.pakistantoday.com.pk/2017/10/11/mainstreaming-militancy-not-surprising-at-all/

56 Pakistan army pushed political role for militant-linked groups, Asif Shahzad, *Reuter*, 16 September 2017. *Jihad Watch*, 17 September, 2017. Robert Spencer. https://www.jihadwatch.org/2017/09/pakistan-army-pushes-political-role-for-islamic-supremacist-groups

57 *Dawn*, 10 September 2014

58 Islamic State a serious threat to Pakistan, Foreign secretary admits. AFP and Reuters, Mateen Haider, *Dawn* newspaper, 23 February, 2015

59 Mr. Yunis Khushi, Department of Social Sciences, Lahore Garrison University, Lahore, Pakistan, *Omics International*, June 26, 2017. https://www.omicsonline.org/open-access/isis-in-pakistan-a-critical-analysis-of-factors-and-implications-of-isisrecruitments-and-concept-of-jihadbilnikah-2151-6200-1000276.php?aid=90682

60 State versus Nations in Pakistan: Sindhi, Baloch and Pakhtun Responses to Nation Building, Ashok K Behuria, Institute for Defence Studies and Analyses, New Delhi (IDSA) Monograph Series, No. 43 January 2015.

Notes to Chapter 1

1   US worried Pakistan's Nuclear-weapons could land up in terrorists' hands: Official, *The Economic Times*, 25 August 2017, https://economictimes.indiatimes.com/news/defence/us-worried-pakistans-nuclear-weapons-could-land-up-in-terrorists-hands-official/articleshow/60220358.cms

2   Nuclear waste must be out of sight, but not out of mind, Rebecca Bell, *the Guardian*, 01 November 2014

3   Pakistan's Nuclear Development 1974-1998: External Pressures, Iram Khalid and Zakia Bano, *Journal of South Asian Studies*, Vol. 30, No.1, January–June 2015

4   Keeping Pakistan's Nuclear Weapons out of the hands of Terrorists, Lisa Curtis, 18 September, 2007, https://www.heritage.org/asia/report/keeping-pakistans-nuclear-weapons-out-the-hands-terrorists

5   Pakistan's Nuclear Weapons: Proliferation and Security Issues, Paul K. Kerr and Mary Beth Nikitin, May 10, 2012, Congressional Research Service.

6   Long Road to Chaghi: The General and the Atomic Toy. Oxford, Islamabad, and New York, Shahidurrahman, Printwise Publications, 1999

7   Pakistan's Nuclear Development (1974-1998): External Pressures, Iram Khalid and Zakia Bano, *Journal of South Asian Studies, Vol. 30, No.1,* January–June 2015

8   Pakistan Says its ready to use Nuclear Weapons—Should India Worry? "We should pray that such an option never arises, but if we need to use them (nuclear weapons) for our survival we will," Asif told *GeoNews*. Zachary Keck. *The National Interest*, 03 November, 2017, http://nationalinterest.org/blog/the-buzz/pakistan-says-its-ready-use-nuclear-weapons%E2%80%94should-india-23034

9   *The Project Alpha*, Pakistan's strategic nuclear and missile industries, Centre for Science and Security Studies, King's College September 2016.

10 *New Yorker*, 1993, Abdul Qadeer Khan article

11 *Telegraph*, 13 December 2001

12 Father of Pakistani Bomb sold Nuclear Secrets, Karen Yourish and Delano D'Souza, Arms Control Association

13 *Daily Times*, 21 January 2004

14 Pakistan Unveil Nuclear Procedure, Kathy Gannon, *Associated Press*, 25 July 2000

15 *Friday Times*, Eating grass: the making of the Pakistani bomb. Feroz Hassan Khan, Stanford University Press, 2012

16 Pakistan's Nuclear Weapons Programme: 5 Things you need to Know, Akhilesh Pillalamarri, *National Interests*, 21 April, 2015

17 India, Pakistan and the Nuclear Race: The Elephant and the Dilemma of Nuclear Force Planning, Vice Admiral (Retd.) Vijay Shankar, Institute of Peace and Conflict Studies, 16 Apr, 2013

18 *New York Times*, 26 December 2004

19 Documents indicate A. Q Khan offere Nucleat Weapons Design to Iraq in 1990: Did he Approach other Countries? David Albright and Corey Hinderstein, 04 February 2004

20 *Indian Express*, Khaled Ahmad, 07 December, 2012

21 Nuclear proliferation claims re-open can of worms in Pakistan, F.M. Shakil June 16, 2017 *Asia Times* reported

22 Pakistan's Nuclear Weapons, Paul K. Kerr, Mary Beth Nikitin Congressional Research Service, 01 August 2016

23 9 EU-Non-Proliferation Consortium, Non-Proliferation Papers, and No. 19 July 2012 Pakistan's nuclear and WMD programmes: status, evolution and risks, Bruno Tertrais.

24 Jalalzai, PP: 25

25 The AQ Khan Revelations and Subsequent Changes to Pakistani Export Controls, *NTI*, 01 December, 2004

26 *Daily Times*, 21 July 2014

27 Ibid

28 Ibid

29 Ibid

30 Ibid

31 Ibid

32 *Dawn*, 16 June 2017

33 Ibid

34 *Dawn*, 16 June 2017, and also Washington Post, quoting a friend of Dr Khan's, reported in February 2004 that Pakistan had good reason to try to bury the issue

35 Possibility of Nuclear Armageddon in South Asia, Zainab Aziz, *Euroasia Review*, 30 March, 2017

36 The Global Regime for Terrorism, Report by International Institutions and Global Governance Program, *Issue Brief*, Council of Foreign Relations, 31 August, 2011.

37 *Reuters*, 14 April 2017

38 On 22 June 2017, Pentagon warned that Pakistan was 'the most influential' external actor affecting Afghan stability and the military alliance's mission

39 Afghan President Ghani Accused Pakistan of State-Sponsored Terrorism in his Country, *ToloNews*, 15 June 2017, *Dawn*

40 06 August 2017, *Dawn*

41 *The Hill*, 05 August 2017

42 Ibid

43 Ibid

44 Trump wants Pakistan's 'paradoxical' policies to change: Anwar Iqbal, *Dawn*, 06 August, 2017

45 28 April, 2017, *Hindustan Times*

46 *ToloNews*, 24 May 2017

47 *Dawn* 29 May 2017

48 Ibid

49 *ToloNews*, 24 May 2017

50 14 July 2017, *ToloNews*

51 *Ibid*

52 *ToloNews*, 14 July 2017, https://www.tolonews.com/index.php/opinion/why-should-pakistan-be

53 Ibid, second document

54 Ibid, meetings of Pakistani intelligence agencies with Taliban groups within the quarters of armed forces.

55 Ibid

56 Ibid

57 Why Should Pakistan Be Added To List of Terrorist States? *ToloNews*, Kabul Afghanistan, 14 July 2016 http://www.tolonews.com/opinion/why-should-pakistan-be-added-list-terrorist-states

58 Jihadist penetration of Pakistani armed forces, Amir Mir, *Asia Times*, June 9, 2016

59 Pentagon Report, *Ariana News*, 21 June 2017, Kabul Afghanistan

60 *Economic Times*, 07 February 2017

61 *Indian Express* 07 February 2017

62 Afghans point finger at Pakistan, *CNN* 01 June 2017

63 Pakistan: The First Domino in the Nuclear Security Dolemma, Julian Reder, *International Policy Digest*, 02 May 2017, https://intpolicydigest.org/2017/05/02/pakistan-first-domino-asian-nuclear-security-dilemma

64 SIS boasts of smuggling nuke from Pakistan through 'porous border' with Mexico, by Barbara Boland, Washington Examiner, 04 June, 2015, https://www.washingtonexaminer.com/isis-boasts-of-smuggling-nuke-from-pakistan-through-porous-border-with-mexico.

65 ISIS boasts of smuggling nuke from Pakistan through 'porous border' with Mexico, by Barbara Boland, *Washington Examiner*, 04 Jun 2015

66 *Dawn*, 16 June 2017

67 Terrorists still raising funds in Pakistan, warns a report of the US State Department, Anwar Iqbal, *Dawn*, 21 July, 2017, https://www.dawn.com/news/1346603

68 The strategic triangular dilemma in South Asia, Zafar Khan, Express Tribune, May 5, 2017

69 The terrifying geography of nuclear and radiological insecurity in South Asia, Hannah E. Haegeland and Reema Verma, *The Bulletin of the Atomic Scientists*, 22 January 2017

70 The Growing Nuclear Club, Kathleen Sutcliffe, Council on Foreign Relations, 17 November 2006

71 On 21 April 2017, Analyst Mr. Todd Royal in his *Asia Times* article warned about the recent escalation of military crisis between India and Pakistan

72 Pakistan's Hand in the Rise of International Jihad, Carlotta Gall, *New York Times*, 6 February, 2016

73 Ibid

Notes to Chapter 2

1   I've sold nuclear secrets to Libya, Iran and North Korea, Ahmed Rashid and Anton La Guardia, The Telegraph London, 03 Feb 2004, https://www.telegraph.co.uk/news/worldnews/asia/pakistan/1453353/Ive-sold-nuclear-secrets-to-Libya-Iran-and-N-Korea.html

2   *The Guardian*, 06 February 2009

3   *Dawn,*30 May 2008

4   30 May 2008, *Dawn NewsTV*

5   *GeoNew TV Channel*, Dr. Abdul Qadeer Khan interview with Sohail Waraich in Islamabad Pakistan

6   The AQ Khan Revelations and Subsequent Changes to Pakistani Export Controls, *NTI-01* December, 2004

7   *Telegraph* 03 February 2004

8   Devjyot Ghoshal, 19 September 2017

9   CRS Report for Congress: Pakistan's Nuclear Proliferation Activities and the Recommendations of the 9/11 Commission: U.S. Policy Constraints and Options January 25, 2005, *Congressional Research Service* ¯ The Library of Congress.

10 Press Release by Inspector General of Police in Relation to Investigation on the Alleged Production of Components for Libya's Uranium Enrichment Programme, Iran Watch, February 20, 2004 https://www.iranwatch.org/library/government/malaysia/royal-police-office/press-release-inspector-general-police-relation-investigation-alleged-production-components-libya%E2%80%99s. Full statement by the inspector general of police, The Star Online, 21 Feb 2004 https://www.thestar.com.my/news/nation/2004/02/21/full-statement-by-the-inspectorgeneral-of-police/

11 Ibid

12 Ibid

13 Ibid

14 Pakistan's nuclear exports: Was there a state strategy? Paper prepared for the Non-proliferation Education Centre Bruno Tertrais, 20 October 2006. PP-1, and 2, also, Simon Henderson, "Nuclear Spinning: The Iran-Pakistan Link", National Review Online, 11 December 2003; Special Report: The AQ Khan Network: Crime... and Punishment? WMD Insights, Issue 03 March 2006. Researcher Mr. David Albright, "A.Q. Khan Network: The Case Is Not Closed", Testimony to the Subcommittee on International Terrorism and Non-proliferation, Committee on International Relations, House of Representatives, US Congress, 25 May 2006. Pakistan's Nuclear Exports: Was there a State Strategy. Paper prepared for the Non-proliferation Education Centre, Bruno Tertrais, 20 October 2006, http://www.npolicy. org/article_file/20061023-Tertrais-Pakistan_310111_0722.pdf.   Pakistan's Nuclear Future: Worries beyond War, Henry D. Sokolski, January 2008.

15 *The Guardian*, 06 February 2009

16 *Congressional Research Service*, Pakistan's nuclear Weapons, Paul K. Kerr, Mary Beth Nikitin, 01 August 2016

17 On 07 July 2011, David E. Sanger, *New York Times*

18 20 September 2009, *Sunday Times*

19 *Times of India*, 21 September 2009

20 Pakistan Received Chinese Nuclear-Weapon Assistance, Khan Letter Asserts, September 24, 2009, *NTI*, http://www.nti.org/gsn/article/pakistan-received-chinese-nuclear-weapon-assistance-khan-letter-asserts/

21 *Dawn*, September 24, 2009

22 Protect: The Security of Pakistan's Nuclear Facilities. Senior Consultant to the Global Security Program of the East West Institute and International Legal Adviser to the International Crisis Group, Mr. Ken Berry in his research paper (2008) noted important facts about the safety and security of Pakistan's nuclear weapons. https://www.eastwest.ngo/sites/default/files/ideas-files/The%20Security%20of%20Pakistan%27s%20Nuclear%20Facilities.pdf

23 Statement by Ambassador Tehmina Janjua, Permanent Representative of Pakistan to the United Nations in Geneva and Conference on Disarmament at the First Committee Thematic Debate on Other Weapons of Mass Destruction, New York, 18 October 2016, https://s3.amazonaws.com/unoda-web/wp-content/uploads/2016/10/18-Oct-Pakistan-OWMD.pdf

24 Ibid

25 Ibid

26 *The News*, 20 April 2016

27 *NBC News* reported.1 On 20 April 2016, Ashraf Ali reported to *NBC News*. On 20 April 2016, Ashraf Ali reported Director General of Pakistan's intelligence bureau (IB), Mr. Aftab Sultan warned that hundreds of fighters from his country were joining ISIS in Syria, generating concerns about their links and activities when they returned home.

28 *Reuter* report

29 Combating Terrorism Center Report 2016

30 *Times of India*, 10 July 2017

31 *Financial Express*, 12 July 2017

32 *Asia Times*, 13 July 2017

33 Ibid

34 Journalist E Jaya Kumar 13 July 2017 reported to *Asia Times* the Hizbul chemical weapons against Indian soldiers or civilians, *Asia Times*.

35 15 January 2017, *Sunday Guardian*

36 26 September 2004, *South Asian Tribune* reported refugees fleeing WANA in South Waziristan were targeted by Pakistan army. Security forces used poisonous gas or a bio-weapon on a large scale against them. M. A Siddiqui noted some important cases, is the Pakistan Army Using Chemical Weapons in WANA Operation by M.A Siddiqui, *South Asia Tribune* from Washington, Washington DC, 26 September, 2004.

37 On 17 May 2017, Mr. Vinayak Bhat in *Outlook magazine* reported Pakistan's new secret nuclear weapons storage facility.

38 *GeoNews*, 11 December, 2014

39 On December 11, 2014, former Interior Minister of Pakistan Mr Rehman Malik told a local news channel that IS had established recruitment centres in Gujranwala and Bahawalpur districts of Punjab province.

40 *ToloNews* 2016

41 In November 2016, *Russian Television* (RT) aired interview of *Wikileaks* founder Mr. Julian Assange with a UK based Australian journalist, Mr. John Pilger. Mr. Assange uncovered important facts about the wealthy officials from Saudi Arabia and Qatar donating money to the Hillary Clinton's Foundation and Islamic State (IS) respectively.

42 In 17 August 2014, Mr. Assange made public an email in which Hillary Clinton urged the then advisor to US President Barak Obama, Mr. John Podesta, to pressure Qatar and Saudi Arabia for funding Islamic State (ISIS)

43 15 November, 2016, Khyber Sarban, *Diplomat Magazine*

Notes to Chapter 3

1   Saudi crown prince warns it will build nuclear bomb if Tehran does the same. *The Guardian*, 15 March 2018, https://www.theguardian.com/world/2018/mar/15/saudi-arabia-iran-nuclear-bomb-threat-mohammed-bin-salman

2   *BBC*, 06 November 2013, and *the Guardian* also reported the deal, 07 November 2013

3   Saudi Arabia's Nuclear Ambitions and Proliferation Risks, Sara Burkhard, Erica Wenig, David Albright, and Andrea Stricker, Institute for Science and International Security, Washington, March 30, 2017 https://isis-online.org/uploads/isis-reports/documents/SaudiArabiaProliferationRisks_30Mar2017_Final.pdf. Saudi Crown Princ Warns Riyadh will Develop Nuclear weapons if Iran builds bomb, Japam Times, 16, 03, 2018, https://www.japantimes.co.jp/news/2018/03/17/world/saudi-crown-prince-warns-riyadh-will-develop-nuclear-weapons-iran-builds-bomb, the Guardian, 15 March 2018.

4   The Pak-Saudi Nuke and How to Stop It. Christopher Clary and Mara E. Karlin, the American Interests, 10 June 2012, https://www.the-american-interest.com/2012/06/10/the-pak-saudi-nuke-and-how-to-stop-it/

5   *The Guardian* London, 07 Nobember 2013

6   *The Telegraph* London, 29 June 2015

7   Saudi nuclear weapons 'on order' from Pakistan, Mark Urban, *BBC*, 6 November 2013, Nuclear war fears: Saudi Arabia looking to get hold of 'nukes to combat Iran', Zoie O'Brien, *Express News*, 01 Apr , 2017, Report: Saudi Arabia Still Seeking Nuclear Weapons Capability, Adam Kredo, 31 March, 2017. http://freebeacon.com/national-security/report-saudi-arabia-still-seeking-nuclear-weapons-capability/, Why Saudi Arabia can't get a nuclear weapon, Fareed Zakaria, *Washington Post*, 11 June, 2015, https://www.washingtonpost.com/opinions/saudi-arabias-nuclear-bluff/2015/06/11/9ce1f4f8-1074-11e5-9726-49d6fa26a8c6_story.html?utm_term=.5f01847e6831,

Report: Saudi Arabia Still Seeking Nuclear Weapons Capability. A new report by the Institute for Science and International Security indicates that "Saudi Arabia is in the early stages of nuclear development" and is expected to "more actively seek nuclear weapons capabilities", Ami Rojkes Dombe, 02 April 2017, *Israel Defence*, http://www.israeldefense.co.il/en/node/29097

8   *BBC*, 18 November 2017

9   *The Guardian* 11 July 2011

10 *Forbes* report, 11 October, 2013

11 *BBC*, 15 July 2015

12 *Dawn*, 10 March 2014, the newspaper reported Prime Minister Nawaz Sharif visit to Saudi Arabia to discuss the issue of bomb transfer.

13 *Daily Star*, 28 March 2014

14 *Dawn*, 10 March 2014

15 *Reuter*, 10 April 2015

16 In March 2015, *Dawn* reported Prime Minister Nawaz Sharif visited Saudi Arabia and discussed issues of mutual understanding.

17 *Dawn*, 08 March 2015

18 Ibid

19 Saudi Investment in Pakistan nuclear weapons, *Daily Times*, 13 November 2013

20 *Al Monitor*, 19 February 2018

21 Prospect of Nuclear Jihad, 2015, the Conversation, 06 March 2018, https://theconversation.com/why-pakistan-has-troops-in-saudi-arabia-and-what-it-means-for-the-middle-east-92613, Why Saudi Arabia needs Pakistan: Pakistan may be Saudi Arabi's best bet for a strong long-term security guarantee. Akhilesh Pillalamarri , March 12, 2015, https://thediplomat.com/2015/03/why-saudi-arabia-needs-pakistan/

22 Ibid

23 *CNN*, 12 December 2017

24 *India Today*, 27 June 2014

25 Ibid

26 *Dawn*, 15 July 2017. Iraqi Ambassador to Pakistan thanked the country miltablishment for its military contribustion, The Baghdad Post, 15 July 2015.

27 Saudi Arabia's nuclear Thinking and the Pakistani Connection, Reshmi Kazi, 07 January, 2014, The Institute for Defence Studies and Analyses (IDSA) http://www.idsa.in/issuebrief/SaudiArabiasNuclearThinkingandPakistan_rkazi_070114

28 Ibid

29 *Dawn* February 2014

30 08 February 2014, *Daily Naya Akhbar*

31 *Ummat Daily*, 08 February 2014

32 Ibid

33 *Dawn*, 07 March 2014

34 *Dawn*, 07 March 2014

35 *Ibid*

36 *The Friday Times*, 21 March 2014

37 *Ibid*

38 *Dawn*, 20 March 2014

39 *Daily Times*, 19 March 2014

40 Battling Terrorism: Legal Perspective on the use of Force and the War on Terror, Jackson Nyamuya Maogoto, Routledge, 2005

41 Ibid

42 *Express Tribune*, 12 May 2011

43 *Reuter* 21 May 2011, *Pakistan Today* 12 March 2011, *AryNews* 13 June 2015, and *The Nation*, 05 February 2015

44 *The Mail*, 21 Febraury 2015

45 *Dawn*, 21 February 2015

46 Ibid

47 *Shiite News*, 02 March 2015, http://www.shiitenews.org/index.php/pakistan/item/14320-riyadh-summon-nawaz-due-to-unveiling-of-saudi-funding-to-pakistani-terrorists

48 *Dawn*, 20 January 2015

49 Ibid

50 *Homeland Security news* Wire,19 February 2015

51 Ibid

52 Issue Brief: The Global Regime for Terrorism, Report by International Institutions and Global Governance Program, Council on Foreign Relations, 31 August 2011

53 *The Guardian*, 18 October 2013

54 *American Thinker*, 2013

55 Ibid

56 *American Thinker* 2013, On 07 September 2012, George Washington University document of US counter terrorism efforts from National Security Archive Electronic Briefing Book No. 388

57 *Jerusalem Post*, 25 June 2014

58 Ibid

59 The Afghan Intel crisis, Musa Khan Jalalzai, New York

60 National Crisis Management Cell of Pakistan, 2013

61 *Daily Times*, 13 November 2013

62 The Afghan Intel crisis, Musa Khan Jalalzai, New York

63 Nuclear Fatwa: Religion and Politics in Iran's Proliferation Strategy, Michael Eisenstadt and Mehdi Khalaji, Washington Institute, September 2011, *Friday Times*, 11 April 2014, Islamic Bomb, Belfer Centre, 1 January 2011, and Arms Control networks, 25 November 2015

64 *Moscow Times*, October 2017

65 *The Independent* 05 October 2017

66 Ibid

67 *The Independent* 13 October 2017

Notes to Chapter 4

1 Pranay Kotasthane, "An Assessment of Indian and Pakistani Nuclear Forces", *Pragati – The Indian National Interest Review*, January 6, 2016.

2 Hans Kristensen and Robert Norris, "Pakistani Nuclear Forces, 2015 and Indian Nuclear Forces, 2015," *Bulletin of the Atomic Scientists*, 2016.

3 H Nayyar and Zia Mian, "Pakistan and the Nasr Missile: Searching for a Method in the Madness," *Economic and Political Weekly*, 50, no. 39, September 2015)

4 Declassified US National Security Council Net Evaluation Committee Reports on "Management and Termination of War with Soviet Union", 1947-63, courtesy Maj Gen P Mullick

5 Lt Gen BS Nangal, "No First Use", *Force Magazine*, December 2014.

6 Christine M Leah, "Tactical Nuclear Weapons and Deterrence", The

Diplomat, June 12, 2015

7 Maj Gen P K Chakravorty, "Tactical Nuclear Weapons in Current Indo-Pak Environment", Vivekananda International Foundation, November 2016.

8 Ali Ahmed, "At the Conventional-Nuclear Interface", IDR Net Edition, August 2014.

Notes to Chapter 5

1 ISIS is now waging a sectarian war in Afghanistan– and even the Taliban oppose it, Milo Comerford, *Independent*, 28 July 2016. https://www.independent.co.uk/voices/isis-in-afghanistan-sectarian-war-taliban-opposes-it-middle-east-islamic-state-islamism-a7158146.html. Country Report on Terrorism, July 2017, US Department of State.

2 *Economist*, 04 October 2001

3 Ibid

4 Cahal Milmo, 08 September 2017, *I News* UK

5 *Time magazine*, 10 April, 2017 http://time.com/4728293/uranium-underworld-dark-secrets-dirty-bombs/

6 *Times of India*, 25 August 2017

7 Ibid

8 *The Diplomat*, 11 January 2018

9 Lowy Institute, 25 October 2017,https://www.lowyinstitute.org/publications/accident-waiting-happen-trump-putin-and-us-russia-relationship

10 Moshe Kantor. *Washington Times*, 23 March, 2017, https://www.washingtontimes.com/news/2017/mar/23/nuclear-terrorism-a-real-threat/

11 Pakistan's Nuclear Weapons: Proliferation and Security Issues. CRS report for Congress, Paul K. Kerr, Diane Publishing, 2010

12 Central Asia: A Nuclear–Terrorism Nexus? Sophie Henderson, 6 April 2017, Proliferation and Nuclear Policy, Central and South Asia, Royal United Services Institute for Strategic Studies, London https://rusi.org/commentary/central-asia-nuclear%E2%80%93terrorism-nexus

13 Nuclear Terrorism: The New Terror of the 21st Century. Reshmi Kazi, *IDSA Monograph series*, December 2013

14 *The Diplomat*, 01 February 2017

15 The Crisis of Britain's Surveillance State, Mus Khan Jalalzai 2014

16 Terrorist Tactics in Pakistan Threaten Nuclear Weapons Safety, Shaun Gregory, Journal of combating Terrorism Centre, Volume 4, Issue 6, June 2011, https://ctc.usma.edu/terrorist-tactics-in-pakistan-threaten-nuclear-weapons-safety/

17 The Atlantic Cover Story: Pakistan, the Ally from Hell, Jeffrey Goldberg, *The Atlantic Magazine*, 04 November 2011, https://www.theatlantic.com/international/archive/2011/11/the-atlantic-cover-story-pakistan-the-ally-from-hell/247886/

18 The Nation, 22 August 2008

19 Ibid

20 *Dawn*,16 August 2012

21 *Dawn*, 18 September 2015

22 Ibid

23 Ibid

24 *The News International*, 22 May 2011

25 Ibid

26 Defence Forum India: The distrust: Can India ever trust Pakistan's religiously zealot polity and its jihadi generals? 19 May 2017. http://defenceforumindia.com/distrust-can-india-ever-trust-pakistans-religiously-zealot-polity-jehadi-generals-2220

27 On 01 April 2016, in the *Australian newspaper*, Catherine Philp report

28 *The New York Times*, 09 August 2013

29 *Express Tribune*, 06 September 2012

30 *Express Tribune*, 01 April 2016, and *Sunday Express*, 30 June 2015

31 02 April 2016, *Defence News*

32 Mr. Joseph V. Micallef in his *Huffpost*, 07 February 2017

33 On 23 May 2015, *Express Tribune* of Pakistan reproduced the Independent article that reported the Islamic State (ISIL) resolve to obtain Pakistan's nuclear weapons within a year

34 23 May 2015, *Express Tribune*

35 30 January 2017, *Small War Journal* research paper, Sajid Farid Shapoo

36 General Pervez Musharraf said terrorists like Osama bin Laden and the Taliban were heroes for Pakistan. Mr. Musharraf admitted that Pakistan supported and trained groups like Lashkar-e-Toiba (LeT) in 1990s to carry out militancy in Kashmir, *Indian Express*, On 28 October 2015

37 Ibid

38 The undeclared war between Afghanistan and Pakistan is intensifying and almost taking the shape of a declared war, President Ashraf Ghani said on his visit to India. On 17 September 2017, *Ariana News* reported Afghan President hammered Pakistan for its undeclared war against Afghanistan, *NDTV* also reported President Ghani remarks.

39 *Reuter*, 16 July 2016

40 Ibid

41 Ibid

42 Ibid

43 Ibid

44 Sanction Pakistan as State Sponsor of Terror, 23 February 2017, Journalist Anders Corr, *Forbes*

45 05 April 2017, JK Verma, *Aviation & Defence*

46 *Daily Times*, 08 June 2015

47 Ibid

48 Pakistan's Nuclear Use Doctrine, Sadia Tasleem, Carnegie Endowment for International Peace, 30 June 2015, http://carnegieendowment.org/2016/06/30/pakistan-s-nuclear-use-doctrine-pub-63913

49 *Express Tribune*, 08 April 2017

50 *India Today*, 29, 08 2016

51 Why Pakistan supports terrorists groups, and why the US finds it so hard to induce change, Vanda Felbab-Brown, Brooking, 05 January 2018, https://www.brookings.edu/blog/order-from-chaos/2018/01/05/why-pakistan-supports-terrorist-groups-and-why-the-us-finds-it-so-hard-to-induce-change/

52 01 April 2016, *the Times*

53 *The National Interest*, 21 April 2015

54 *Daily Times*, 08 June 2915

55 Ibid

56 *Pajhwok Afghan News*, 06 June 6, 2015

Notes to Chapter 6

1 *Dawn*, 01 October 2017

2 The ISI Role in Pakistan's Politics, Dr. Bidanda M. Chengappa, Senior Fellow, IDSA, https://www.idsa-india.org/an-feb00-2.html

3 India's former National Security Advisor, Shiv Shankar Memon told Indian Express that increasing risk to Pakistan nuclear weapons was from army not terrorists. *Indian Express*, 13 October 2016.

4 On 13 October 2016, *Hindustan Times* reported India's former National Security Advisor, Shiv shankar Memon told Indian Express that increasing risk to Pakistan nuclear weapons was from army not terrorists.

5 Are Nuclear Weapons Pushing India and Pakistan Towards War? Preteek Joshi, *The National Interests*, 08 December 2016, http://nationalinterest.org/blog/the-buzz/are-nuclear-weapons-pushing-india-pakistan-towards-war-18664

6 Ibid

7 On 17 April 2017 *Dawn* reported Director General of Inter-Services Public Relations (ISPR), Maj Gen Asif Ghafoor, announced that Mr. Ehsanullah Ehsan, former spokesperson of the Tehreek-e-Taliban Pakistan (TTP) and a senior leader of the Jamaat-ul-Ahrar, had turned himself in to Pakistan's security agencies

8 *Daily Times*, 17 April 2017

9 *The News International*, 30 April 2017, Azaz Syed, https://www.thenews.com.pk/print/201621-Ehsan-returned-on-terms-of-revealing-Taliban-secrets

10 *Dawn*, 26 April 2017

11 *Ibid*

12 Transcript of Ehsanullah Ehsan's 'confession', *the Hindu newspaper*, 26 April 2017

13 Why the surrender of Ehsanullah Ehsan is important for Pakistan, Marvi Sirmed, *Daily Times*, 20, April 17, http://dailytimes.com.pk/pakistan/20-Apr-17/why-the-surrender-of-ehsanullah-ehsan-is-important-for-pakistan

14 Ibid

15 In 2015, *International Crisis Group* (ICG) hammered Pakistan's counter-

terrorism measures

16 *The Friday Times*, 07 July 2017

17 On 06 January 2015, *Dawn*

18 *The News*, 04, September 2013

19 *Express Tribune*, 12 October 2017

20 *Dawn*,Prime Minister Nawaz Sharif speech in General Assembly, 2014

21 *The Diplomat*, 10 July 2017

22 Ibid

23 *Egypt Indpendent*, 01 December 2017

24 *The National Bureau of Asian Research*, Arun Sahgal, 2012

25 Uphill Challenges: China's Military Modernization and Asian Security, Ashley J. Tellis, *The National Bureau of Asian Research*

26 Is Narendra Modi's government unravelling? Soutik Biswas, *BBC News*, 26 February 2016

27 *Global Solutions*, Preventing Nuclear Terrorism: Nuclear Security, the Nonproliferation Regime, and the Threat of Terrorist Nukes, Samuel Kane, https://globalsolutions.org/files/public/documents/Sam-Kane-Preventing-Nuclear-Terrorism.pdf

28 Fighting Religious Extremism, Farooq Tariq, International Institute of Research and Education–Manila, 2017

Notes to Chapter 7

1 Talking to a local TV Channel, *GeoNews*, 17 September 2016

2 Khawaja Asif speech in a book launching ceremony in 2016, *The News* reported

3 *Daily Times*, 08 June 2015

4 Ibid

5 Ibid

6 Ibid

7 Council on Foreign Relations report, 17 August 2017

8 On 01 August 2016, The US Congressional Research Service in its paper reported Pakistan's three civilian power reactors

9 The new nuclear age, the *Economist*, 15 March 2015, https://www.economist. com/news/leaders/21645729-quarter-century-after-end-cold-war-world-faces-growing-threat-nuclear

10 *Dawn*, 04 March 2015

11 *Wall Street Journal*, 11 March 2015

12 The Four Faces of Nuclear terrorism Making the Bom, Lose material and Know How, Charles D. Ferguson, William C. Potter, Routledge, 21 Aug 2012

13 Calculating new Global terrorism Threat, International Atomic Energy Agency, 27 October 2001 https://www.iaea.org/newscenter/pressreleases/calculating-new-global-nuclear-terrorism-threat

14 10 June 2014, terrorists were facilitated by their colleagues within the army to enter the Karachi airport. Once again, the law enforcement and intelligence apparatus were shown to be inadequate.

15 Researchgate, Rajesh M. Basrur and Prof. Friedrich Steinhäusler paper

16 The Changing Dimensions of Security: India's Security Policy Options. Dr. Suresh R. Vij Books, India, 01 January 2016

17 James E. Doyle, 2013 Why Eliminate Nuclear Weapons?, *Survival*

18 Jihadists and Weapons of Mass Destruction, Gary Ackerman, Jeremy Tamsett, CRC Press, 03 Feb 2009

19 Deterring nuclear terrorism: Reflections from Islamabad, Sadia Tasleem, 5 June 2013, Bulletin of Nuclear Scientists, http://thebulletin.org/nuclear-deterrence-and-terrorism-implications-global-security/deterring-nuclear-terrorism

20 What Can Destroy Strategic Stability: Nuclear Terrorism Is a Real Threat, Vladimir Dvorkin, Belfer Center for Science and International Affairs, 21 September, 2012. http://www.belfercenter.org/publication/what-can-destroy-strategic-stability-nuclear-terrorism-real-threat

21 It's mostly about N-Pakistan, Munir Akram, *Dawn* 02 February, 2014, https://www.dawn.com/news/1084338

22 *BBC*, 10 July 2014

23 The Possibility of WMD Terrorism, Mushfiq Murshed, *Criterion*, 31 October 2013, Vol 8 No 4, WMD, http://www.criterion-quarterly.com/the-possibility-of-wmd-terrorism/

24 Researchgate, Rajesh M. Basrur and Prof. Friedrich Steinhäusler paper, https://www.researchgate.net/publication/228896301_Nuclear_and_Radiological_Terrorism_Threats_for_India_Risk_Potential_and_

Countermeasures

25 *Outlook India*, 24 January 2004

26 Terrorism and Weapons of Mass Destruction, Gabriel H. Oosthuizen and Elizabeth Wilmshurst, Chatam House, September 2004, https://www.chathamhouse.org/sites/files/chathamhouse/public/Research/International%20Law/ILP0904bp.

27 Dengue, Measles and Polio, Weapons of Bioterrorism in Pakistan, November 25, 2014, Dr. Agha Inamullah Khan,http://www.zemtv.com/2014/11/25/dengue-measles-and-polio-weapons-of-bio-terrorism-in-pakistan/

28 *Global Policy Journal*, 2013

29 Bioterror in the 21st Century: Emerging Threats in a New Global Environment, Daniel Gerstein, Naval Institute Press, 07 Dec 2010

30 Central Asia, Kashmir Face New Jihadi Threat; Concerns in Russia, by Ramtanu Maitr, 29 Oct 2013

31 Extremist, Nuclear Pakistan: An Emerging Threat? Subodh Atal, CARO Institute,March 5, 2003, https://www.cato.org/publications/policy-analysis/extremist-nuclear-pakistan-emerging-threat

Notes to Chapter 8

1 Country Reports on Terrorism 2016

2 Ibid

3 Whose army, PP: 17 and 18

4 BMD and MIRV Technology in South Asia and Implication for Region, Asma Khalid, EuroAsia Review, 17 April 2017, https://www.eurasiareview.com/about-2/

5 Nuclear battles in South Asia, Pervez Hoodbhoy and Zia Mian, Bulletin of the Atomic Scientists, 04 May 2016, *Bulletin of the Atomic Scientists*, http://thebulletin.org/nuclear-battles-south-asia9415

6 South Asian nuclear arms race accelerates amid India-Pakistan standoff, By Sampath Perera, 28 February 2017, *World socialist Website.*

7 India successfully tested Prothvi defence Vehicle, a new missile killer system, Franz Stefan Gady, 15 February 2017, https://thediplomat.com/2017/02/india-successfully-tests-prithvi-defense-vehicle-a-new-missile-killer-system/

8 India's Gilgit Baltistan Problem-Part one: Pakistan's dependence on Gilgit

Baltistan, Vikas Kumar, 11 July 2017, FDI Associates

9   Professor Dr. Hoodbhoy, 28 May 2011. Bioterrorism Threat in south Asia, *Daily Times*, 06 October 2014

10 *Daily Times*, 06 October 2014

11 Ibid

12 Ibid

13 On 26 September 2014, *Dawn* reported the outgoing Peshawar corps commander Gen Khalid Rabbani expressed deep concern about the militancy problem in Pakistan.

14 India's First Secretary address to the UN General Asembly 29 December 2014

15 Nuclear terrorism Prevention at crossroads, Kenneth N, and Luongo Kenneth, Reuters, March 24, 2014, http://blogs.reuters.com/great-debate/2014/03/23/nuclear-terrorism-prevention-at-a-crossroads/

16 Bioterrorism Threat In south Asia, Daily Times, 06 October 2014

17 Dr. Pervez Hoodbhoy, *Express Tribune*, 28 May 2011

18 16 May, 2009, Israeli website, *Debka* report

19 July 2012, the EU non-proliferation consortium non- proliferation paper No: 19

20 Pakistan's nuclear and WMD programmes: status, evolution and risks, Bruno tertrais, *EU Non-Proliferation Consortium*, Non-Proliferation Papers, No-19, July 2012. https://www.files.ethz.ch/isn/151272/brunotertrais5010305e17790.pdf

21 *IDSA Monograph Series*, No. 27 October 2013, nuclear terrorism: The New terror of the 21st century, Reshmi Kazi. Islamic State (ISIS) in Pakistan would be to obtain fissile material necessary to construct a Nuclear Explosive Device, and use it against civilian or military installations.

22 Ibid

23 James Martin Centre for Non-proliferation studies, 13 November 2012

24 On 03, March, 2014, *Daily Dawn* reported a London based scholar's remarks about Pakistan's nuclear danger. The author voiced alarm about Pakistan's nuclear arsenal, the world's fastest growing, which he said would likely expand until at least 2020.

25 Ibid

Notes to Chapter 9

1   *The Mail*, 16 September 2016

2   *Al Jazeera*, 07 February 2015

3   The changing nature of state sponsor terrorism, Daniel L. Byman, Analysis paper number-6, 16 May 2008

4   Ibid

5   Taliban and Islamic State: Enemies or Brothers in Jihad? Dr. Antonio Giustozzi, Centre for Research and Policy Analysis, 14 December, 2017

6   Pakistan Transports its Nukes in everyday Vans, John Hudson, 04 November 2011, *The Atlantic*, https://www.theatlantic.com/international/archive/2011/11/pakistan-transports-its-nukes-everyday-vans/335924/

7   *Daily Times*, 03 October 2013

8   Ibid

9   *Daily Times*, 03 October 2013

10 Ibid

11 Ibid

12 Islamic State could steal Pakistan's nuclear weapons and make 'dirty bomb', defence analysts warn, Ashraf Ali, *ABC News*, 20 Apr 2016, http://www.abc.net.au/news/2016-04-20/growing-concerns-is-could-steal-nuclear-weapons/7342722

13 *Daily Times*, 03 October 2013

14 The Evolution of Cooperative Threat Reduction: Issues for Congress, Mary Beth D. Nikitin, Amy F. Woolf, Congressional Research Service, 13 June, 2014

15 Ibid

16 *Daily Times*, 03 October 2013

17 Ibid

18 *Dawn*, 26 March 2018

19 The Nuclear Tipping Point: Prospects for a World of Many Nuclear Weapons States, Mitchell B. Reiss

20 *Daily Times*, 03 October 2013

21 *Hindustan Times*, 19 June 2014

22 Ibid

23 The Afghan Intel Crisis, Musa khan Jalalzai, new York

24 Nuclear arms race in South Asia, Musa Khan Jalalzai, *Daily Times*, 06 July 2015

25 Ibid

26 Ibid

27 Journalist Ramesh Thakur, *Japan Times*, 07 October 2016

28 Ibid

29 Possibility of Nuclear Armageddon in South Asia, Zainab Aziz, 30 March 2017.

30 *Dawn*, 29 September 2014

31 Ibid

32 Four Disturbing Questions about the Mumbai Terror Attack: Despite extensive evidence and a U.S. indictment, Pakistani authorities haven't moved to arrest accused masterminds in the 2008 massacre or explain the alleged involvement of officers in Pakistan's spy agency. Sebastian Rotella, Propublica, 22 February 2013.

33 *Daily Times*, 28 September 2014

34 Ibid

35 Nuclear arms race in South Asia, Musa Khan Jalalzai, *Daily Times*, 06 July 2015

36 Ibid

37 *Express Tribune*, 27 September 2013

38 *NDTV*, 10 October 2014

39 *Indian Express*, 07 May 2017

40 *The Star*, 09 October 2014

41 *Dawn*, 09 October 2014

42 Ibid

43 *Daily Mail*, 09 October 2014

44 Ibid

45 India, Pakistan and the Nuclear Race Institute of peace and conflict studies,

04 April 2013

46 Ibid

47 How Pakistan and China are strengthening nuclear ties, Krista Mahr, *Time Magazine*, 02 December 013

48 Pakistan and India: Race to the End, Tom Hundley, Pulitzer Centre, 05 September 2012, https://pulitzercenter.org/reporting/pakistan-and-india-race-end

49 *Japan Times*, 19 April 2013

50 Ibid

51 *The Indian Express*, 22 March 2016

52 On May 2015, an article in the official magazine of ISIS claims that the terror army has the financial wherewithal to purchase a nuclear weapon, possibly from corrupt officials in Pakistan.

53 North Korea's Bomb Made in Pakistan, Madhav Nalapat, *Sunday Guardian*, 25 September, 2016, http://www.sundayguardianlive.com/investigation/6641-north-korea-s-bomb-made-pakistan

54 Former Chinese nuclear engineer: 'We've been transferring nuclear technology to Pakistan', 28 February 2017, *NDTV* News reported indirect Chinese nuclear technology cooperation with Pakistan.

55 The China-Pakistan axis gathers momentum, Prof. Harsh V. Pant, *Japan Times*, 28 April 2016, http://www.japantimes.co.jp/opinion/2016/04/18/commentary/world-commentary/china-pakistan-axis-gathers-momentum.

56 *Asia Programme Paper* ASP PP 2012/01, the China-Pakistan, Alliance: Rhetoric and Limitations. Rosheen Kabraji

57 Pakistan's Tactical Nukes: Relevance and Options for India, Arka Biwas, 05 October 2017, https://www.tandfonline.com/doi/abs/10.1080/016366 0X.2017.1370355?src=recsys&journalCode=rwaq20, Pakistan's Nuclear Weapons Programme: 5 Things you Need to Know, Akhilesh Pillalamarri, The National Interests, 21 April 2015, https://www.tandfonline.com/doi/abs/10.1080/0163660X.2017.1370355?src=recsys&journalCode=rwaq20

58 *Insight & Opinion*, Syed Fazl-e-Haider, 01 September 2014

59 *Wall Street Journal*, 15 November 2012

60 Ibid

61 Ibid

62 The Diplomat, 15 February 2015

63 *Dawn*, 24 November 2014

64 President Barack Obama and Prime Minister Narendra Modi meeting in New Delhi on 25 January 2015

65 Indian Prime Minister Narendra Modi and US president Barack Obama have announced they have reached an agreement to break the deadlock that has been stalling a civilian nuclear power agreement. ANC News, 25 January 2015. Obama and Modi agree to limit US liability in case of nuclear disaster, Decision set to lead to contracts worth billions of dollars but hopes for a US-China-style air pollution deal are dashed, Dan Roberts, *the Guardian*, 25 January 2015

66 Ibid

67 Ibid

68 The US War in Afghanistan-1999-2019. The Taliban insurgency remains resilient sixteen years after US-led forces toppled its regime in what led to the United States' longest war. Council of Foreign Relations

69 The Chemical, Biological, Radiological, and Nuclear Terrorism Threat from the Islamic State, Carole N. House, 2016

70 *Daily Times*, 21 July 2014

71 Ibid

72 ISIS storms Saddam-era chemical weapons complex in Iraq, Facility containing disused stores of sarin and mustard gas overrun by jihadist group, *Telegraph*, 19 Jun 2014, Times, Iraq Militants Seize Old Chemical Weapons Facility, Noah Rayman, Jun 19, 2014, http://time.com/2901562/iraq-isis-chemical-weapons/, The Politics of Weapons Inspections: Assessing WMD Monitoring and Verification Regimes, Nathan E. Busch, Joseph F. Pilat, Stanford University Press, 21 Mar 2017

73 Security Council Urges Greater Collective Efforts to Prevent Terrorists from Acquiring Weapons, Unanimously Adopting Resolution 2370-2017, SC/12938 SECURITY COUNCIL 8017TH MEETING (AM), 2 AUGUST 2017, https://www.un.org/press/en/2017/sc12938.doc.htm

74 Telegraph, London, 02 April 2017

75 Ibid

76 *Daily Times*, 21 July 2014

77 *Daily Times*, 21 July 2014

78 Ibid

79   Ibid

80   Ibid

81   *APP news agency*

82   Ibid

83   Ibid

84   On 05 May 2006, Baloch militants attacked the dumping site near Baghalchur Uranium mine in Dera Ghazi Khan District. In 2007, terrorists attacked two air force facilities in Sargodha, associated with nuclear installations. There are two F-16 squadrons in Sargodha. On 21 August 2008, terrorists attacked Ordinance Factories in Wah. In July 2009, a suicide bomber struck a bus that may have been carrying A.Q Khan Research Laboratory scientists. In this incident 30 people injured

85   Nuclear jihad in Pakistan, Musa Khan Jalalzai, 2015, New York

86   TAC Nukes in South Asia, Michael Krepon Arms Control Work, 18 April, 2012

87   Ibid

88   IPCS Debate: India, Pakistan and Tactical Nuclear Weapons: Irrelevance for South Asia, Amit Gupta, 06 January, 2014

89   Ibid

90   Pakistan's Tactical Nuclear Weapons. Conflict Redux, Gurmeet Kanwal, K.W Publisher, 2013

91   *The Diplomat*, 02 January 2013

92   Nuclear Notebook: Pakistan's nuclear forces, 2011, Hans M. KristensenRobert S. Norris, 04 JULY 2011. *The Bulletin of the Atomic Scientists*, http://thebulletin.org/background-and-mission-1945-2017

93   On 12 September 2013, *Reuter* reported think tank at the International Institute for Strategic Studies, in which experts panel expressed deep concern on the safety and security of nuclear weapons in South Asia

94   Ibid

95   Ibid

96   Ibid

97   Illicit Radiological and Nuclear Trafficking, Smuggling and Security Incidents in the Black Sea Region since the Fall of the Iron Curtain – an Open Source Inventory, by Alex P. Schmid & Charlotte Spencer-Smith,

Perspectives on Terrorism is a *journal of the Terrorism Research Initiative and the Center for Terrorism and Security Studies, Vol 6, No 2,* 2012. http://www. terrorismanalysts.com/pt/index.php/pot/about

98   *Bloomberg-TV*, April 2014

99   Ibid

100   Ibid

101   22 June 2014, *Daily the Frontiers Post*

102   Ibid

103   Ibid

104   Future World of Illicit Nuclear Trade Mitigating the Threat, David Albright, Andrea Stricker, Houston Wood, July 29, 2013, Institute for Science and International Security, http://isis-online.org/uploads/isis-reports/documents/Full_Report_DTRA-PASCC_29July2013-FINAL.

105   Pakistan nuclear weapons at risk of theft by terrorists, US study warns, Julian Borger, the Guardian, Mon 12 Apr 2010

106   A Scenario for Jihadist Revenge: The Greatest Threat, Edward A. Friedman, Federation of American Scientists (FAS), 05 June 2014

107   *World Affairs Journal,* 2011, Neil Padukone

108   Preventing Nuclear Terrorism: Nuclear Security, the Non-proliferation Regime, and the Threat of Terrorist Nukes, Samuel Kane, Preventing Nuclear Terrorism: Nuclear Security, the Non-proliferation Regime, and the Threat of Terrorist Nukes" was drafted by Samuel Kane as a project conducted in the summer of 2012 while serving as a Research Associate at GlobalSolutions.org. https://globalsolutions.org/files/public/documents/Sam-Kane-Preventing-Nuclear-Terrorism.pdf

109   Too Close for Comfort Cases of near Nuclear Use and Options for Policy, April 2014, Dr Patricia Lewis, Sasan Aghlani, also, Nuclear Black Markets: Pakistan, A.Q. Khan and the Rise of Proliferation Networks – A Net Assessment, (London: The International Institute for Strategic Studies, 2007, Nuclear Black Markets: Pakistan, A.Q. Khan and the Rise of Proliferation Networks, International Institute for Strategic Studies, 2007, and Mr. Umer Farooq, "Pakistan Tests New Missile and Revises Command Structure," *Jane's Defence Weekly*, 16 February 2000, https://www.chathamhouse.org/publications/papers/view/199200

110   Nuclear Pakistan: Implications for National and International Security, Paper no.429. 2002, Dr. Rajesh Kumar Mishra, *South Asia Analysis Group*

111   The Iran deal and South Asia, Asif Ezdi, *the News International*, 03 August

2015, Mr. Asif also elucidated India's desire to be regarded as a rival of China for influence in Central Asia and has been making hectic plans to catch up with its northern neighbour. To match China's 'One Belt One Road' initiative for a network of infrastructure and energy projects to link China with Europe and the Middle East over land and by sea, Asif sees Delhi's revived plans for a transit corridor to Europe and Russia through Iran as a new development. https://www.thenews.com.pk/print/54378-the-iran-deal-and-south-asia

Notes to Chapter 10

1   *BBC*, 23 November 2016

2   Ibid

3   Pakistan 'Unprepared' for refugees fleeing operation against Taliban, Jon Boone. *The Guardian*, 26 Jun 2014

4   Nuclear Jihad in South Asia, Algora, 2015, new York

5   Lt General Aslam resigns after being superseded, Pakistan Today, 28 November 2013, and Lt General Aslam resigns after he fails to become Pakistan Army Chief, The Economic Times,28 Nov, 2013,

6   Ibid

7   Nuclear Jihad in Pakistan, Musa Khan Jalalzai, 2015

8   A Pakistani general steps into the middle of the Iran and Saudi firestorm, Bruce Riede, *the Daily Beast*, 10 may 2017

9   Pakistan Supreme Court Rules ousted PM Sharif cannot Lead his Party, Kay Johnson, Asif Shahzad, *Reuter*, 21 February 2018

10 *Dawn*,28 July 2017

11 Ibid

12 *The Bloomberg*, 28 July 2017

13 *Dawn*,28 July 2017

14 Ibid

15 Pakistan's Internal Security Challenges: Will Military Cope? Issue Brief, The Institute of Peace and conflict Studies (IPCS), 06 August 2013

16 Defenders of human rights in Balochistan in need of defence, Angelika Pathak, August 2011, http://reliefweb.int/sites/reliefweb.int/files/resources/AHRC-PRL-035-2011-01.pdf

17 *Dawn*, On 25 September 2017

18 Ibid

19 *Dawn*, 25 September 2017

20 The missing debate, I.A. Rehman, *Dawn*, September 10, 2017 1 Comment.

21 The United Nations counter-terrorism Complex: Bureaucracy, political Influence and Civil Liberties, United Nations, 23 February, 2017

22 *Dawn*, 28 August 2017

23 Ibid

24 *The News International*, 10 Sep 2017, Mr. Sher Ali Khalti noted important facts of missing persons in Baluchistan and Khyber Pakhtunkhawa provinces.

25 *India Today* 02 September 2016

26 *Dawn*, 25 August 2016

27 Samar Abbas, Enforced disappearances continue in Pakistan, *International Press Agency*, 16.July 2017

28 30 August 2017, World Sindh Congress and Asian Human Rights Commission (AHRC), Voice of Baloch Missing Persons (VBMP) and Rightsnow joint report.

29 *Dawn*, 30 July 2017

30 Ibid

31 Enforced Disappearances and Extrajudicial killings of Workers in Pakistan, The Indian Panorama, 04 August 2017, https://www.theindianpanorama.news/unitedstates/enforced-disappearances-extra-judicial-killings-workers-pakistan/

32 *The News*, 30 July 2017, Amnesty International, 06 November 2017

33 Human Rights Commission of Pakistan Report, 2009

34 Ibid, and also US Department of State, 2009 Country Reports on Human Rights Practices, Report, 11 March 2010

35 The mass graves of Baluchistan, Malik Siraj Akbar, *Huffpost*, https://www.huffingtonpost.com/malik-siraj-akbar/the-mass-graves-of-baloch_b_5696642.html

36 Ibid

37 Ibid

38 Assassinations Decimate Pakistan's Tribal Leadership, May 06, 2014, https://gandhara.rferl.org/a/assassinations-decimate-pakistans-tribal-leadership/25374570.html, and also reported by; Foreign Affairs, How War Altered Pakistan's Tribal Areas: Cultural Change Comes to FATA, Umar Farooq, 06 October, 2017, https://www.foreignaffairs.com/articles/pakistan/2017-10-06/how-war-altered-pakistans-tribal-areas

39 15 November 2017, *Dawn report*

40 Ibid

41 Ibid

42 *Dawn*, 25 September 2016

43 Major Challenges For Pak Army 29 Decembe, 2014, Manish Rai, *The Times of Israel*, http://blogs.timesofisrael.com/major-challenges-for-pak-army/

44 Musa Khan Jalalzai, The Afghan Intel crisis, 2017, New York

Notes to Chapter 11

1   National Action Plan: Implementation Gaps & Successes, Shakeel Ahmed Ramay, Sustainable Development Policy Studies, October 2016).

2   Is Pakistan's National Action Plan Actually Working? Two years after Pakistan unveiled its strategy for fighting terrorism, the results are mixed. Zeeshan Salahuddin, *the Diplomat*, December 24, 2016.

3   Ibid

4   Pakistan's National Security Adviser on Counterterrorism: Lt. Gen. Janjua speaks about his strategy and his views on current progress in Pakistan's fight on terror. Zeeshan Salahuddin, April 07, 2017

5   Ibid

6   Pervez Musharraf forms 'Grand Alliance' of 23 political parties. The grand alliance named Pakistan Awami Ittehad (PAI) will be headed by 74-year-old Musharraf, while Iqbal Dar has been appointed as Secretary General, 11 November 2017. http://www.freepressjournal.in/world/pervez-musharraf-forms-grand-alliance-of-23-political-parties/1168747.Also, Countering Violent Extremism: Evaluating Pakistan's Counter Radicalization and De radicalization Initiatives, Abdul Basit, *IPRI Journal* XV, no. 2. 2015

7   Security experts view these counter-measures as flawed and brutal for the reason that this unprofessional security approach cannot restore the confidence of minorities, ethnicities and political parties. The Afghan Intelligence crisis, Musa Khan Jalalzai, Algora, New York, 2017

8   The prospect of Nuclear Jihad in Pakistan, PP; 143

9   Ibid

10 Ibid

11 Pakistan's military is waging a quiet war on journalists: As activists and journalists are kidnapped, entire regions of the country are going silent. Kiran Nazish, 27 March 2018

12 The Afghan Intelligence Crisis, Musa Khan Jalalzai, New York, 2017

13 Ibid

14 Ibid

15 Role of Pakistan Police in Counterinsurgency, Hassan Abbas, Research Fellow, Belfer Centre, Harvard University, Brookings Counterinsurgency and Pakistan Paper Series, No. 5 Terrorism & Political Islam: Origin, Ideology, and Methods. A Counterterrorism Textbook, 2nd Edition, Erich Iviarquartd, and Christopher Heffelfinger https://www.aclu.org/files/fbimappingfoia/20111019/ACLURM000540.pdf

16 The Afghan Intel Crisis, Musa Khan Jalalzai

17 A Bullet has been chosen for you: Attacks on journalist in Pakistan. Amnesty International 2014, https://www.amnesty.org.uk/files/pakistan_journalists_300414.pdf

18 Agha Khaild, 29 August 2013, the News International Pakistan

19 *The News International*, 26 August 2013

20 Agency men found involved in kidnapping of traders. *The News International*, 29 August 2013, Pakistan. https://www.thenews.com.pk/archive/print/632694-agency-men-found-involved-in-kidnapping-of-traders

21 Dawn, 01 April 2018

22 I.A Rehman, *Dawn*, 16 March 2017

23 Ibid

24 *Dawn*, 06 January 2017

25 *Dawn*, 12 October 2017

26 Ibid

27 *Outlook India*, 30 October 2017

28 The Unrepresented Nations and People Organization (UNPO), and the Frontline Defenders organizations condemned their disappearance,

Pakhtunkhawa Times, 02 November 2017; Jalazai's book also reported it (The Prospect of Nuclear Jihad in Pakistan, Musa Khan Jalalzai, Algora Publishing, New York.

29 UNPO Strongly Condemns the Enforced Disappearance of Baloch Activists' Families. 02 Nov, 2017. The Unrepresented Nations and People Organization (UNPO) is an international, nonviolent and democratic membership organisation. American Friends of Baluchistan (AFB) statement on attacks on Baloch and Pashtun students on Punjab University campus, Lahore, 24 January 2018

30 *South Asia Terrorism Portal*, March 2017

31 Baloch leader claims abduction of women, children part of Pak propaganda, Hyrbyair Marri also said both China and Pakistan were trying to annihilate the Baloch nation to strengthen their grip on its soil. Deccan Chronicle, Nov 2, 2017, https://www.deccanchronicle.com/world/europe/021117/baloch-leader-claims-abduction-of-women-children-part-of-pak-propaganda. html. Baloch women, children abduction part of Pak's campaign of enforced-disappearances. *Business Standard*, November 2, 2017, http://www.business-standard.com/article/news-ani/baloch-women-children-abduction-part-of-pak-s-campaign-of-enforced-disappearances-117110200501_1.html

32 Ibid

33 International Convention for the Protection of All Persons from Enforced Disappearance (ICPPED), United Nations Human Rights statement. States must put an end to widespread practice of enforced disappearances, International justice, 30 August 2017.

34 No More "Missing Persons": The Criminalization of Enforced Disappearance in South Asia, August 2017, International Commission of Jurists.

35 Ibid

36 Amnesty International in its report, 06 November 2017

37 *Dawn*, 07 December 2017

38 *Reuter*, 11 January 2017

39 *Dawn*, 07 December 2017

40 Ibid

41 Pakistan: Don't Reinstate Secret Military Courts: Fight Militancy by Reforming Justice System, Upholding Rule of Law. Human Rights Watch, 20 March, 2017 https://www.hrw.org/news/2017/03/20/pakistan-dont-reinstate-secret-military-courts, Dawn 24 January 2016, Military courts convicted 40 terrorists so far, The Nation, 09 January, 2016, Pakistan's

military courts: What did they achieve? A Pakistani law allowing military courts to try civilians on terror charges has expired. It's unclear if the government will extend the law, after criticism of the courts' legality and of their failure to curb terrorism. Pakistan's military courts: What did they achieve? *Deutsche Welles*, 07, 01, 2017.

42 Asian Human Rights Commission that celebrated the International Day of Victims of Enforced Disappearance on 30 August 2016 spotlighted Pakistan as a notorious country for enforced disappearances of individuals

43 20 September 2017, *Outlook India*

44 Ibid

45 Ibid

46 *Outlook India*, 20 September 2017. Risks to the lives of media men have increased the last few years. Moreover, war in Baluchistan, Khyber Pakhtunkhwa, Waziristan, Aurakzai and Karachi along with sectarian and ethnic terrorism and actions of 'murder squad' of the intelligence agencies have also led to the killings of local journalists.

47 *Dawn*, 09 February 2018

48 Ibid

49 Ibid

50 *Dawn*, 09 February 2018. In Baluchistan, the army used helicopter gunships, bombarded villages and destroyed the houses of the poor Baloch.

51 *Daily Times*, 19 February 2018

52 Ibid

53 The Afghan Intelligence Crisis, Musa Khan Jalalzai, 2017, New York

54 Ibid

55 Did Pakistani security agents kidnap bloggers to make a point? Pamela Constable *Washington Post* 14, 2017, https://www.washingtonpost.com/world/asia_pacific/did-pakistani-security-agents-kidnap-bloggers-to-make-a-point/2017/02/12/3f672d72-ed66-11e6-a100-fdaaf400369a_story.html?utm_term=.f1745c9c2267. Abducting social activists, Dr. Pervez, Hoodbhoy, Dawn 14 January, 2017, https://www.dawn.com/news/1308254

56 *Indian Express*, 10 September 2017

57 *Dawn*, 26 January 2018

58 *Tribune India*, 02 February 2018

59 *Dawn*, 26 January 2018

60 *The News International*, 26 January 2018

61 Ibid

62 *Afghanistan Times* Editorial: Pashtun Long March—soon to bear result 13 February, 2018

63 *Dawn* Investigation: Rao Anwar and the killing fields of Karachi: What kind of law-enforcement system accommodates and protects cops like the former Malir SSP? Fahim Zaman | Naziha Syed AliU, February 18, 2018

64 *Daily Times*, 19 February 2018

Notes to Chapter 12

1   *Dawn*, 14 August 2015

2   Ibid

3   Ibid

4   *Dunya News*, 14 August 2015

5   Ibid

6   26 September 2017, *Dawn report*

7   *NDTV* 26 September 2017

8   *The news International*, 26 September 2017

9   *The Nation*, 26 September 2017

10 *Dawn*, 26 September 2017

11 Ibid

12 The petition was filed on Sept 22, 2017 by Malik Asad.*Dawn* 01 October, 2017

13 Ibid

14 *Dawn*, 30 September 2017

15 *GeoNews*, 30 September 2017

16 *The News international* 30 September 2017

17 *Dawn*, 28 September 2017, Dawn

18 Ibid

19   *The Nation*, 29 September 2017

20   Cabinet assails 'fake news' about Nawaz Sharif's order to Intelligence Bureau, *Dawn*, 27 September, 2017.

21   Ibid

22   *Express Urdu News*, 06 October 2017

23   *Dawn*, 06 October 2017

24   *The Friday Times* 20 March 2011

25   Daily Times, 23 September 2017

26   Indian FM said: 'Pakistan export factory for terror', *Daily Times*. 23 September, 2017.

27   *Daily Outlook Afghanistan*, 06 October 2017

28   Pakistan military admits ISI has links to militant. *Times of India*, 06 October 2017

29   Academia's collaborative role in fostering Pakistani terror, *Asia Times*, F.M. Shakil 30 September 2017

30   *Express Tribune* 08 October 2017

31   *Dawn*, 10 October 2017

Notes to Postscript

1   The Prospect of Nuclear Jihad in Pakistan, PP: 145

2   Ibid

3   The Prospect of Nuclear Jihad in South Asia: Pakistan's Army, Extra-judicial Killings, and the Forceful Disappearance of Pashtuns and Balochs. Musa Khan Jalalzai, Algora Publishing, 01 Oct 2015

4   Ibid

5   The Afghan Intelligence Crisis, Musa Khan Jalalzai, Algora, New York, 2017

6   Ibid

7   Pakistan, Taliban and the Afghan Quagmire, Bruce RiedelSaturday, Brookings, August 24, 2013, https://www.brookings.edu/opinions/pakistan-taliban-and-the-afghan-quagmire/

8   Pakistan: reorganisation of intelligence infrastructure. Daily Times, Musa Khan Jalalzai, 24 March, 2014. In my argument on Pakistani agencies, I

warned that the agencies do not accept the authority of Parliamnet. The ISI and MI so often proved that they are stronger than the country's parliament; they can make parliament, and they can dissolve it. In one of my articles in Daily Times, I argued that the case of Mr Nawaz Sharif is not so different from the case of former President Asif Zardari, who received serious threats from the country's secret agencies. He was warned that an ambulance was ready to shift him to hospital. A decade-long war among civilian and military intelligence agencies has deeply impacted their professional intelligence mechanism. For example, the IB never liked receiving instructions from the ISI and military intelligence agencies. From 1977 to 1999, ISI and MI confiscated the secret record of the federal and provincial offices of the IB and police Special Branches (SB) time and again. This civilian and military intelligence war caused great anger in the police and other law enforcement agencies. In a nine-page statement before the Supreme Court, former Intelligence Bureau chief Masud Sharif Khattak revealed that former Prime Minister Benazir Bhutto extensively increased the budget of the IB, because the ISI was not willing to report to the Prime Minister.

9   Tackling Sunni Muslim ultra-conservatism: A Pakistani-US collision in the making, James M. Dorsey, *Huffpost*, 12 August 2017, https://www.huffingtonpost.com/entry/tackling-sunni-muslim-ultra-conservatism-a-pakistani_us_5a2a585ee4b0d7c3f26221ab

10 Pakistan's Security Challenges and Problems in the Next Decade, Salma Malik, E-International Relations, 04 February,2016,http://www.e-ir.info/2016/02/04/from-cinderella-to-beauty-and-the-beast-dehumanising-world-society/, Canadian Security Intelligence Service report "Pakistan's Security-Today and Tomorrow" has spotlighted several complex challenges of Pakistan's national security: "Pakistan faces several complex and interdependent challenges: The Intel Service's role of providing timely information, analysis and advice to government decision-makers is vital to Canada's security. In carrying out this role, the men and women of CSIS are committed to the values and best interests of Canada and its citizens. https://www.csis.gc.ca/bts/index-en.php

11 Pervez Hoodbhoy, *Dawn*, December 16, 2017

12 *Dawn*, 14 December 2017

13 *Daily Outlook Afghanistan*, 25 December 2017

14 Mr. Zamir Kabulov, Russia's special presidential envoy for Afghanistan said that Moscow was worried about an increasing foothold of Daesh militants in northern Afghan provinces bordering Tajikistan and Turkmenistan. "Russia was among the first to sound the alarm in connection with the emergence of Daesh in Afghanistan ... Daesh has significantly increased its power in the country recently. *Press TV*, 09 February 2018.

15   Russia Says about 10,000 IS Militants Now in Afghanistan, Ayaz Gul, Voice of America Radio, 23 December, 2017, The Russian envoy alleged helicopters "without identifying insignia" are transferring fighters and delivering "Western [military] equipment" to the Afghan branch of the terrorist group. https://www.voanews.com/a/russia-afghanistan-islamic-state/4176497. html. Moscow Wants Kabul to Engage in Constructive Dialogue with Armed Opposition, Russian Special Presidential Envoy for Afghanistan and Foreign Ministry's Director of the Second Asian Department Zamir Kabulov in an interview to Sputnik spoke about the situation in Afghanistan and possibility of peace talks between Kabul and Taliban. Sputnik International, Asia & Pacific, 23.December 2017, https://sputniknews.com/asia/201712231060262185-russia-afghanistan-taliban-dialogue-opposition/, VI Moscow conference on international security, Ministry of Defence of the Russian Federation, 26–27 April 2017, http://www.pircenter.org/media/content/files/14/15106553510.pdf

16   *TOLONews*, 6 October 2016

17   Ibid, 18 January 2018, Afghan President Ashraf Ghani questioned Pakistani mullah's FATWA against terrorism in Pakistan

18   Pakistan Assessment of 2017, *South Asia terrorism Portal*

19   *Dawn*, 08 January 2018

20   *Dawn*, January 28th, 2018

21   *ToloNews*, 30 January 2018

22   *NDTV*, 30 January 2018

23   *Afghanistan Times*, 31 January 2018

24   Nothing but lies and deceit': Trump launches Twitter attack on Pakistan, US president tweets saying Pakistan is providing 'safe haven to terrorists' and America was 'foolish' to give $33bn in aid. *The Guardian*, 01 January 2018, and the Independent, 01 January 2018.

25   *Dawn*, 30 December 2017

26   *Express Tribune*, 04 January 2018

27   *NDTV*, 28 October 2015

28   *The news International*, 17 January 2018

29   *The Financial Daily*, 17 January 2018

30   Azizullah Hamdard, Pajhwok Afghan News, 02 February, 2018, https://www.pajhwok.com/en/2018/02/02/11-suspects-linked-recent-attacks-detained-ghani

31 *Dawn*, 31 January 2018

32 Ibid, 01 February 2018

33 F.M. Shakil, *Asia Times*, 10 February, 2018

Bibliography

Abbas Hassan. 2004. Pakistan's Drift into Extremism: Allah, the Army and America's War on Terror. M.E Sharp Inc.

Abid, Abdur Rehman, 22 April, 2009, "Buner Falls into the Hands of Swat Taliban," *Dawn* Karachi

Abrams Herbert L. 1991, "Human Reliability and Safety in the Handling of Nuclear Weapons," Science and Global security

Abrahamson, James L and Paul H. Carew, 2002, Vanguard of American Atomic Deterrence, the Sandia Pioneers, Westport, Praeger

Abrams, Herbert L., 1991, Human Reliability and Safety in the Handling of Nuclear Weapons, Science & Global Security

Alexander, Yonah and Milton Hoenig, 2001, Super Terrorism: Biological, Chemical and Nuclear. Ardsley, NY: Transnational Publishers

Alexander, Yonah and Stephen D. Prior, 2001, Terrorism and Medical Responses: U.S. Lessons and Policy Implications. Ardsley, NY: Transnational Publishers

Abraham, Itty, 2009. South Asian Cultures of the Bomb: Atomic Publics and the State in India and Pakistan. Bloomington, IN: Indiana University Press

Abrahamson, James L. and Paul H. Carew, 2002, Vanguard of American Atomic Deterrence: The Sandia Pioneers, 1946-1949. Westport, CT: Praeger

Ackland, Len. 1999, Making a Real Killing: Rocky Flats and the Nuclear West. Albuquerque, NM: University of New Mexico Press

Acton, James. 2010, Deterrence during Disarmament: Deep Nuclear Reductions and International Security. New York: Routledge

Adams, Ruth and Susan Cullen, 1981, the Final Epidemic: Physicians and Scientists on Nuclear War. Chicago, IL: Educational Foundation for Nuclear Science

Ahmad Khalid. 2011. Sectarian War: Pakistan's Sunni Shia Violence and its Links to the Middle East, Oxford University Press.

Albright David, 2002, "Al Qaeda's Nuclear Program: Through the Window of Seized Documents." Policy Forum on Line, No. 47, November, 6, Nautilus Institute Berkeley, USA

Allen James S. 1952. Atomic Imperialism, International Publisher, New York, USA

Alley, William M and Rosemary Alley, 2013, Too Hot to Touch, the Problem of High Level Nuclear Waste, Cambridge University Press

Arnold, Lorna and Mark Smith, 2006, Britain, Australia and the Bomb: The Nuclear Tests and Their Aftermath. New York: Palgrave Macmillan.

Aron, Raymond. 1965. The Great Debate: Theories of Nuclear Strategy. Garden City, New York.

Ayson, Robert. 2004. Thomas Schelling and the Nuclear Age: Strategy as Social Science. New York. Frank Cass.

Albright, David, 2002, Al Qaeda's Nuclear Program: Through the Window of Seized Documents," Policy Forum On-line, Special Forum No. 47, November 6, Nautilus Institute, Berkeley, CA

Basrur, Rajesh, October 2002, "Kargil, Terrorism, and India's Strategic Shift," India Review

Basrur, Rajesh, "September 2003, Nuclear India at the Crossroads," Arms Control Today

Badash, Lawrence. 1994. Scientists and the Development of Nuclear Weapons. Atlantic Highlands, NJ: Humanities Press.

Bashkar Roy. 2008, "China Unmasked—What Next"? South Asian Analysis group Paper No. 2840.

Basrur Rajesh and Rizvi Hassan Askari.2003, "Nuclear Terrorism and South Asia;"Occasional Paper 25 Cooperating Monitoring Centre

Badash Lawrence, 1994. Scientists and the Development of Nuclear Weapons, Atlantics Highlands, Humanitarian Press

Bartone, John C. 1999. Biological Warfare and Chemical Gases: Index of New Information and Research Reference Book. Washington, DC: Abbe Publishers Association

Bermudez, Joseph S. 1998, Chemical and Biological Weapons and Deterrence: Case Study 5, North Korea. The Deterrence series, case study 5. Alexandria, VA: Chemical and Biological Arms Control Institute

Bester, William T. 1998, A New Enemy: Silent, Lethal, and Invisible. Carlisle Barracks, PA: U.S. Army War College

Baylis, John and Robert O'Neill, 2000, Alternative Nuclear Futures: The Role of Nuclear Weapons in the Post-Cold War World. Oxford, UK: Oxford University Press

Bernstein, Barton J. 1976. The Atomic Bomb: Critical Issues. Boston, MA: Little, Brown & Co

Bernstein, Jeremy. 2008. Nuclear Weapons: What You Need to Know. New York: Cambridge University Press

Bernstein, Jeremy. 2009. Plutonium: A History of the World's Most Dangerous Element. Ithaca, Cornell University Press, New York

Black, Samuel. 2010. The Changing Political Utility of Nuclear Weapons: Nuclear Threats from 1970 to 2010. Washington, DC: Henry I. Stimson Centre

Bellany LAN. 2007. Terrorism and Weapons of Mass Destruction: Responding to the Challenge. Routledge Global Security Studies

Brachman.Jarret M and William F. McCant, 2006, Stealing al Qaeda's Playbook, West Point, US Military Academy, Combating Terrorism Center

Byman Daniel. 2008. The Five Fronts War: The Better Way to Fight Global Jihad, Hoboken, Wiley.

Bellamy Alex J. 2008. Fighting Terror: Ethical Dilemmas, Zed Books, USA and UK

Cameron Gavin. 1999. Nuclear Terrorism: A Threat Assessment for the 21st Century. St. Martin's Press New York

Bailes, J. 2013. Weapon of the strong: conversations on U.S. state terrorism. London: Pluto Press.

Burt, Richard R. 1982. "Use of Chemical Weapons in Asia: Laos, Cambodia, and Afghanistan." US Department of State Bulletin

Burgess, Lisa. 1998. "Initiative Expands Guard's Role in Bio-Chem Defense." Army Times, April 6.

Caldicott, Helen. 2002, The New Nuclear Danger: George W. Bush's Military– Industrial Complex. New York: The New Press.

Carlotta Gall, 2014. The Wrong Enemy: America in. Afghanistan 2001–2014. Houghton Mifflin Harcourt, New York.

Chalmers Malcolm. 2012. Less is better: Nuclear Restraint at Low Numbers. Royal United Services Institute for Strategic Studies London.

Clarke, J.W.2007. Defining danger: American assassins and the new domestic terrorists, New Brunswick, N.J.: Transaction Publishers.

Carruthers S. 2000. The Media at War: Communication and Conflict in the 21st Century. St.Martin's Press. New York.

Crenshaw P, 1981, Psychology of Terrorism: An Agenda for the 21st Century. Wesleyan University

Carey Schofield. 2010. Inside Pakistan army: A Women Experience in the Frontline of the War on Terror. Biteback

Cole, B, 2011, the changing face of terrorism: How real is the threat from biological? Chemical and nuclear weapons London: I.B. Tauris.

Chandran D. Suba 2008, "Violence against Women in Swat, Why Blame only Taliban"? IPCS Issue Brief, No. 97, India

Clarke Richard. 2004. "Against All Enemies: America's War on Terror," Free Press, New York, USA.

Coll Steve. 2004. Ghost Wars: The Secret History of the CIA, Afghanistan and Bin Laden, from the Soviet Invasion to September 10, 2001, Penguin Publishers. USA.

Dahl Robert, 1985, Controlling Nuclear Weapons: Democracy versus Guardianship. Syracuse University Press, New York.

Dando Malcolm. 2001. The New Biological Weapons: Threat,

Proliferation and Control. Lynne Rienner Publishers, London

Dark Sun. 1995, the Making of the Hydrogen Bomb, by Richard Rhodes, Simon & Schuster, New York

Davies Philip H. J and Gustafson Kristian C, 2013; Intelligence Elsewhere: Spies and Espionage outside the Anglo sphere. Georgetown University Press, Washington DC USA

Eager Paige Whaley, 2008, From Freedom Fighters to Terrorists: Women and Political Violence, Ashgate, Hampshire

Editorial Dawn, "Deployment of Troops Begins in South Waziristan." 21 February, 2004.

Editorial the Nation, 21 February, 2004. Troops Moved Towards Angoor Adda. Falk Richard and David Krieger, 2008, At the Nuclear Precipice: Catastrophe or Transformation? Palgrave MaCmillan, USA.

Farmelo Graham. 2009. The Strangest Man: The Hidden Face of Paul Dirac, Mystic of the Atom. Basic Books, New York USA

Faruqui Ahmad, 2001. The Complex Dynamics of Pakistan Relationship with China, Policy Research, Islamabad

Farmelo Graham. 2013. Churchill's Bomb: How the United States Overtook Britain in the First Nuclear Arms Race. Basic Books, New York, USA

Ferguson Charles D, William C. Potter. 2004. The Four Faces of Nuclear Terrorism, Monterey Institute of International Studies.

Frank P. Harvey. 2008. The Homeland Security Dilemma: Fear, Failure and the Future of American Insecurity. Routledge, London.

Frederic Volpi, 2008. Transnational Islam and Regional Security, Routledge, London.

Freedman Lawrence, 2003.The Evolution of Nuclear Strategy Palgrave, UK,

Freedman Lawrence, 2013, Disarmament and Other Nuclear Norms, Washington Quarterly.USA

Fair C. Christine. 2007. Militant Recruitment in Pakistan: A New Look at the Militancy–Madrasa Connection, Asian Policy.

Fresch Hillel & Inbar Efraim, 2008, Radical Islam and International Security, Routledge,

First Brian, 2009, Terrorism, crime, and public policy, Cambridge: Cambridge University Press.

Frost, Robin M. 2005. Nuclear terrorism after 9/11, Abingdon: Routledge for the International Institute for Strategic Studies.

Gerstein, Daniel M. 2009. Bioterrorism in the 21st century: emerging threats in a new global environment. Annapolis, Md.: Naval Institute Press.

Fuhrmann, Matthew. 2012. Atomic assistance: how "atoms for peace" programs cause nuclear insecurity. Ithaca: Cornell University Press.

Gavin, Francis J. 2012. Nuclear statecraft: History and Strategy in America's Atomic Age. Cornell University Press

Gibson, David R. 2012. Talk at the brink: deliberation and decision during the Cuban Missile Crisis. Princeton: Princeton University Press.

Graham, Allison T. and Philip Zelikow, 1999, Essence of Decision: Explaining the Cuban Missile Crisis, Longman, New York

Graham, Allison T. 2004. Nuclear Terrorism: The Ultimate Preventable Catastrophe. Henry Holt & Co, New York

Guhar Altaf, 1996, Ayub Khan: Pakistan's First Military Ruler, Oxford University Press.

Ganguli Sumit and S. Paul Kapur, 2009. Nuclear Proliferation in South Asia: Crisis Behavior and the Bomb. Routledge, New York.

Harvey, Frank P. 2008. The Homeland Security Dilemma: Fear, Failure, and the Future of American Insecurity. Contemporary Security Studies

Howie Luke. 2012. Witnesses to terror: understanding the meanings and consequences of terrorism. Basingstoke: Palgrave Macmillan.

Howitt, Arnold M 2003, countering terrorism: dimensions of preparedness. Cambridge, Mass.: MIT Press.

Han Henry Hyunwook. 1993. Terrorism & Political Violence: Limits

& Possibilities of Legal Control, Oceana Publications, New York, USA.

Hoffman Bruce. 1998. inside terrorism, Columbia University Press. New York.

Husband Mark. 1998. Warriors of the Prophet: The Struggle for Islam. Westview Press.

Hurley Jennifer A. 1999. Weapons of Mass Destruction: Opposing Viewpoints. San Diego, Greenhaven Press.

Ikle Fred Charles. 2006. Annihilation from Within: The Ultimate Threat to Nations. Columbia University Press, 2006

Itty, Abraham. 2009, South Asian Cultures of the Bomb: Atomic Publics and the State in India and Pakistan, Indiana University Press.

Iversen, Kristen. 2013. Full Body Burden: Growing Up in the Nuclear Shadow of Rocky Flats. New York: Random House

Jahan Rounaq. 1972. Pakistan: Failure and National Integration, Columbia University Press. New York.

Jalal Ayesha, 2011. The Past and Present in Pakistan: Beyond the Crisis State, Columbia University Press, New York.

Jenkins Brian Michael. 2008. Will Terrorist Go Nuclear? Promethus Book. New York.

Jaspal Zafar Nawaz. 2009. "Threat of Extremism and Terrorist syndicate Beyond FATA." Journal of Political Studies

Jeremy Bernstein. 2008, Nuclear Weapons: What You Need to Know. Cambridge University Press

Kellman Barry 2007. Bioviolence: Preventing Biological Terror and Crime. Cambridge University Press, New York.

Kenneth N.Luongo and Naeem Salik, December, 1, 2007. "Building Confidence in Pakistan's Nuclear Security," Arms Control Today

Kenneth D. Bergeron. 2002, Tritium on Ice: The Dangerous New Alliance of Nuclear Weapons and Nuclear Power. Cambridge, MIT Press.

Khan Saira. 2009. Nuclear Weapons and Conflict Transformation (The Case of India– Pakistan). Routledge (Taylor and Francis Group), London.

Krepton Michael. 2009. Better Safe than Sorry: The Ironies of Living with the Bomb. Stanford University Press, USA.

Krotz Ulrich and Schild Joachim. 2013. Shaping Europe: France, Germany, and Embedded Bilateralism from the Elysee Treaty to Twenty-First Century Politics. Oxford University Press, UK.

Lan Bellany. 2007. Terrorism and Weapons of Mass Destruction: Responding to the Challenge. Routledge, London

Lian W. 2010. Talibanization in the Tribal Area of Pakistan, Journal of Middle Eastern and Islamic Studies

Lewis, Jeffrey. 2014. Paper Tiger: China's Nuclear Posture. International Institute for Strategic Studies, London

Lichbach M.I. 1989. "An Evaluation of "Does Economic Inequality Breed Political Conflict"? A Quarterly Journal of International Relations.

Lindholm C. 1986 Jan. 1. "Leadership Categories and Social Process in Islam: The Case of Dir and Swat." Journal of anthropological Research.

Martinage Robert C. 2008. The Global War on Terrorism: An Assessment. Centre for Strategic and Budgetary Assessments. Washington DC.

Mehra Parshotam. 1998. The North West Frontiers Drama, 1945–47: A Re-assessment. Manohar Publisher, New Delhi, India

Mir Amir. 2009. Talibanization in Pakistan, Pentagon Security International, Publisher, India.

Nawaz Shuja. 2009. FATA: The Most Dangerous Place, Centre for Strategic and International Studies. USA.

Omand David. 2010. Securing the State. Hurst & Company, London.

Osama W.M. 2002, the Case of US Leadership in Rebuilding of Afghanistan, Analysis from East West Centre.

Perez Margaret Gonzalez. 2008. Women and Terrorism: Female activities in Domestic and International Terror Groups, Routledge, London and New York.

Pape R.A. 2003. "The Strategic Logic of Suicide Terrorism," American Political science Review.

Philip H. J. Davies and Kristian C. Gustafson, 2013, Intelligence Elsewhere: Spies and Espionage outside the Anglo sphere. Georgetown University Press, USA

Pinault D. 2003. "Shia–Sunni Relations in Contemporary Pakistan." Journal of South Asian and Middle Eastern Studies

Raza Rumi. 2010–2011.The rise of Violent Extremism. Extremism Watch, Mapping

Conflict trends in Pakistan, Jinnah Institute Islamabad. Raza Rumi is the editor of Daily Times Pakistan

Rhodes, Richard, 1986. The Making of the Atomic Bomb, Simon & Schuster, New York

Rid, Thomas.2013. Cyber War Will Not Take Place. Hurts & Company London

Satu Limaye, Robert Wirsing & Mohan Malik. 2004. Religious Radicalization and Security in South Asia. Honolulu Asia Pacific Centre for Security Studies

Shulsky Abram N. and Schmitt. Gary J. 2002. Silent Warfare: Understanding the World of Intelligence. Potomac Books Washington, USA

Siddiqa Ayesha, Military Inc.: Inside Pakistan's Military Economy, Pluto Press 20 Apr 2007.

Taj Farhat. 2012. Taliban and Anti Taliban, Cambridge Scholars Publishing.

Weller George. 2006. First into Nagasaki: The Censored Eyewitness Dispatches on Post-Atomic Japan and its Prisoners of War, Crown, New York

Wellock Thomas R. 1998. Opposition to Nuclear Power in California, 1958–1978.

Madison, University of Wisconsin Press.

Wenger, Andreas, and Reto Wollenmann, 2007, Bioterrorism: Confronting a Complex Threat, Lynne Rienner, London.

Whitney Craig R. 2005. "The WMD Mirage: Iraq's Decade of Deception and America's False Premises for War," Journal of Public Affairs,

New York

Yoshihara Toshi and James R. Holmes. 2012. Strategy in the Second Nuclear Age: Power Ambitions and the Ultimate Weapon. Georgetown University Washington DC

Younger Stephen M. 2010. The Bomb: A New History. ECCO, New York.

Yusafzai Hamid Iqbal. 2011. The US Factor in Pak–Afghan Relations Post 9/11. Lambert Academic Publishing, Germany

Yusufzai, Rahimullah, "Fall of the Last Frontier?" Monthly Newline Magazine (Karachi), June 2002.

Zaeef, Abdul Salam, 2009. My Life with the Taliban, London: Hurst and Company.

Index